Text Analytics
for
Business Decisions

TEXT ANALYTICS

FOR

BUSINESS DECISIONS

A Case Study Approach

Andres Fortino, PhD

MERCURY LEARNING AND INFORMATION

Dulles, Virginia
Boston, Massachusetts
New Delhi

Publisher: David Pallai
MERCURY LEARNING AND INFORMATION
22841 Quicksilver Drive
Dulles, VA 20166
info@merclearning.com
www.merclearning.com
1-800-232-0223

A. Fortino. *Text Analytics for Business Decisions: A Case Study Approach.*
ISBN: 978-1-68392-666-5

Library of Congress Control Number: 2021936436
212223321   Printed on acid-free paper in the United States of America.

Dedicated to
my sister, Catalina

Contents

Preface   *xiii*

Chapter 1 Framing Analytical Questions   **1**

Data is the New Oil   3

The World of the Business Data Analyst   4

How Does Data Analysis Relate to Decision Making?   6

How Do We Frame Analytical Questions?   7

What are the Characteristics of Well-framed Analytical Questions?   8

Exercise 1.1 – Case Study Using Dataset K: Titanic Disaster   10

What are Some Examples of Text-Based Analytical Questions?   13

Additional Case Study Using Dataset J: Remote Learning
Student Survey   14

References   16

Chapter 2 Analytical Tool Sets   **17**

Tool Sets for Text Analytics   19

Excel   19

Microsoft Word   20

Adobe Acrobat   20

SAS JMP   20

R and RStudio   21

Voyant   22

Java   22

Stanford Named Entity Recognizer (NER)   23

Topic Modeling Tool   23

References   24

Chapter 3 Text Data Sources and Formats   **25**

Sources and Formats of Text Data   27

Social Media Data   28

Customer opinion data from commercial sites   28

Email	29
Documents	30
Surveys	30
Websites	31
Chapter 4 Preparing the Data File	**33**
What is Data Shaping?	34
The Flat File Format	35
Shaping the Text Variable in a Table	39
Bag-of-Words Representation	39
Single Text Files	40
Exercise 4.1 – Case Study Using Dataset L: Resumes	41
Exercise 4.2 – Case Study Using Dataset D: Occupation Descriptions	44
Additional Exercise 4.3 – Case Study Using Dataset I: NAICS Codes	46
Aggregating Across Rows and Columns	46
Exercise 4.4 – Case Study Using Dataset D: Occupation Descriptions	47
Additional Advanced Exercise 4.5 – Case Study Using Dataset E: Large Data Files	49
Additional Advanced Exercise 4.6 – Case Study Using Dataset F: The Federalist Papers	53
References	54
Chapter 5 Word Frequency Analysis	**55**
What is Word Frequency Analysis?	56
How Does It Apply to Text Business Data Analysis?	57
Exercise 5.1 – Case Study Using Dataset A: Training Survey	58
Exercise 5.2 - Case Study Using Dataset D: Job Descriptions	71
Exercise 5.3 - Case Study Using Dataset C: Product Reviews	77
Additional Exercise 5.4 - Case Study Using Dataset B: Consumer Complaints	83

Chapter 6 Keyword Analysis   **85**

Exercise 6.1 – Case Study Using
Dataset D: Resume and Job Description   87

Exercise 6.2 - Case Study Using
Dataset G: University Curriculum   101

Exercise 6.3 - Case Study Using
Dataset C: Product Reviews   115

Additional Exercise 6.4 - Case Study Using
Dataset B: Customer Complaints   118

Chapter 7 Sentiment Analysis   **119**

What is Sentiment Analysis?   120

Exercise 7.1 - Case Study Using
Dataset C: Product Reviews – Rubbermaid   121

Exercise 7.2 - Case Study Using
Dataset C: Product Reviews-Windex   129

Exercise 7.3 – Case Study Using
Dataset C: Product Reviews-Both Brands   134

Chapter 8 Visualizing Text Data   **139**

What Is Data Visualization Used For?   140

Exercise 8.1 – Case Study Using
Dataset A: Training Survey   141

Exercise 8.2 – Case Study Using
Dataset B: Consumer Complaints   147

Exercise 8.3 – Case Study Using
Dataset C: Product Reviews   154

Exercise 8.4 – Case Study Using Dataset E: Large Text Files   161

References   163

Chapter 9 Coding Text Data   **165**

What is a Code?   167

What are the Common Approaches to Coding Text Data?   168

What is Inductive Coding?   168

Exercise 9.1 – Case Study Using Dataset A: Training   169

Exercise 9.2 - Case Study Using Dataset J: Remote Learning   172

Exercise 9.3 - Case Study Using Dataset E: Large Text Files 178

Affinity Diagram Coding 181

Exercise 9.4 - Case Study Using
Dataset M: Onboarding Brainstorming 181

References 184

Chapter 10 Named Entity Recognition **185**

Named Entity Recognition 186

What is a Named Entity? 187

Common Approaches to Extracting Named Entities 188

Classifiers – The Core NER Process 188

What Does This Mean for Business? 188

Exercise 10.1 - Using the Stanford NER 189

Exercise 10.2 – Example Cases 191

Exercise 10.2 - Case Study Using
Dataset H: Corporate Financial Reports 195

Additional Exercise 10.3 - Case Study Using
Dataset L: Corporate Financial Reports 200

Exercise 10.4 – Case Study Using Dataset E: Large Text Files 200

Additional Exercise 10.5 – Case Study Using
Dataset E: Large Text Files 203

References 203

Chapter 11 Topic Recognition in Documents **205**

Information Retrieval 206

Document Characterization 207

Topic Recognition 208

Exercises 209

Exercise 11.1 - Case Study Using
Dataset G: University Curricula 209

Exercise 11.2 - Case Study Using
Dataset E: Large Text Files 216

Exercise 11.3 - Case Study Using
Dataset E: Large Text Files 220

Exercise 11.4 - Case Study Using
Dataset E: Large Text Files 226

Exercise 11.5 - Case Study Using
Dataset E: Large Text Files 230

Additional Exercise 11.6 - Case Study
Using Dataset P: Patents 235

Additional Exercise 11.7 - Case Study Using
Dataset F: Federalist Papers 235

Additional Exercise 11.8 - Case Study Using
Dataset E: Large Text Files 236

Additional Exercise 11.9- Case Study Using
Dataset N: Sonnets 236

References 237

Chapter 12 Text Similarity Scoring **239**

What is Text Similarity Scoring? 240

Text Similarity Scoring Exercises 243

Exercise 12.1 – Case Study Using
Dataset D: Occupation Description 243

Analysis using R 254

Exercise 12.2 - Case D: Resume and Job Description 254

Reference 258

Chapter 13 Analysis of Large Datasets by Sampling **259**

Using Sampling to Work with Large Data Files 260

Exercise 13.1 - Big Data Analysis 260

Additional Case Study Using
Dataset E: BankComplaints Big Data File 268

Chapter 14 Installing R and RStudio **271**

Installing R 272

Install R Software for a Mac System 272

Installing RStudio 277

Reference 279

Chapter 15 Installing the Entity Extraction Tool   **281**

Downloading and Installing the Tool   282

The NER Graphical User Interface   283

Reference   283

Chapter 16 Installing the Topic Modeling Tool   **285**

Installing and Using the Topic Modeling Tool   286

Install the tool   286

For Macs   286

For Windows PCs   286

UTF-8 caveat   287

Setting up the workspace   287

Workspace Directory   287

Using the Tool   289

Select metadata file   292

Selecting the number of topics   294

Analyzing the Output   295

Multiple Passes for Optimization   295

The Output Files   295

Chapter 17 Installing the Voyant Text Analysis Tool   **297**

Install or Update Java   298

Installation of Voyant Server   298

The Voyant Server   299

Downloading VoyantServer   299

Running Voyant Server   301

Controlling the Voyant Server   304

Testing the Installation   305

Reference   306

Index   **307**

Preface

With the rise in data science development, we now have many remarkable techniques and tools to extend data analysis from numeric and categorical data to textual data. Sifting through the open-ended responses from a survey, for example, was an arduous process when performed by hand. Extend the data set from a few hundred survey responses to tens of thousands of social media postings, and now you have an impossible task unless it is automated. The result is the rise in the need and the solutions for text data mining. It is essential in the business world, where we want to quickly extract customer sentiment, for example, or categorize social media postings.

Accelerating advances in natural language processing techniques was the response. They have now come out of the lab and become mainstream in use. It is now widespread and even imperative to analyze text variables in a data set alongside techniques to mine information from numeric and categorical variables. This book aims to make the emerging text analytical techniques accessible to the business data analyst.

This book was written for business analysts who wish to increase their skills in extracting answers from text data in order to support business decision-making. Most of the exercises use Excel, today's most common analysis tool, and R, a popular analytic computer environment. Where appropriate, we introduce additional easy to acquire and use tools such as *Voyant*, and many natural language processing tools available as open source. The techniques covered in this book range from the most basic text analytics, such as word frequency analysis, to more sophisticated techniques such as topic extraction and text similarity scoring.

The book is organized by tool or technique, with the basic techniques presented first and the more sophisticated techniques presented later. The book is not meant to explain the origins or characteristics of each method thoroughly. Instead, at the heart of the book is a series of exercises putting the technique or tool to work for different business situations. We leave it for other authors and other texts to present the theoretical and explanatory understanding of the tools. A significant contribution of this book is a curated database of text-based data files which should provide plenty of practice.

Using the CRISP-DM data mining standard, the early chapters discuss conducting the preparatory steps in data mining: translating business information needs into framed analytical questions and data preparation. Chapter 1 gives plenty of practice of framing analytical questions applied to text data. Chapter 2 briefly covers the most common tools for data preparation and data mining. Chapter 3 explores where text data may be found in business databases and situations, and the forms it might take. Chapter 4 covers data preparation and shaping the data set for analysis.

The next eight chapters cover basic text analytics techniques. Chapter 5 presents techniques and practical exercises on word frequency analysis. It is a basic approach used for subsequent techniques. Chapter 6 follows by applying Chapter 5 techniques to extract keywords from the text. Chapter 7 carries this further by categorizing and scoring frequent words to measure sentiments expressed in the text. Chapter 8 covers techniques for visualizing text data, from word clouds to more sophisticated techniques.

The last five content chapters cover advanced techniques. Chapter 9 presents the traditional approach to analyzing text data by coding. It uses affinity techniques and qualitative coding methods. Chapter 10 covers named entity extraction, where we tabulate the frequency of certain types of data (names, dates, places, etc.) Chapter 11 presents tools for extracting the main topics in a corpus of texts. Topic extraction makes use of sophisticated machine learning algorithms. We round out the section by showing text similarity scoring in Chapter 12. We score several texts in a corpus to exemplify text, based on similarity—a powerful technique.

The rest of the book has utility chapters. They deal with the installation and use of tools. Chapter 13 helps with big data files by sampling, in order to extract a representative smaller set of text for preliminary analysis or for use by tools (like Excel) that are limited to the size of the data set. Chapter 14 guides the reader on installing the R and RStudio platforms. Chapter 15 is a guide for the installation of the Entity Extraction tool from MIT. Chapter 16 presents how to install the Topic Modeling Tool from Harvard. Lastly, Chapter 17 covers the installation of the Voyant text analysis platform on the reader's computing environment, rather than using the cloud-based version for added security.

On the Companion Files

The exercises require the data sets used in analyzing the cases. They may be accessed on the companion disc with the book or for downloading by writing to the publisher at info@merclearning.com. A folder, *Case data*, has all the files referenced in the exercises. They are organized by a folder titled, *Lab Data.zip*, found in the same repository, which can be downloaded to make data available on a local drive. The solution folders within each exercise folder contain some illustrative charts and tables as well as solution spreadsheets.

Acknowledgements

This book was a personal journey of discovery, both as a student exploring the emerging field of extracting information from text data and as a translator for my students so they could also master the field. I had a great deal of help from my students, for which I am grateful, including the preparation and class-testing of the exercises. I am most grateful to Ms. Yichun Liu and Mr. Luke Chen, for your staunch support and assistance. Their working right alongside me developing exercises for the book were an integral part of the finished product you see before you. I also wish to thank many other students who collaborated with me in exploring text data mining and co-authoring many papers in the area, some award-winning. Thank you primarily to Qitong Zhou for exemplary scholarship and for mentoring of your peers as we struggled to learn and to co-create excellent research. And thank you, Sijia Scarlett Fang, for writing the wonderful similarity scoring algorithm and the Web front-end we discuss in Chapter 12. I want to acknowledge my graduate students at the NYU School of Professional Studies, and the many American Management Association professionals who attended my AMA seminars, with whom I shared these techniques. I also wish to thank my colleague Dr. Roy Lowrance, a world-class data scientist. He has been my collaborator in researching text data mining with my students. He was always there to advise and keep me straight when trying to understand some obscure AI concepts.

The entire team of editors and artists at Mercury Learning was terrific. They have my gratitude. A special thanks to Jim Walsh, my editor, who kept asking for more and helped shape an excellent book.

Finally, I wish to acknowledge my loving and patient wife, Kathleen. This book was written in the middle of a worldwide tragedy – the COVID virus pandemic. I can say with certainty that it helped to have all that time indoors and locked up to finish the book. But having Kathleen by my side with her infinite patience and constant encouragement helped me survive the pandemic and complete this book in peace.

Dr. Andres Fortino
April 2021

## CHAPTER 1

FRAMING ANALYTICAL QUESTIONS

Analytical efforts in support of a business must begin with the business's purpose in mind. (We use the word "business" here to mean all the operational and strategic activities of any organization used to run itself, be it for-profit, non-profit, or governmental.) This chapter presents the practical aspects of the preparatory processes needed to apply analytical tools to answer business questions. We start with the stated business's informational needs, which drive the framing of the analytical problems. For the analysis to be effective, it is essential to do some homework first. An analysis of the context of the informational needs must be conducted. Discovering the key performance indicators (KPIs) driving the needs and the current gaps in performance in those indicators must motivate our work. That way, we ensure we fulfill the immediate information requests and shed light on the underlying KPI gaps.

The CRISP-DM (Cross Industry Standard Process for Data Mining) reference model is a useful and practical process for any data mining project, including text data mining. The model was developed by the CRISP-DM consortium [CRISP-DM99]. The first step in the process is to ascertain and document a business understanding of the problem to be analyzed. Wirth and Hipp [Wirth00], two of the project originators, summarized the method as follows: "This initial phase focuses on understanding the project objectives and requirements from a business perspective and then converting this knowledge into a data mining problem definition, and a preliminary project plan designed to achieve the objectives."

This chapter is a practical approach to the discovery of the business needs driving the text analytics project. The exercises provided in this chapter help the reader acquire the necessary skills to ensure the business needs drive their analytics projects.

Data is the New Oil

In today's business environment, we often hear: "Data is the new oil." (The phrase was coined by Clive Humby in 2006 [Humby06].) It is a useful metaphor underscoring the need for management to embrace data-driven decision making. For us, it is an appropriate metaphor for the process of distilling data into knowing what to do. Let's see what that means for the analyst. The elements of the metaphor and their equivalencies are summarized in Figure 1.1.

	Oil Industry	Business	Knowledge Management
	Raw Material: Crude Oil	Data	Raw data is collected in databases and flat files. ERPs, CRM, RDBMS data warehouses, Excel spreadsheets.
	Distillates: Gasoline	Information	Through analysis data is converted to information, a collection of facts. We draw conclusions. At the end of the process we are informed.
	Conversion to energy: Gasoline Engine	Knowledge	The facts become the basis for decision making: "Data driven decision making". Convert facts to decisions. Now we know what to do, what action to take.

FIGURE 1.1 "Data is the new oil"

In the oil industry, the raw material is crude oil; in business, the raw material is data. Just like oil, in and of itself, data does not provide any significant benefit. It must be processed to produce beneficial effects. The oil must be extracted from the surrounding environment (rocks and soil) and collected, transported, and stored. It is the same with data. It must be cleaned, shaped, and adequately stored before we can apply analytical tools to extract useful information.

The raw material is most useful when it is distilled into byproducts that can be readily consumed and easily converted to energy. Thus, we distill various products from raw oil: crude oil, gasoline, kerosene, and other useful distillates, like benzene. The data must also be distilled to yield useful information products. The data distillation process is *data analysis*. Some analysis processes are straightforward descriptive statistical summaries using pivot tables and histograms. Others are more elaborate and refined analyses, such as predictive analytic products, which require sophisticated techniques such as decision trees or clustering. In the end, applying analysis to data yields information that we encapsulate into facts and summarize into conclusions.

Oil distillates by themselves don't generally produce useful work. They can be burned to produce heat (home heating furnace) and light (kerosene lamp). But the most useful conversion process is a gasoline-burning engine, which generates mechanical power. Either way, we need a mechanism to transform oil distillates into work. It's the same with information distilled from data. It is nice to know the facts, but when they are converted into action, they become very powerful. In the case of business, it's the decision-making engine of the organization that does the converting. Whether it is a single executive, a manager, or a committee, there is a business decision-making process that consumes analysts' information and generates decisions useful to the business. Information processed by the now informed decision-making organizational engine becomes *knowing what to do*. Analysts are the transformers or distillers of data through their analysis process, and they generate facts and conclusions. They feed the decision-making engine of the organization, the managers, and the executives responsible for taking action.

The World of the Business Data Analyst

Data analysis in a business context supports business decision-making. But to be useful, data analysis must be driven by well-framed analytical questions. There is a well-developed process for creating well-framed questions. It is a fundamental task of the data analyst to translate the organization's information needs into computable framed questions. With expertise in their analysis, knowing what can be done and knowing what the results might look like after analysis, the data analyst is the best-placed person to create computable tasks based upon information needs. Information needs are those questions formulated by business managers and staff who require the facts to make their decisions. Figure 1.2 shows some of the steps followed by the business data analyst to present the results of their investigations.

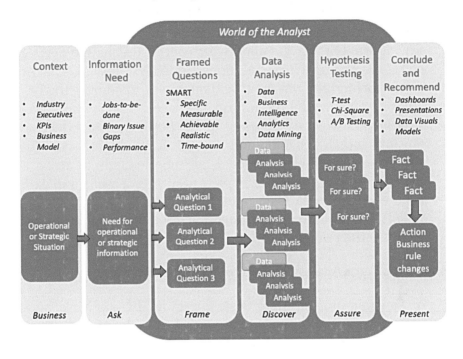

FIGURE 1.2 The world of the analyst: the process of business information need analysis

Although the diagram shows the *business information needs* following the *context* step, ascertaining the information need is usually the first step in the process. A manager or fellow staff approaches the business analyst with an information request to discover the answer to some pressing business issues. That request, called the *business information need,* is often expressed in nebulous terms: "Are we profitable this month?"; "Why do you think shipments have been late in the past six months?"; or "Are we over budget?"

The analyst cannot give an immediate answer. Those questions are not posed in ways in which they can be immediately computed. Thus, the analyst must translate the need into questions that can be used in computation. These are termed *framed analytical questions.*

In addition, it is the analyst's responsibility to investigate the *business context* driving the information need. That way, answering the framed analytical questions goes beyond the immediate need and provides support for the underlying context driving the need. So, as well as creating analytical questions, the analyst must look back to the context behind the questions and analyze it to address the business issues that motivated the information need. The context has to do with the industry the business is in, the business model the company is using, and the current status of the KPIs driving management. The process of thinking through all the elements to arrive at the point of framing questions is presented rather well by Max Shron in his *Thinking with Data* book [Shron14]. He presents a CoNVO model – (Co) *context*, (N) *information need*, (V) *vison* for the solution including the framed questions, and the (O) *outcome*.

How Does Data Analysis Relate to Decision Making?

We answer framed analytical questions by applying analytical techniques to the datasets that we collect and shape. Applying the analysis to the data yields information: we, as analysts, become informed. At the end of our analysis process, we have become subject matter experts on that business issue, the most informed person on the topic at the moment. We communicate our findings as facts and conclusions, and perhaps venture some recommendations, to our colleagues and managers. Using our findings, they are then in the best position to take action: they know what is to be done. So, the data, upon analysis, becomes information (*we become informed*), which then becomes the basis of knowledge (*knowing what to do*). As data analysts, it is our task to convert data into information and offer the resulting facts to our business colleagues for decision making. Figure 1.3 describes this process in detail.

- **Data** – pieces of information, measurements, transactions, opinions, items we collect into a database and becomes the basis for answering questions

- **Information** – once we *analyze* data by answering questions and drawing conclusions, we *become informed*

- **Knowledge** – we can now make informed choices as to what to do – make recommendations on taking action, *we know what to do*

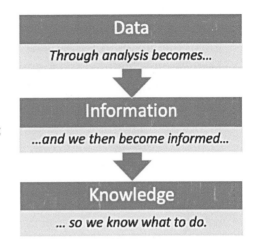

FIGURE 1.3 The data-driven decision-making process

As another example, consider a company that just launched a campaign to make employees more aware of the new company mission. After a period of time, an employee survey asks the open-ended question: "Can you tell us what you think the company mission statement is?" By doing a word frequency analysis of the mission statement and comparing it to the word frequency analysis of the employees' responses, we can gauge the success of the socialization of the mission statement through an education awareness campaign.

How Do We Frame Analytical Questions?

The translation of a nebulous, probably not well-formed, information need into computable, well-framed questions is a critical step for the analyst. One of the "raw materials" of the analysis process is the information need. It must be parsed and taken apart word-for-word to derive its actual meaning. From that parsing process comes a thorough understanding of what must be computed to bring back a good answer. In the parsing process, the analyst asks each element of the request, "What does this mean?" We are seeking definition and clarity. The answers also yield an understanding of elements of the data that will need to be collected.

The parsing process brings an understanding of the other elements of the analysis: (a) "What is the population (rows of our data table) that needs to be studied?", (b) What variables or features of the population (columns) must populate the database to be collected?", and most importantly, (c) What computations will be needed to use these variables (the framed questions)?".

As the analyst begins to understand the meaning of the elements of the request, questions form in the mind that need to be answered in the analysis process. The quantitative questions (what, who, how much, and when) will yield to the analysis tools at the command of the analyst. These are questions that can be answered by tabulating categorical variables or applying mathematical tools to the numerical variables. In our case, we add the use of text analytic tools to text data. These become the framed analytical questions.

At this stage, generating as many computable questions as possible yields the best results. Before starting the analysis, the list of questions is prioritized, and only the most important ones are tackled. It often happens that as the analysis work progresses, new vital framed questions are discovered and may be added to the work. Therefore, the initial set of framed questions needs to be complete. Even so, care must be taken to get a reasonably good set of framed questions.

What are the Characteristics of Well-framed Analytical Questions?

Well-framed analytical questions exhibit the same characteristics we have come to associate with well-framed goals and objectives: they must be SMART. Generally, SMART goals and objectives are

- *Specific*   Target a specific area for improvement or goal to be achieved.
- *Measurable*   Quantify, or at least suggest an indicator of progress towards that goal.
- *Assignable*   Specify who will do it, and who is involved.

- *Realistic*   State what results can realistically be achieved, given the available resources.
- *Time-related*   Specify when the result(s) can be achieved.

When applied to framing analytical questions, the concepts translate as (see Figure 1.4)

- *Specific*   The framed question must be focused and detailed.
- *Measurable*   The framed question must be computable.
- *Attainable*   The framed question must be able to be answered by the techniques known to the analyst who will do the analysis.
- *Relevant*   The answers to framed question must apply to the business.
- *Time-related*   Some element of time should be considered in the analysis.

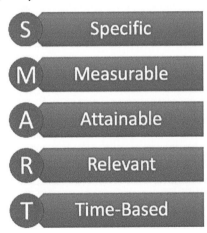

FIGURE 1.4 SMART well-framed analytical questions

Information needs are often expressed in nebulous un-specific terms. Thus, information needs by their nature, are not following the SMART rules. Some information needs are specific and may be computed without further analysis. But in general, additional specific framing is needed.

Exercise 1.1 – Case Study Using Dataset K: Titanic Disaster

The Case

Imagine that you work for a famous newspaper. Your boss is the news editor of the newspaper. It's almost the 100th anniversary of the Titanic disaster. The editor assigned a reporter to cover the story. The reporter submitted an article that states "the crew of the Titanic followed the law of the sea in responding to the disaster." The editor is concerned that this may not be true and assigned you to fact-check this item. You decide to approach it from an analytic point of view. Your analysis of the assignment should yield the following:

The Information Need

Did the crew of the Titanic follow the law of the sea in responding to the disaster?

The Context

This is a newspaper; it prints articles of interest to the general public as the end result of its business processes; its revenue sources are subscription fees, but mostly advertising revenue.

The KPI and Performance Gaps

The editor is concerned that the articles in the newspaper be as truthful as possible, which is why there is such emphasis on fact-checking. There is a concern that the public trusts the paper to publish truthful information, or there will be a loss of readership, resulting in a reduction in subscriptions, but more importantly, a loss in advertising revenue.

Parsing the Information Needs

To translate the information needs into frame questions, we need to ascertain the following. Figure 1.5 describes the parsing process.

a. What do we mean by "the crew?" Who are these people? What was their mindset at the time they had to make decisions on who to put on the lifeboats?

b. What does it mean for the crew to "follow the law of the sea?"

c. What is "the law of the sea?"

d. What do we mean by *responding*? When we say responding to the disaster, what does the response look like? What were the actions taken by the crew in response to the disaster?

e. What is "the disaster?" Was it when the iceberg struck? Was it when the crew realized the ship was going to sink? Was it when the boat sank and lifeboats were away?

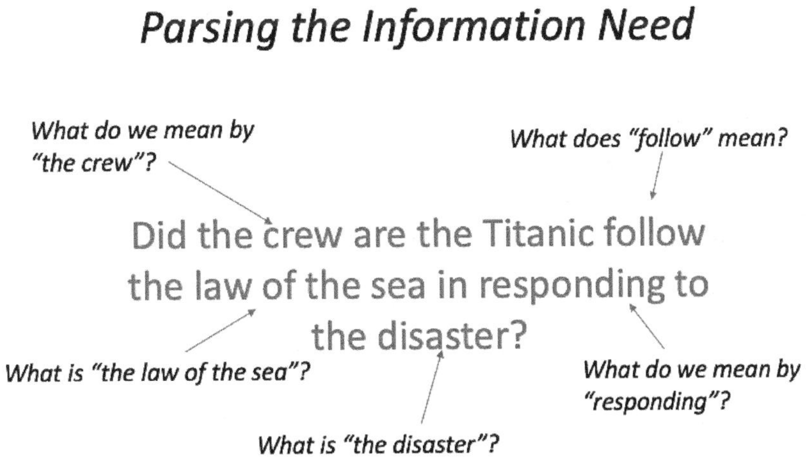

Parsing the Information Need

What do we mean by "the crew"?

What does "follow" mean?

Did the crew are the Titanic follow the law of the sea in responding to the disaster?

What is "the law of the sea"?

What do we mean by "responding"?

What is "the disaster"?

FIGURE 1.5 Parsing the request

We determined that the crew assigned to each lifeboat decided who got on the lifeboats. They were ordinary seamen assigned by their officers to serve as gatekeepers to the lifeboats. Since there weren't enough boats for everybody on the Titanic, this decision making needed to be done. The decision probably followed the well-known "law of the sea," meaning "women and children first." The seamen were charged with filling the boats with women and children before any men got aboard. Did that happen? If you find a positive answer, then we can tell the editor the reporter is truthful in the story. The facts will either support the decision to run the story as is or to change it before it prints.

The Dataset

The critical dataset for our purposes is the Titanic's passenger manifest *(https://public.opendatasoft.com/explore/embed/dataset/titanic-passengers/table/)*.

This publicly available dataset shows the 1,309 passengers, their names, ages (for some), passenger class, and survival status. These features or variables in our dataset should help us form and answer some well-framed questions. A copy of the dataset can also be found in the *Analysis Cases* data repository for this book under the *Case K Titanic Disaster* folder.

Knowing all the facts about the information needs and the context that drives those needs, we are now prepared to frame some analytical questions and begin our analysis. Keep in mind these questions must be SMART: specific, measurable (computable), attainable, relevant, and have some time element in them.

The Framed Analytical Questions

We determined that there are some computations we could undertake that would support a positive or negative answer to the information need.

> *What is the survival rate of women, and how does it compare to the survival rate of men?*

> *What is the survival rate of children, and how does it compare to the survival rate of adults?*

They certainly would give us a powerful indication of whether the crew was following the law of the sea. That would be the question our editor was looking to answer. But we could find a more valuable answer if we included additional information. We could analyze the survival rates for men, women, and children, and break those rates down by passenger class.

> *What are the survival rates of men, women, and children broken down by class?*

The answer to this question might result in useful insights for the editor and the reporter, who could add to the story and make it more interesting. For example, it could give a competitive edge to the story versus the stories published in competing magazines. This is how an analyst adds value to the work they do: bringing back in-depth answers that go beyond the original information needs and support the KPIs driving that need.

What are Some Examples of Text-Based Analytical Questions?

Suppose that in pursuing the story, the reporter conducted interviews of everyday people to ask them questions about the disaster. Some questions yielded categorical or numerical data, as many surveys do. But as is often the case, there was an open-ended question posed at the end of the survey: "How do you feel about the operators of the ocean liner not supplying enough lifeboats for everyone to be saved?" This is an example of a possible question that the reporter may have asked. Typically, reporters will collect answers to that question from a few individuals as a small sample of how "the general public feels." In this case, the survey was conducted electronically through social media, and it collected hundreds of responses. The reporter was overwhelmed and sought your help as an analyst to extract meaning from this larger dataset.

Parsing the information need: This is about the feelings of each respondent, their conception of the operators of ocean-going cruises, exemplified by the Titanic, which is supported by their experience or knowledge of cruises.

Framed analytical questions: We determine that there is some text analysis we could undertake to extract meaning for the collected responses.

> *Do the people posting comments about the disaster feel positively or negatively towards the operators of the Titanic?*

> *What keywords are mostly used to express their opinion?*

> *Is there a visual that can easily represent these keywords and their sentiment?*

Additional Case Study Using Dataset J: Remote Learning Student Survey

The Case: During the Pandemic of 2020, many universities and colleges were forced to cancel face-to-face instruction and move their courses online *en masse*. This was an abrupt decision that had to be implemented practically overnight in March 2020. Many students were familiar with online learning and some were taking classes in that form alreday; nevertheless, it was a sudden change and caused many dislocations. To try to gauge the reactions from the students, some faculty polled their students several weeks into the new all-remote environment. They asked what was working and what was not. The faculty wanted to make course corrections based on how the students were coping with the new mode of learning. A faculty member with expertise in data analysis is asked by a colleague who collected the data to help to make sense of the answers.

The Information Need: From the point of view of the students affected, we need to know what is working and what is not working to guide the necessary pedagogical changes.

The Context: University teaching. Faculty are concerned that students would be upset with using a modality they are not familiar with. This could affect their performance in the class, including grades. More importantly, for the faculty, course evaluations may suffer, reflecting poorly on the teacher. On the other hand, classes were continuing, even in light of the potential health risks.

Parsing the information need:

> *For the students affected, what is working and what is not working in their learning that can guide faculty to make needed pedagogical changes*

Parse the information need to extract the meaning of the important elements. What questions does your parsing raise?

The Dataset: A survey was taken of 31 students in two classes who had previously attended face-to-face classes and then had to continue attending remotely. Only one survey question was asked:

> *Compare and contrast learning in a physical classroom versus learning remotely, as a substitute, during this time of crisis. Tells us what you like and what you don't like, what works and what does not work.*

The responses were open-ended and text-based.

The Framed Analytics Questions: What framed analytical questions may be derived from the information need and the nature of the data?

References

1. [Humby06] Humby, Clive. "Data is the new oil." *Proc. ANA Sr. Marketer's Summit. Evanston, IL, USA* (2006).

2. [Shron14] Shron, Max. *Thinking with Data: How to Turn Information into Insights.* "O'Reilly Media, Inc.", 2014.

3. [CRISP-DM99] *The CRISP-DM process model* (1999), *http://www.crisp-dm.org/.*

4. [Wirth00] Wirth, Rüdiger, and Jochen Hipp. "CRISP-DM: Towards a standard process model for data mining." In *Proceedings of the 4th International Conference on the Practical Applications of Knowledge Discovery and Data Mining*, vol. 1. London, UK: Springer-Verlag, 2000.

## CHAPTER 2

ANALYTICAL TOOL SETS

There are many commercial products available for text data analysis, and they work very well. If you have the means and you have many projects, by all means, avail yourself of these wonderful products. In this book, we take a different approach. We opt for using open-source or readily available products found on any computer or downloaded at no additional cost. We favor open-source products for the most part (R and Java-based tools), which can be downloaded and installed on most computers today (Windows and Macs). We also rely on Microsoft products (Excel and Word), which are also readily available.

The only exception is the inclusion of the SAS JMP program. It is not common in corporate environments, but many universities provide access to the full version to their students and faculty via a virtual platform. Often, the relationship between SAS and the university comes with a student or faculty's ability to download and install a full version of JMP on their laptops for a small annual fee. JMP has many text analysis features, and we include it here for completeness. There are other excellent data-mining programs with text analytics functionality, such a RapidMiner, which are available fully functional as academic versions. All the exercises in this book can also be executed on RapidMiner.

Tool Sets for Text Analytics

There are a few accessible tool sets available for the practical data analyst who has to accomplish straightforward text analysis tasks. Here, we describe some of the more common tool sets, either free or as part of a common set of software in use in most businesses and universities.

Excel

We start with an essential tool: Excel. Excel is probably the most ubiquitous office software program available for data analysis. There are quite a few text analytics tasks we can perform with Excel, but it soon runs out of capability. Excel can perform word counts using COUNTIF and other functions. In Chapter 5, we use Excel to perform word frequency analysis (also called Term Frequency analysis) using the COUNTIF function. We follow up in Chapter 6 where we do keyword analysis, a more refined approach to word frequency analysis. In Chapter 7, we add lists of "positive" and "negative" words to perform sentiment analysis. Word clouds, a powerful text visualization tool, are not available in Excel as-is, but we make do by visualizing word frequency with a Treemap, covered in Chapter 11. Treemaps are a recent addition to the visualization repertoire in Excel.

Excel is an excellent tool for cleaning and shaping the data file. We make full use of this tool in Chapter 4. In that respect, and because we deal with so much text, Word, another Microsoft product, is a useful companion tool to Excel to shape text data. Combined use of these two tools, Excel and Word, should suffice for any text data-wrangling needs of the average data analyst.

Other spreadsheet software is equally useful if you have the skills to work with it. Google Sheets may be used in place of Excel, but it does not offer any particular advantage. Use whichever spreadsheet program most familiar to you to create the necessary tables of data.

Microsoft Word

Word is the workhorse text manipulation platform for our purposes. First, it is ubiquitous and readily available. Second, because of its ubiquity, most professionals are skilled in its use. These skills can be put to work for our text data manipulation needs. Creative uses of the *Edit -> Find -> Replace* function can go a long way to shaping data that has been scraped from a document or a Website and convert it into a text form usable for analysis.

Adobe Acrobat

Some of our text data comes in the form of a PDF document (Adobe Acrobat Portable Document Formatted (.pdf) document.) Having access to the Adobe Acrobat Pro set of tools helps convert the PDF document to a text file ready to be processed with text tools. It requires an Adobe Acrobat Pro subscription. It is a relatively inexpensive way to add text export capability for PDF documents if you need to do conversions frequently. Microsoft Word can import many PDF documents into a Word document, but it does not always work well. It is not a foolproof conversion method, such as when some of the PDF textual elements are transformed into images rather than text. An inexpensive strategy is first to try converting the PDF file into Word format using Word. If that fails, then escalate to the use of the Adobe Acrobat Pro service. Or purchase a separate program that does the conversion.

SAS JMP

The SAS Institute makes some very powerful analysis tools. SAS provides a statistical software suite for data management, advanced analytics, multivariate analysis, business intelligence, and predictive analytics. SAS offers Enterprise and JMP versions of its analysis software. The Enterprise platform has text analytics capability, the SAS Text Miner. We do not use that product here. We use the text analysis capability of their ad-hoc analysis tool, JMP.

The JMP analysis tool has a graphical user interface. It is very useful and powerful for ad-hoc analysis. It can also be programmed (we use that capability to program a script in Chapter 12 for similarity scoring), but we generally use the *Analyze -> Text Analysis* function, which was recently added. Not all versions of JMP have this capability. A free version of JMP is available for students (the JMP Student Edition) to learn basic statistical analysis techniques. It does not have text analysis capabilities. You need to have at least the standard edition, and then in version 12 or above for basic text mining functionality (what they call a *bag of words* analysis). That's the edition we use in this book. There is a JMP Pro version that includes an additional text mining analysis capability not available in the standard version: latent class analysis, latent semantic analysis (LSA), and SVD capabilities. We use the standard edition for text mining.

R and RStudio

In this book, we use the R advanced analytics environment. R itself is a programming language often used for statistical computing, and more recently, for more advanced analysis such as machine learning. R comes with a programming interface that is command-line driven. It needs to be programmed to perform any analysis. There are graphical user interfaces that offer pull-down menus (a GUI) to make R easier to use, such as R-commander (or Rcmdr.) The Rcmdr program enables analysts to access a selection of commonly used R commands using a simple interface that should be familiar to most computer users. However, there is no simple graphic interface for the text analytics capabilities in R (the tidiytext package) [Silge16]. We must still invoke the R functionality via the command line to use the powerful text analytics capabilities in R.

Although R can be run stand-alone, we find it useful to run it under an Integrated Development Environment (IDE). An IDE is essentially software for building applications that combines common developer tools into a single graphical user interface (GUI). RStudio is probably the most popular IDE for R. RStudio, however, must be used alongside R to function correctly. R and RStudio are not separate versions of the same program and cannot be substituted for one another. R may be used without RStudio, but RStudio may not be used without R.

As we will make extensive use of R, we suggest you install it together with RStudio. Chapter 14 has instructions on how to install and run these programs. There is a cloud version of RStudio (RStudio Cloud), which is a lightweight, cloud-based solution that allows anyone to run R programs, share, teach, and learn data analysis online. Data can be analyzed using the RStudio IDE directly from a browser. This lightweight version is limited to the size of the data files. All the exercises in this book, and associated datasets, will work well with RStudio Cloud.

Voyant

Voyant Tools is an open-source, Web-based application for performing text analysis [Sinclair16]. It supports scholarly reading and interpretation of texts or a corpus, particularly by scholars in the digital humanities, but can also be used by students and the general public. It can be used to analyze online texts or any text uploaded by users. We use Voyant throughout this book as an alternative analysis platform for textual data. It can be used via a Web interface, or for those who are security-minded and don't want their text data uploaded to an unknown Web server, we show you how to download and install a version on your computer in Chapter 17.

Java

Java is the name of a programming language created by Sun Microsystems. As of this writing, the latest version is Java 15, released in September 2020. It is a programming platform that runs on almost all computer operating systems. Some of the program interfaces for the tools we use here (the Stanford NER and the Topic Extraction Tool) are written in Java. Thus, it is important the latest version of Java is installed on your computer to properly run these tools.

The Java program is currently being managed by the Oracle corporation. Instructions for downloading and upgrading Java may found at the Java website: *https://www.java.com/en/*. Visit the site and download the proper version of Java for your operating system.

Stanford Named Entity Recognizer (NER)

Named Entity Recognition (NER) is an application of Natural Language Processing (NLP) that processes and understands large amounts of unstructured human language. A NER System is capable of discovering entity elements from raw data and determines the category the element belongs to. Some examples of these named entities are names, dates, money, places, countries, and locations. The system reads sentences from the text and highlights the important entity elements in the text. Stanford scientists have produced a very good version of such a program, and we use it here.

The Stanford NER is a Java implementation of a Named Entity Recognizer. The NER labels sequences of words in a text, which are the names of things, such as person and company names or gene and protein names. It comes with well-engineered feature extractors for Named Entity Recognition and many options for defining feature extractors. We use it in Chapter 11. We show you how to install it in Chapter 15. Jenny Finkel [Finkel00] created the original code, and the feature extractor we use was created by Dan Klein, Christopher Manning, and Jenny Finkel [Klein00].

Topic Modeling Tool

Topic models provide a simple way to analyze large volumes of unlabeled text. A "topic" consists of a cluster of words that frequently occur together. Using contextual clues, topic models can connect words with similar meanings and distinguish between uses of words with multiple meanings. Topic modeling software identifies words with topic labels, such that words that often show up in the same document are more likely to receive the same label. It can locate common subjects in a collection of documents – clusters of words with similar meanings and associations – and discourse trends over time and across geographical boundaries.

The tool we use here is a point-and-click (GUI) tool for creating and analyzing topic models and is a front end to the MALLET topic modeling tool. The Java GUI front end was developed by David Newman and Arun Balagopalan [Newman00]. We show you how to use it in Chapter 10 and how to install it in Chapter 16. MALLET is a natural language processing toolkit written by Andrew McCallum [McCallum00].

References

1. [Ripley01] Ripley, Brian D. "The R project in statistical computing." *MSOR Connections. The newsletter of the LTSN Maths, Stats & OR Network* 1, no. 1 (2001): 23-25.

2. [Silge16] Silge, Julia, and David Robinson. "tidytext: Text mining and analysis using tidy data principles in R." *Journal of Open Source Software* 1.3 (2016): 37.

3. [Finkel05] Finkel, Jenny Rose, Trond Grenager, and Christopher D. Manning. "Incorporating non-local information into information extraction systems by Gibbs sampling." *Proceedings of the 43rd Annual Meeting of the Association for Computational Linguistics (ACL'05).* 2005.

4. [McCallum02] McCallum, Andrew Kachites. "MALLET: A Machine Learning for Language Toolkit." *http://mallet.cs.umass. edu* (2002).

5. [Shawn12] Graham, Shawn, Scott Weingart, and Ian Milligan. *Getting started with topic modeling and MALLET*. The Editorial Board of the Programming Historian, 2012.

6. [Sinclair16] Sinclair, Stéfan and Rockwell, Geoffrey, 2016. *Voyant Tools*. Web. http://voyant-tools.org/.Voyant is a web-based and downloadable program available at *https://voyant-tools.org/ docs/#!/guide/about*. The code is under a GPL3 license and the content of the Web application is under a Creative Commons by Attribution License 4.0, International License.

## CHAPTER 3

TEXT DATA SOURCES AND FORMATS

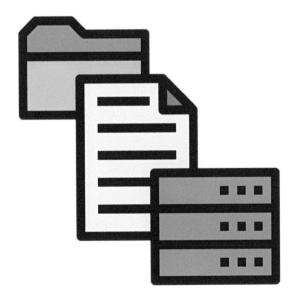

Analysts must deal with many data sources and formats (Figure 3.1 shows the most common types). The most common types of data we gather from business transactions are numeric and categorical. Computerized data is first collected and then stored to analyze financial transactions. The emphasis in analysis is often on summarizing numeric data, which can easily be done with mathematical tools such as the averages, sum, average, maximum, and minimum. Summarizing by categorical data used to be difficult. Initially, about the only thing we could do with categories was to tabulate them, counting the occurrence of each category. It was not until the advent of the Excel pivot table analysis that evaluating categorical data become as easy and commonplace as analyzing numerical data.

Text data was much harder to evaluate. We still had to count words, but much of this work required tabulation and quantization by hand. We developed some very laborious measures to do so. We show you how to code qualitative text data in Chapter 9. Not until the advent of social media and electronic commerce, when we began to be flooded with textual data, did we need to go further and automate quantizing to make sense of text data. This chapter presents the many forms and sources of text data.

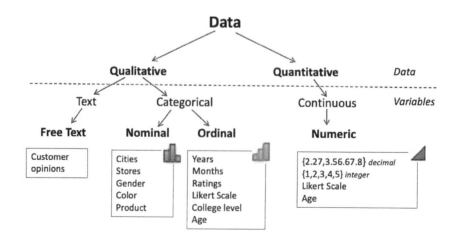

FIGURE 3.1 Categorizing the types of data formats and resulting variable types

Sources and Formats of Text Data

Numerical and categorical data are the most common data types. We use standard techniques to work with these data types, such as pivot tables and numerical summarization functions. With the advent of social networks and the development of sophisticated data tools, text data analysis is now more commonplace.

Business managers often want to know about certain aspects of the business, such as "What is the meaning of what people are saying about our company on Twitter or Facebook?" or "Does our use of keywords on the site match or surpass that of our competitors?" In other words, "Do we have the right keywords or enough of them for search engines to classify the company website higher in search returns than our competitors (search engine optimization, SEO analysis)?" These types of questions require that analysts do a thorough job analyzing the web page content text.

In customer conversational interactions it is essential to look at the text that a person wrote. Why? We already know that a combination of keywords and phrases is the most important part of a post. Before we do an analysis, we need to know what words and phrases the people are using. This analysis is accomplished by looking at the texts in terms of word frequency, sentiment, and the keywords.

It is essential to know where text data is found and in what form to optimize the scraping and shaping process and ultimately produce it in the right format for analysis. In this chapter, we discuss the various forms in which it comes across our desk. In the next chapter, we investigate extracting the data from its native format and shaping it into a form that can be easily analyzed with our tools. In this chapter, we also cover some of the techniques you may need to employ to acquire the data.

Social Media Data

Prominent examples of social media data sources are Facebook, Twitter, and LinkedIn. They can be excellent sources of customer text data. For example, if you have a conversation about a new product release with a client on Facebook or Twitter, that client tells you about what they're thinking about or planning to do. If a business relies on Twitter to gain feedback, a business in the early phases may wish to focus primarily on how customers perceive their product or service on Twitter to deduce the right product roadmap.

These social media sources generate data in real time. In that case we can do one of two things: process the stream in real time or download a portion of the stream for later processing. Analyzing the text stream in real time requires specialized software and is beyond the scope of this book. We limit ourselves to downloading the data stream into a fixed file for post-processing. Once we have the customers' text data plus the metadata about each tweet or Facebook post, we can process it as a flat file. Don't forget to add the metadata to the tweet or Facebook post's payload, as it contains additional information and puts the customer's comments in context.

If there's a need to extract sentiment or term frequency analysis, or even keywords in real time from these data streams, there are many of commercially-available programs that can do that. You might want to investigate these types of tools rather than attempting to modify the modest tools described in this book to manage real-time data.

Customer opinion data from commercial sites

There are significant amounts of customer feedback data from online shopping. This data is available as text and can be evaluated using the techniques in this book. Customer reviews and customer opinions are other excellent sources of product and service feedback available in text form. Again, as with social media data, commercial programs may be used to scrape, clean, and analyze these types of data. In our case, we assume that you don't analyze customer opinions from commercial sites regularly, but only have the occasional need. In that case, applying the simple tools presented in the book makes sense, but you will need to perform a significant amount of data cleaning and shaping.

The techniques described in Chapter 4 are useful after you scrape the data and paste it into an editor. Typically, that editor is a program like Word, where most of the shaping of the scraped data into a CSV file is done. (This approach requires significant effort and it is not often required. It can occasionally be a good solution). The endpoint of scraping and shaping is a CSV file that we can import into a table, with one of the columns containing the customer's opinion or feedback. We can then process the table containing our customer's comments using the tools presented in this book.

Email

Emails are another interesting source of text data. The stream of emails can be analyzed in real time as we would with social media data, but again, that would require the use of sophisticated commercial software. In our case, we need to scrape and shape the stream of emails into a flat file that can be processed as a table. The email's metadata is collected in the variables about the email, and the body of the email is captured into a text variable in the table. Then we process the static file to extract information from the text field.

Email presents us with another interesting opportunity for analysis. We can make each email into a separate document extracted and saved in the UTF-8 text format. Then we can upload the emails as a set of documents in a table so we can perform our analysis across the documents. Keep in mind that a group of documents in the text field of the table is called a *corpus*. A program such as Voyant can analyze texts in a corpus uploaded as a group of individual text files to give us more information. We can extract topics from the corpus (Chapter 10) and categorize emails by topic. We can extract named entities from each email and tabulate the frequency of appearance across the corpus. Emails can be analyzed as a monolithic file or a corpus of documents for cross-document comparisons and analysis.

Documents

Documents are another source of text data, and may be in the form of contracts, wills, and corporate financial reports. Some examples of text data that will yield to the analysis types presented in this book are the books found at project Gutenberg, patents from the United States Patent and Trademark Office, corporate financial reports filed with the Securities and Exchange Commission, and documents written by the United States Founding Fathers (The Federalist Papers).

Each document can be analyzed alone or as part of a corpus. We show you how to do both and how to extract topics across a corpus of texts, discover keywords across documents, and perform simple word frequency analysis. A powerful tool we cover in Chapter 12 is text similarity scoring, where we compare the frequency words in one text to those in a corpus of many texts. We try to discover the most similar text within the corpus to our target text.

Surveys

When we conduct surveys, we have specific questions in mind, and we are very careful about how we ask those questions. Typically, the answer to those questions yields either categorical or numerical data, which can be analyzed using standard techniques. Very often, surveys include question "Do you have anything else to tell us?" We're expecting a sentence or two of freeform text with the respondent's opinion.

In the past, we would have to laboriously read through these texts to extract significant themes, code all the survey responses by hand, and attempt to extract meaning. We show you this conventional approach, called *coding*, in Chapter 8. With the advent of natural language processing tools, we more powerful techniques to extract information from text data. We show you how the methods of word frequency analysis, sentiment analysis, keywords, and text similarity scoring can be profitably applied to what respondents write. In the case where we have more than a few dozen survey responses (of the order of 10,000 or 100,000 responses), we can process that larger volume of data more effectively than manually coding and tabulating it.

Websites

Websites are a good source of text data. We may want to do a similarity scoring of a page on our company's website against that of our competitors or perform a keyword analysis of our page to improve our standing with respect to search engines (search engine optimization). We may want to do a keyword analysis of our site and that of our competitors to see the similarities and differences in the presence of keywords. We can do a named entity extraction (Chapter 9) on our Website and topic analysis (Chapter 10). As websites contain a significant amount of text, their analysis using text tools can be very informative.

## CHAPTER 4

PREPARING THE DATA FILE

This chapter covers the essential and time-consuming process of shaping the text document or text variables into a form that can be analyzed. The result of our scraping, cleaning, and shaping will be the production of simple text files ready to be aggregated into a corpus (collection of text documents) or as data elements in the cells of a spreadsheet. The flat file format is popular for preparing data for analysis. Here, we describe the format and present examples of files that are in the flat file format. Flat files are also popular for data input when programming in the R language. They are called *data frames*. We also show how to shape text variables by concatenating text data cells for aggregation. We introduce the powerful Excel function COUNTIF. We make extensive use of this tool throughout the book. Lastly, we describe a text data file model called the *Bag-of-Words* model, also used throughout the book. We sometimes need to explicitly shape the file into a Bag-of-Words format when we use Excel for text analysis (Chapters 5 and 6). Other times, the various programs we employ implicitly translate the text data files into this format for us.

What is Data Shaping?

Data comes to us in many shapes and sizes, as we saw in the previous chapter. For most of our analytical tools, the data should be in a tabular format. Shaping the dataset is the transformation from whatever shape the data is acquired in (such as a report, an SQL query output, a CSV file, or an Excel file) into the proper format ready for analysis with our tools.

Data analysts spend the great majority of their time cleaning and shaping the dataset. A survey conducted by the data science company Crowdflower in 2016 shows the breakdown in tasks and the time needed to complete each (Figure 4.1).

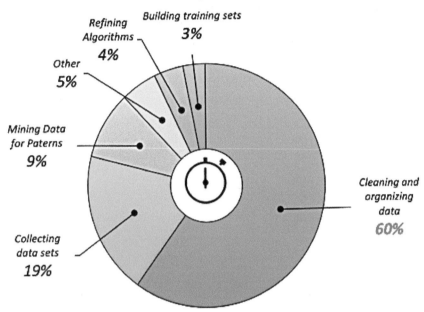

What Do Data Scientists Spend The Most Time Doing

Building training sets 3%

Refining Algorithms 4%

Other 5%

Mining Data for Paterns 9%

Cleaning and organizing data 60%

Collecting data sets 19%

FIGURE 4.1 Typical proportions for cleaning, shaping, and analysis [Crowdflower16].

The Flat File Format

Storing data in a simple structure of rows and columns is common today, often done with an Excel spreadsheet. This format has many limitations that may be overcome with sophisticated structures, such as Relational Database Management Systems (RDBMSs), which include indexing, economy of storage, easier retrieval, and additional massive datasets. Corporate data may sometimes be found stored in these more complex systems, but to use the data to answer questions, we extract the data from them and present it to the analysis in the form of a flat file of rows and columns.

A flat file can also be considered a database, albeit a simple one, with data stored uniformly. Records (the rows) follow a consistent format, and there are no structures for indexing or recognizing relationships between records. Columns are the named variables. The file is simple. A flat file can be a plain text file or a binary file. Relationships may be inferred from the data in the file, but the table format itself does not make those relationships explicit. Typically, all the rows are about the same population, such as orders, customers, patients, companies, or payments.

We often use spreadsheets as a form of database or as container for data. We usually load these spreadsheets with many non-data elements not useful for data analysis. For example, a particular spreadsheet may be a report with titles, page numbers, and the coloring of specific cells to make it for easier humans to read and interpret the information. Some of this is metadata (data about the dataset). To make the analysis more straightforward, we need to remove all of these human interface elements out of the spreadsheet and format the remaining data into a row and column format. Some of the summarization tools in spreadsheets, such as name pivot tables, require us to format the file into this format.

Moreover, the programming language for statistical analysis, R, readily ingests data in this form. In R, we refer to this format of data as *data frames*. In most cases, the flat file format is a convenient structure for analysis. Figure 4.2 shows a spreadsheet in the flat file format.

Each column is a variable, a "feature", of the data set, or attributes of the population

	A	B	C	D	E
1	name	age	sex	height	weight
2	KATIE	12	F	59	95
3	LOUISE	12	F	61	123
4	JANE	12	F	55	74
5	JACLYN	12	F	66	145
6	LILLIE	12	F	52	64
7	TIM	12	M	60	84
8	JAMES	12	M	61	128
9	ROBERT	12	M	51	79
10	BARBARA	13	F	60	112
11	ALICE	13	F	61	107
12	SUSAN	13	F	56	67
13	JOHN	13	M	65	98

Each row is an example, or "instantiation" of the population

FIGURE 4.2 The flat file format showing the elements of the rows and columns

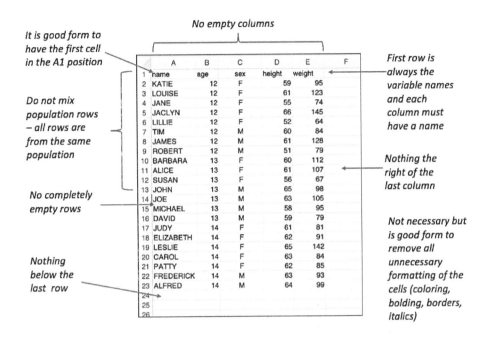

FIGURE 4.3 The elements of a flat file

Before applying an analysis tool to a file, remember always to ask: "Is this dataset in the flat file format?" Shaping the dataset results in a tabular format, with our desired text data as a column (or columns) in the flat file formatted table. Figure 4.3 is an excellent example of a table in such a format.

	A	B	C	D	E	F
1	PIZZA	BAKERY	SHOES	GIFTS	PETS	
2	80	150	48	100	25	
3	125	40	35	96	80	
4	35	120	95	35	30	
5	58	75	45	99	35	
6	110	160	75	75	30	
7	140	60	115	150	28	
8	97	45	42	45	20	
9	50	100	78	100	75	
10	65	86	65	120	48	
11	79	87	125	50	20	
12	35	90			50	
13	85				75	
14	120				55	
15					60	
16					85	
17					110	
18						
19	Business Startup Costs					
20						
21	The following data represent business startup costs (thousands of dollars) for shops.					
22	PIZZA = startup costs for pizza					
23	BAKERY = startup costs for baker/donuts					
24	SHOES = startup costs for shoe stores					
25	GIFTS = startup costs for gift shops					
26	PETS = startup costs for pet stores					
27	Reference: *Business Opportunities Handbook*					
28						

FIGURE 4.4 A data file not in the flat file format

Let's consider the table given in Figure 4.4. Apply the flat file format criteria to the table. Is this table in the flat file format? In Figure 4.4, we see that there are two variables in the dataset, one variable is the type of store that was being started, and the other variable is the starting capital needed to open that type of store. One variable is categorical. The other variable is numerical. In reality, there should be a two-column, or two-variable, table with each row of the table being a particular store type needing individual capital cost datasets. It would require significant shaping to put the data in this table into the flat file format. If there are many tables that need to be reshaped into flat files, this process could be automated with a macro or even a VBA script.

Shaping the Text Variable in a Table

Most of the case files used in this book have already been cleaned and shaped into the flat file format. When working with text data, we are often confronted with an additional issue: the text itself needs further processing or *pre-processing*. Before entering it into a table, a text variable may need to be shaped further. Some of the shaping may be done with complementary tools, such as Microsoft Word, or other text manipulation tools. Analytics programs, such as R, have routines that allow us to clean and shape the data, but it's often expeditious to use the most familiar tools, such as Microsoft Word. In our case, we will use the most commonly available platform to clean text data.

Bag-of-Words Representation

The Bag-of-Words model is a representation of textual data used in natural language processing (NLP) and information retrieval (IR). In this model, text (such as a sentence or a document) is represented as the bag (multiset) of its words, without regard to grammar and word order, but with the multiplicity of the words maintained (for later counting, for example). One of the main problems that can limit this technique's efficacy is the existence of prepositions, pronouns, and articles in our text. These words likely appear frequently in our text, but they lack information about the main characteristics and topics in our document. These common, uninteresting words, (called stopwords) are removed in the process of creating a Bag-of-Words text data file or data element. Chapter 5 demonstrates techniques to remove these unwanted terms as part of the analysis.

The Bag-of-Words model is commonly used in document classification methods, including many of the tools we use in this book. Before applying the tools presented here, it is essential to convert the text into a Bag-of-Words representation (shown in Figure 4.5), whether entering the text data into a spreadsheet's cells under a text variable or as stand-alone text documents.

| | Text | Bag of Words | Term Frequency |

FIGURE 4.5 A Bag-of-Words representation of text data

Single Text Files

Let's see how to change a document containing text into a Bag-of-Words text file, cells in a text variable in a flat file, or a single stand-alone file. We start with a single document containing text that needs to be prepared for analysis. It's essential to keep in mind the end result of the cleaning and shaping: a single text of words coded in the most basic ASCII character set (UTF-8). If this text string of words is entered into an Excel worksheet cell or is part of a formatted table, such as a CSV formatted table. The text string must be devoid of carriage returns.

Exercise 4.1 – Case Study Using Dataset L: Resumes

1. Access the repository of case files, and in the folder *Dataset L: Resumes,* open the resume *AFORTINO.pdf.* This document was downloaded from LinkedIn, and it is typical of such resume scrapings. If you have a LinkedIn account, you may try this process for your resume or the resume of any of your colleagues. An Adobe Acrobat file (an example of a scraped LinkedIn resume) is shown in Figure 4.6.

FIGURE 4.6 An Adobe Acrobat PDF file of a resume extracted from LinkedIn.

2. There are two ways of producing a simple text file from this Adobe Acrobat document. One approach is to use the Adobe Acrobat Premium services (which requires a purchase).

3. If these services are available, click on "Tool" and select "Export pdf," as shown in Figure 4.7.

FIGURE 4.7 The Export tool in Adobe Acrobat

4. Under "More formats," select the text option. Clicking on the settings wheel brings you to a dialog box where are you should select "UTF-8" as the export format from the pulldown menu under encoding. Figure 4.8 shows the choices. Click the "OK" button and then "Export" to yield a UTF-8 coded version of the resume, which we can save under the same name to any folder we wish.

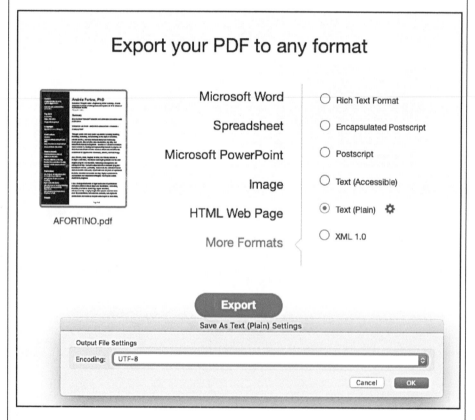

FIGURE 4.8 Choices for exporting the PDF version of the resume as a UTF-8 encoded plain text file

5. Upon examination of the resulting text file, we see that the file still contains many carriage returns, which will cause us problems if we try to enter the text into an Excel spreadsheet cell. It will require further processing with a tool to remove the carriage returns. Using MS Word, we can post-process it into the desired file, as shown in Figure 4.9.

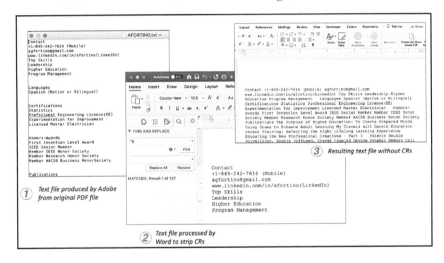

FIGURE 4.9 Use of MS Word to further process the text document into a text file

6. A more direct approach, and one that does not require additional cost, is to open the .pdf file in Adobe Acrobat and copy the entire text into the computer buffer by selecting it. Then paste it into Word as pure text. Remove the carriage returns, as shown earlier, and save the file as a plain UTF-8 encoded text file.

Aggregation

Sometimes the elements of the final text variable are distributed over many cells. We may need to combine them into one text variable. This is the simple case of aggregating two columns into one. Sometimes the text that needs to be aggregated spans several columns.

Exercise 4.2 – Case Study Using Dataset D: Occupation Descriptions

1. Let's start with a file that contains two text variables that need to be combined into one. Locate the folder *Dataset D: Occupation Descriptions* and load the *Occupations.xlxs* spreadsheet into Excel.

2. Note that there are two columns: one is a categorical variable called *Title*, which for this exercise, we will consider to be pure text, and the other is a text variable called *Description*. Figure 4.10 shows the raw flat file.

	A	B	C	D
1	O*NET-SOC Code	Title	Description	Full Description
2	11-1011.00	Chief Executives	Determine and formulate policies and provide overall direction of companies or private and public sector organizations within guidelines set up by a board of directors or similar governing body. Plan, direct, or coordinate operational activities at the highest level of management with the help of subordinate executives and staff managers.	
3	11-1011.03	Chief Sustainability Officers	Communicate and coordinate with management, shareholders, customers, and employees to address sustainability issues. Enact or oversee a corporate sustainability strategy.	
4	11-1021.00	General and Operations Managers	Plan, direct, or coordinate the operations of public or private sector organizations. Duties and responsibilities include formulating policies, managing daily operations, and planning the use of materials and human resources, but are too diverse and general in nature to be classified in any one functional area of management or administration, such as personnel, purchasing, or administrative services.	
5	11-1031.00	Legislators	Develop, introduce or enact laws and statutes at the local, tribal, State, or Federal level. Includes only workers in elected positions.	
6	11-2011.00	Advertising and Promotions Managers	Plan, direct, or coordinate advertising policies and programs or produce collateral materials, such as posters, contests, coupons, or give-aways, to create extra interest in the purchase of a product or service for a department, an entire organization, or on an account basis.	

FIGURE 4.10 Raw occupational O*NET data file with a created variable, *Full Description*, where we will aggregate the *Title* and *Description* fields

1. We create a third variable in our table that combines both the position title and the position description. When analyzing this text, we have a full description of the occupation that includes both the title and the occupation description.

2. Start by inserting an empty column right after the *Description* column. Using the CONCATENATE excel function, aggregate the occupation title and occupation description into one, as shown in Figure 4.11. Make sure to add a space between variables as shown below:

```
=CONCATENATE (B2,", "C2)
```

fx =CONCATENATE(B2," ",C2)			
	B	C	D
C Code	Title	Description	Full Description
	Chief Executives	Determine and formulate policies and provide overall direction of companies or private and public sector organizations within guidelines set up by a board of directors or similar governing body. Plan, direct, or coordinate operational activities at the highest level of management with the help of subordinate executives and staff managers.	=CONCATENATE(B2," ",C2)

FIGURE 4.11 Aggregating the occupation *Title* and *Description* variables into a *Full Description* variable using the CONCATENATE Excel function

3. The resulting file will be populated with the aggerated new variable, as shown in Figure 4.12.

B	C	D
Title	**Description**	**Full Description**
Chief Executives	Determine and formulate policies and provide overall direction of companies or private and public sector organizations within guidelines set up by a board of directors or similar governing body. Plan, direct, or coordinate operational activities at the highest level of management with the help of subordinate executives and staff managers.	Chief Executives Determine and formulate policies and provide overall direction of companies or private and public sector organizations within guidelines set up by a board of directors or similar governing body. Plan, direct, or coordinate operational activities at the highest level of management with the help of subordinate executives and staff managers.
Chief Sustainability Officers	Communicate and coordinate with management, shareholders, customers, and employees to address sustainability issues. Enact or oversee a corporate sustainability strategy.	Chief Sustainability Officers Communicate and coordinate with management, shareholders, customers, and employees to address sustainability issues. Enact or oversee a corporate sustainability strategy.
General and Operations Managers	Plan, direct, or coordinate the operations of public or private sector organizations. Duties and responsibilities include formulating policies, managing daily operations, and planning the use of materials and human resources, but are too diverse and general in nature to be classified in any one functional area of management or administration, such as personnel, purchasing, or administrative services.	General and Operations Managers Plan, direct, or coordinate the operations of public or private sector organizations. Duties and responsibilities include formulating policies, managing daily operations, and planning the use of materials and human resources, but are too diverse and general in nature to be classified in any one functional area of management or administration, such
Legislators	Develop, introduce or enact laws and statutes at the local, tribal, State, or Federal level. Includes only workers in elected positions.	Legislators Develop, introduce or enact laws and statutes at the local, tribal, State, or Federal level. Includes only workers in elected positions.

FIGURE 4.12 The aggregated new variable, *Full Description*

Additional Exercise 4.3 – Case Study Using Dataset I: NAICS Codes

1. As an additional practice exercise, aggregate the *Title* and the *Description* into a *Full Description* text variable.

2. Locate the folder *Dataset I: NAICS Codes* and load the *2017_NAICS_Description (short).xls* spreadsheet into Excel.

3. Note that there are two columns of text, one is a categorical variable called *Title*, which for this exercise we will consider to be pure text, and a text variable called *Description*, which is a text variable.

4. Create a new text variable by aggregating the *Title* and the *Description* into a *Full Description* text variable.

Aggregating Across Rows and Columns

There are times when we may want to aggregate data that spans across columns and over several rows of data. One way to do it is to create a column with a variable that identifies the rows we want to aggregate and then invoke the concatenate function across those rows. The next exercise gives you one possible way to accomplish this task.

Exercise 4.4 – Case Study Using Dataset D: Occupation Descriptions

1. Locate the folder *Dataset D: Occupation Descriptions* and load the *Task Statements.xlsx* spreadsheet into Excel.

2. Note that there are two columns of text, one is a categorical variable called *Title*, which is pure text, and a text variable called *Tasks*, which is a text variable.

	A	B	D
1	O*NET-SOC Code	Title	Task
2	11-1011.00	Chief Executives	Direct or coordinate an organization's financial or budget activities to f
3	11-1011.00	Chief Executives	Appoint department heads or managers and assign or delegate responsil
4	11-1011.00	Chief Executives	Analyze operations to evaluate performance of a company or its staff in
5	11-1011.00	Chief Executives	Direct, plan, or implement policies, objectives, or activities of organizat
6	11-1011.00	Chief Executives	Prepare budgets for approval, including those for funding or implement
7	11-1011.00	Chief Executives	Confer with board members, organization officials, or staff members to
8	11-1011.00	Chief Executives	Implement corrective action plans to solve organizational or departmen
9	11-1011.00	Chief Executives	Direct human resources activities, including the approval of human resc

FIGURE 4.12 Raw task O*NET data file ready to aggregate the *Title* and *Tasks* fields across rows by Title

3. We create a new text variable by aggregating the *Title* and the *Task* into an *All Tasks* text variable.

4. Start by adding two new columns to the table's right: label one column *Change* and the other *All Tasks*. In the *Change* column, we note whether the *Title* has changed from one row to another. We code a change as a "1" and no change as a "0." Use this formula:

```
=IF(B2=B1,0,1)
```

5. Now we have a marker to signify a change in *Title*. In the *All Tasks* field, aggregate across the rows while keeping the *Title* variable the same. Use this formula:

```
=IF(I4=1,D4,CONCATENATE(D4," ",J3))
```

6. Figure 4.13 shows the resulting aggregation.

fx =IF(I4=1,D4,CONCATENATE(D4," ",J3))

B	D	I	J
		Change	
Title	Task		All Tasks
Chief Executives	Direct or coordinate an organization's financial or budget activities to fi	1	Direct or coordinate an organization's financial or budget activities to func
Chief Executives	Appoint department heads or managers and assign or delegate responsi	0	Appoint department heads or managers and assign or delegate responsibi
Chief Executives	Analyze operations to evaluate performance of a company or its staff ir	0	=IF(I4=1,D4,CONCATENATE(D4," ",J3))
Chief Executives	Direct, plan, or implement policies, objectives, or activities of organizat	0	Direct, plan, or implement policies, objectives, or activities of organization
Chief Executives	Prepare budgets for approval, including those for funding or implement	0	Prepare budgets for approval, including those for funding or implementati

FIGURE 4.13 Task O*NET data file with aggregated *Tasks* rows by *Title*

7. To only retain the last row in each *Title* series, which contains the aggregated *Tasks* for that *Title*, we need another market. Create a variable called *Keep* and code it as a 0 for all rows with the same *Title* except for the last one in the *Title* series, coded as 1. Use this formula:

```
=IF(B2=B3,0,1)
```

8. Then sort the table by the *Keep* variable in descending order. All the "1" rows move to the top, select them and move to another worksheet. You now have a table with aggregated tasks by position.

Additional Advanced Exercise 4.5 – Case Study Using Dataset E: Large Data Files

This is a travel book of Darwin's journey around the world in 1831. Today he would use social media and post daily blogs of his observations as he travelled. Back then, he had to wait to get home, compile his notes, and publish a book. We can use his book as a stand-in for today's blogging or social media postings. Our purpose for shaping this data file into a form for text analysis is to answer the question:

Where in his voyages did Darwin see or write about volcanoes?

This could be a useful question to ask for any text variable that has location or data information associated with it. We aggregate the text into separate Excel cells and then look for the occurrences of the word "volcano." We then use a function we will encounter again in Chapter 5, the COUNTIF function. Let's continue with our exercise.

1. Locate the folder *Dataset E Large Text Files* and load the *VoyageOfTheBeagleDarwin.txt* text file into a text editor. Notice that this a book-length text file with many pages and over 200,000 words.

2. Note that the text, as saved from the open-source Guttenberg server, has carriage returns at the end of roughly 10-15 words of text. Figure 4.14 shows the beginning of the text file.

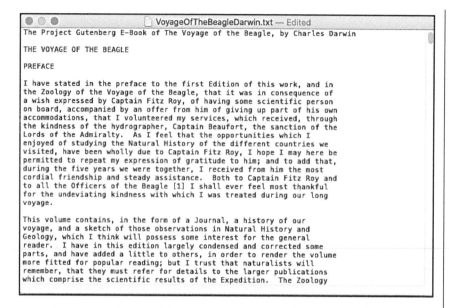

FIGURE 4.14 The raw *Voyage of the Beagle* book as a text file

3. We have a perfect source of text. We can search for "volcanoes" line by line and then try to correlate it to where he was on the day of the sighting, but that becomes difficult. Since each chapter of the book deals with a different location and they are in chronological order, we confine ourselves to see in which chapter (which point to the location) Darwin talks about volcanoes.

4. Scrape the text into the computer buffer, open an Excel spreadsheet, and paste it into one of the worksheets. Label it *Raw Data*. Notice that each line of the text goes into a separate cell in column A.

5. As we have done before, we introduce several marker columns. Add a *CHAPTER* column in column B after labeling column A as *TEXT*.

6. Use the following formula to label the start of each chapter. We also have to identify the *Preface* and the use of the recurrence of the *Title* of the book. This procedure adds a "1" for chapter changes.

```
=COUNTIF(A2, "*CHAPTER*")+ COUNTIF(A2,"*PREFACE*")+
COUNTIF(A2,"*THE VOYAGE OF THE BEAGLE*")
```

7. Add another column named *BLANK* to get rid of the blank lines. Use the following formula, which adds in one for each blank line.

```
=COUNTIF(A2,"")
```

8. *BLANK* is now sorted in ascending order, bringing all the blank lines to the top and deleting them. After you use the *BLANK* column, delete it.

9. Then follow our aggregation process, as shown in previous exercises, to collect all lines belonging to each chapter into one cell by chapter. Use the following formula:

10. Now that we have aggregated all lines for each chapter into the last line before each chapter change, we need to delete all but those lines. Add a maker column in column D and label it *KEEP*. Use the following formula:

```
=IF(B2=1,A2,CONCATENATE(C1," ",A2))
```

11. Copy all the rows and paste them into another worksheet and label it *Final Table*.

12. Sort the rows by the *KEEP* column in ascending order. Delete all but the rows that contain a "1" and only those that contain the text data from each chapter (delete rows with titles). Delete the *TEXT* and *CHAPTER* columns. Label the text of each chapter column *CHAPTER TEXT*.

13. You should have 22 rows of data, one for each chapter and one for the preface.

14. Now we can count the instances of the word *volcano* in each chapter. Use the following formula:

```
=COUNTIF(A2,"*volcano*")
```

15. Figure 4.15 shows the resulting table and the results of discovering where in the book Darwin discusses volcanoes. We see that it happens in Chapters I and II as he crosses the Atlantic from Cape Verde to Rio de Janeiro, and then once again as he travels up the coast of Chile. The year 1832 was a spectacular year for volcanoes, as many of them along the Andes were erupting. He talks about volcanoes when he visits the Galapagos Islands and Tahiti, and then again at the end of the book, when he summarizes his voyage.

	A	B
1	CHAPTER TEXT	VOLCANO
2	PREFACE I have stated in the preface to the first Edition of this work, and in the	0
3	CHAPTER I ST. JAGO--CAPE DE VERD ISLANDS Porto Praya--Ribeira Grande--Atm(	1
4	CHAPTER II RIO DE JANEIRO Rio de Janeiro--Excursion north of Cape Frio--Great I	1
5	CHAPTER III MALDONADO Monte Video--Excursion to R. Polanco--Lazo and Bola	0
6	CHAPTER IV RIO NEGRO TO BAHIA BLANCA Rio Negro--Estancias attacked by the	1
7	CHAPTER V BAHIA BLANCA Bahia Blanca--Geology--Numerous gigantic Quadrup	0
8	CHAPTER VI BAHIA BLANCA TO BUENOS AYRES Set out for Buenos Ayres--Rio Sa	0
9	CHAPTER VII BUENOS AYRES AND ST. FE Excursion to St. Fe--Thistle Beds--Habit:	0
10	CHAPTER VIII BANDA ORIENTAL AND PATAGONIA Excursion to Colonia del Sacra	0
11	CHAPTER IX SANTA CRUZ, PATAGONIA, AND THE FALKLAND ISLANDS Santa Cruz	0
12	CHAPTER X TIERRA DEL FUEGO Tierra del Fuego, first arrival--Good Success Bay-	0
13	CHAPTER XI STRAIT OF MAGELLAN.--CLIMATE OF THE SOUTHERN COASTS Strait	0
14	CHAPTER XII CENTRAL CHILE Valparaiso--Excursion to the Foot of the Andes--Str	1
15	CHAPTER XIII CHILOE AND CHONOS ISLANDS Chiloe--General Aspect--Boat Excur	1
16	CHAPTER XIV CHILOE AND CONCEPCION: GREAT EARTHQUAKE San Carlos, Chilo	1
17	CHAPTER XV PASSAGE OF THE CORDILLERA Valparaiso--Portillo Pass--Sagacity o	0
18	CHAPTER XVI NORTHERN CHILE AND PERU Coast-road to Coquimbo--Great Loac	0
19	CHAPTER XVII GALAPAGOS ARCHIPELAGO The whole Group Volcanic--Numbers	1
20	CHAPTER XVIII TAHITI AND NEW ZEALAND Pass through the Low Archipelago--T;	1
21	CHAPTER XIX AUSTRALIA Sydney--Excursion to Bathurst--Aspect of the Woods--	0
22	CHAPTER XX KEELING ISLAND:--CORAL FORMATIONS Keeling Island--Singular ap|	1
23	CHAPTER XXI MAURITIUS TO ENGLAND Mauritius, beautiful appearance of--Gre;	1

FIGURE 4.15 Final table of the *Voyage of the Beagle* text by chapter with an indication of where Darwin writes about volcanoes

16. Excel has a limit to the number of characters it can allow into any one cell (32,767 is the character maximum). Many of the chapters are very large, and they don't fit into a cell when aggregated. Therefore, much of the text has been left out of the chapter aggregations above.

17. Let's examine the preface. It only has 4,034 characters, and they are in the cell for the preface. But Chapter I has 3,934, and only 32,767 have been aggregated into the cell in our table. So at best, the results above are an approximation, and not an exact result. There may be other techniques we could use, but we reserve them for future chapters.

Additional Advanced Exercise 4.6 – Case Study Using Dataset F: The Federalist Papers

The American founding fathers wrote these documents over 250 years ago to advocate for adopting the Constitution that was being ratified by the states. There are 77 of these, which are the founding documents of the US government. They are all present in the text file, which has been scraped from an Internet source. We'd like to do the same thing to this file as was done to the *Voyage of the Beagle* book in the previous exercise. Our purpose for shaping this data file into a form for text analysis is to answer the question:

Which papers explained the roles and powers of the presidency and which founding father had the most to say about it?

1. Locate the folder *Dataset F: Federalist Papers* and load the *Federalist Papers.txt* text file into a text editor.

2. Each Federalist Paper in our aggregated text is broken up with many carriage returns. As with the *Beagle* text, we must aggregate by paper and place the results into a flat file with the text in a column by paper, together with the author and perhaps a few more variables for each paper, such as where it appeared in print.

3. Shape the text file and create an Excel table of the text for the Federalist Papers. Compute which founding father wrote the most about the office of the president and in which of the papers we would find their thoughts.

References

1. [Jurafsky13] Jurafsky, Daniel, and James H. Martin. *Speech and language processing: Pearson new international edition*. Pearson, 2013.

2. [CrowdFlower16] CrowdFlower, *2016 Data Science Report*.

## CHAPTER 5

WORD FREQUENCY ANALYSIS

In this chapter, we discuss the most basic technique in text analysis: counting words. It is the starting point for most investigations. We assume that the most frequently-appearing words hold some meaning: they are somewhat more important than other words. We tabulate their frequency because they likely have some greater significance in the context of our text. We ignore nuances, such as grammatical structure (for example, is the word a noun or a verb?) and how a term is used (Sarcasm? Irony? Fact?). We also know that not all words carry significant meaning, such as propositions or conjunctions (for example, "and," "beside," "at," or "in.") We assume we can safely ignore these and remove them from the text using a list of words with less meaning (stopwords). We strive to create a Bag-of-Words text data file (document) or text data field (data point in a cell of a spreadsheet). Then we count the most meaningful words to determine which are more important and which are less important.

We use a variety of tools and different types of data in these exercises. We demonstrate how to perform word frequency analysis, first with Excel, then with SAS JMP, and then the Web-based tool Voyant. Lastly, we demonstrate it using the programming language R. There are examples with text data as data elements in a text variable in a table as well as whole documents. We demonstrate how to aggregate the text in a column of data into a Bag-of-Words bundle (as we did in Chapter 4) and then parse it into its individual words so we can count them. The process is transparent when using Excel and R, but involves "hidden" computations when using JMP and Voyant.

What is Word Frequency Analysis?

Word frequency analysis is a way to enumerate the occurrences of interesting words in a document or text field. This technique is also called *Term Frequency* (TF) analysis.

It helps us quickly extract meaning from the text being analyzed. We count the occurrence of each word in the document. For business purposes, we are not interested in an in-depth linguistic analysis of the text but to quickly get a sense of what is contained in it and what it means. We want the most salient topics and themes.

Not all words are of interest when looking for meaning, so we often remove the most common words in a *stopword list*. Words such as "an," "it," "me," and "the" are all words that are usually found on such a list. Once removed, looking at the frequency of occurrence of the remaining words could be very informative. If, for example, we removed the stop words and analyzed the word frequency of the *Little Red Riding Hood* fable, we would have a very informative table (Figure 5.1). It gives us an excellent picture of the story in the fable.

Words	Count of Words
Little	16
wolf	14
Riding	12
Red	12
Grandmother	12
Hood	10
mother	5
door	5
pot	5
cake	5
butter	5
bobbin	4
bed	4
child	4

FIGURE 5.1 A word frequency analysis of the *Little Red Riding Hood* fable

How Does It Apply to Text Business Data Analysis?

We can use this technique in several ways. Say we surveyed what customers wanted in a product. Besides asking quantitative questions (such as "on a scale of 1 to 5…"), we also ask open-ended questions (such as "Is there anything else you want us to know…"). Doing a word frequency analysis of the text responses to the open-ended question and comparing it to the word frequency analysis of the product description tells us if we are meeting expectations. The more often the two-word frequency tables match, the more we are matching the customer's expectations.

As another example, consider a company that launched a campaign to make employees more aware of the new company mission. After some time and using an employee survey, we ask the open-ended question: "Can you tell us what you think the company mission statement is?" By doing a word frequency analysis of the mission statement and comparing it to the frequency analysis of the employee's responses, we can gauge how successful our awareness campaign has been.

Exercise 5.1 – Case Study Using Dataset A: Training Survey

Suppose you were just hired to teach a course on data analysis. You would want to know what your audience desires to know. You send each participant a simple three-question survey: (1) What do you want to get out of the class?; (2) How would you rate your Microsoft Excel skill level?; and (3) What is your official title? The last two questions can be analyzed using standard methods, being that the variables are categorical. The first question is free form text and difficult to categorize. We use word frequency analysis to discover what they want to learn. In subsequent chapters, we analyze the text responses by coding (Chapter 9) and visually (Chapter 8). In this chapter, we use the word frequency analysis to answer the following questions:

What are the most frequent words that signify the essence of what the trainees want to learn in this seminar?

How do the most frequent words on the course Website compare to the employee survey input?

Word Frequency Analysis Using Excel

1. Access the case files' repository and in the folder *Dataset A: Training Survey,* and open the file *Attendee PreSurvey Results in Data.csv* with Excel. Save it as *Attendee PreSurvey Results Data.xlxs.*

2. You will see the textual responses from 17 attendees in the second column. Our first step is to aggregate all these comments into one cell. Copy the column into another worksheet and label the tab as *Text of Responses*. Delete the first row that contains the variable name (which in this case is the question that was asked). You should have something that looks like what is shown in Figure 5.2.

	A	B	C	D	E	F	G
1	I'm looking to learn how to better present grants and budget data so that interpreting and tr:						
2	To better understand quantitative analysis and how to translate data into easily readable for						
3	Skills in Quantitative and Qualitative Data Analysis would enable me to make recommendat						
4	I am looking to gain tools and information to allow for proficient data analysis in the future						
5	I am interested in learning different approaches to organizing, summarizing and interpreting						
6	As an aspiring Budget Analyst, I want tools that I can use to organize, summarize and interpr						
7	I am seeking a refresher on data analysis tools within Microsoft Excel. I am interested in pivc						
8	I am hoping that the class will help me with data visualization. I would like to be able to pre						
9	I'm looking to get more creative/faster for reporting, applying, examining and understanding						
10	My center has gone through a realignment and I have been reassigned as an analyst. So, und						
11	I am looking for strategies to better present portfolio analysis data						
12	To improve my Data Analysis skills.						
13	I would like to learn what this course offers in terms of quantitative tools and methods for a						
14	What others do with respect to Data Analysis						
15	I would like to get more comfortable with data analysis in Excel and to learn new tricks. I wc						
16	I am looking to gain a better understanding of how to interpret and analyze data patterns an						
17	How to manipulate excel to analyze data quickly with the use of formulas and macros.						

FIGURE 5.2 The raw text responses as a column of data

3. Next, we aggregate the responses all into one cell. In cell B1, copy the data from cell A1. Starting in B2, we concatenate the data that is in the cell above with the data that is directly to the left with the following formula:
```
=CONCAT(B16, " ", A17)
```

4. Copy that formula to the bottom of column B. We should be at B17. The compiled responses are now in cell B17.

5. Copy the content of B17 into another worksheet and label it as *Bag of Words*. Use *Paste Special -> Values* when you paste the data into A1 in the new worksheet, or you will get an error in copying the formulas and not just the data's values.

6. Now we parse the text into a list of words, each in its cell. Copy the text in A1 to A3 (just to preserve our text intact before we further process it). Use the *Data -> Text to Columns* function on the text in A3, and you will see it being parsed into one word per column. Your text-to-column wizard should be set up as shown in Figure 5.3 to turn the text into a *Bag of Words* (it's the technical definition for text devoid of punctuation, just words). We removed all periods, commas, and most other punctuation marks.

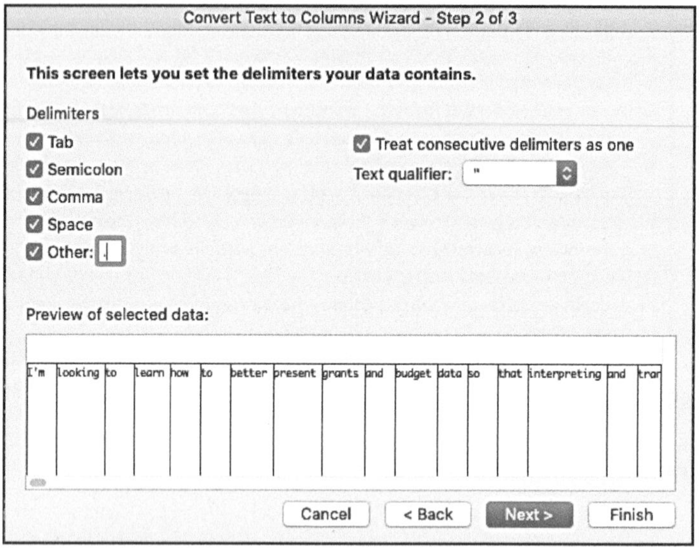

FIGURE 5.3 Use the conversion *Text to Column* wizard to yield a parsed set of words from our Bag-of-Words

7. Select the entire row containing the parsed words and paste it into another worksheet. Paste it as a column by transposing the paste, as shown in Figure 5.4. Label this new worksheet *Frequent Words*. Label the column *TEXT*.

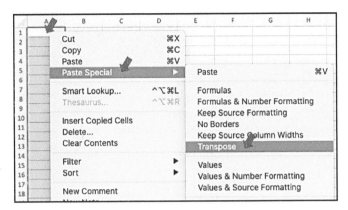

FIGURE 5.4 Creating a column of the words in the text by pasting and transposing

8. Counting common words, such as "a," "and," "it," and "to," is of no interest to us in this case. We want to enumerate the essential words that covey most of the meaning of what the trainees desire to learn. We remove these words by creating a label for each word in another column as to whether we want to count this word or not. We use a commonly accepted list of stop words to do this.

9. In the *Tools* file folder, under the *Stopwords* folder, find the file *StopWords.xlxs*. Open it in Excel and copy the A column. It contains all the stop words. In the future, it is to this file you will add any other words you want the analysis program or process to ignore.

10. Now insert the copied stop word column into our analysis worksheet. For convenience, insert it to the left of our text words. You should see two columns of words, as shown in Figure 5.5.

	A	B
1	STOP WORD	TEXT
2	a	I'm
3	about	looking
4	above	to
5	across	learn
6	after	how
7	again	to
8	against	better
9	all	present
10	almost	grants
11	alone	and
12	along	budget
13	already	data
14	also	so
15	although	that
16	always	interpreting

FIGURE 5.5 The *TEXT* column of attendee input with the *STOP WORD* list inserted to its left

11. We now use the Excel COUNTIF function twice. The first time is to generate the count of occurrences of each word within the column of text data:

```
=COUNTIF(B$2:B$662,B2)
```

12. The second instance of COUNTIF is used in another column labeled STOP to flag the common words to filter them out:

```
=COUNTIF($A$2:$A$430,B2)
```

13. Once the two columns are created, insert a pivot table with the selected range: $B$1:$D$662. You can insert the pivot table on the same worksheet, for example, at location F3. Figure 5.6 shows all the parameters to create the pivot table; use the filter to select words not on the stop word list, and sort by the most frequent words.

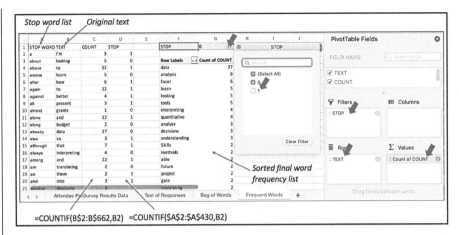

FIGURE 5.6 The resulting pivot table, its parameters, and the frequent word list sorted by frequency

14. We can repeat steps 1 through 13 to discover what in the description of the course attracted the attendees (the most frequent words) to compare whether their expectations will be met or changes are needed.

15. In the dataset *Data* repository, in the *Dataset A Training Survey* folder, find the course description text file *Data Analysis Fundamentals.docx*. First, we convert it into a text file using the techniques in Chapter 4. Save it as *Data Analysis Fundamentals.txt*.

16. Open the text file in a text editor and copy it into a fresh spreadsheet. Follow the procedure outlined above to

- Paste the text into cell A1.

- Parse it into a set of words

- Copy the data into a column by transposing.

- Add the stop words column and create the COUNT and STOP columns using the COUNTIF function, as explained in steps 11 and 12.

- Create a pivot table and create a sorted most frequent word list.

17. We are now ready to compare the two frequent word lists to see if what the attendees are asking matches the course description. Figure 5.7 shows the top 24 most frequent words from both lists. There are 15 direct matches, and we can conclude that they appear well matched.

Attendee Survey Responses		Course Description	
Row Labels	Count of COUNT	Row Labels	Count of COUNT
data	27	Data	39
analysis	9	business	14
Excel	6	Analysis	11
learn	5	questions	10
looking	5	tools	8
tools	5	decisions	6
interpreting	4	value	6
quantitative	4	using	5
analyze	3	organization	4
decisions	3	analyzing	4
understanding	3	Answer	4
Skills	2	interpreting	4
methods	2	goes	4
able	2	information	3
future	2	methods	3
project	2	apply	3
gain	2	basic	3
translating	2	analyze	3
understand	2	address	3
Analyst	2	insights	3
hoping	2	Create	3
Overall	2	Issues	3
Information	2	analytical	3
analyzing	2	quantitative	3

FIGURE 5.7 Word frequency lists for attendee survey responses and the course description to show they are well matched

Word Frequency Analysis Using SAS JMP

TSAS JMP has a built-in stop word list and performs advanced techniques (we will encounter one such method in Chapter 12, text similarity scoring). For now, we perform a simple word frequency analysis.

1. Access the repository of *Case Data* files and in the folder *Dataset A: Training Survey,* and open the file *Attendee PreSurvey Results Data.csv* with JMP.

2. Click *Analyze*, select *Text Explorer*. Drag the attendee's comments variable into the *Text Column* box and press *OK.* Figure 5.8 shows the proper choices.

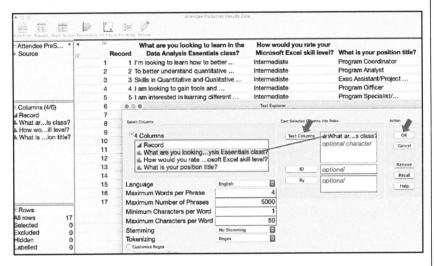

FIGURE 5.8 Setting up the term frequency analysis

3. The resulting term frequency analysis is shown in Figure 5.9. Note that you get the single word frequencies and the most frequent phrases, which is a bonus.

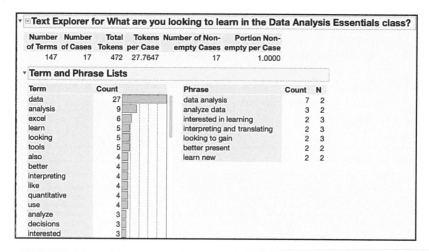

FIGURE 5.9 Word frequency results in JMP for attendee survey responses

4. Now we compute the word frequencies for the course description's text and see how well they match.

5. In the *Case Data* repository, in the *Dataset A: Training Survey* folder, find the course description text file *Data Analysis Fundamentals.docx*. First, we convert it into a text file using the techniques in Chapter 3. Save it as *Data Analysis Fundamentals.txt*.

6. Open the text file in a text editor and copy it to your computer.

7. Open a new JMP analysis table. Paste the course description into the first cell in the first column. Label the column *Course Description*.

8. Click *Analyze*, select *Text Explorer*. Drag the course description into the *Text Column* box and press *OK*. Figure 5.10 shows the resulting word frequencies for the course description. Compare this list to the attendees' requests in Figure 5.8.

Text Explorer for Course Description

Number of Terms	Number of Cases	Total Tokens	Tokens per Case	Number of Non-empty Cases	Portion Non-empty per Case
183	2	663	331.5	1	0.5000

Term and Phrase Lists

Term	Count		Phrase	Count	N
data	39		data analysis	8	2
business	14		business questions	6	2
analysis	11		value of using data	3	4
questions	10		value of using	3	3
tools	8		address business	3	2
decisions	6		business decisions	3	2
value	6		every day	3	2
right	5		using data	3	2
using	5		ability to solve problems	2	4
analyzing	4		address business issues explain	2	4
answer	4		analysis to explore proven	2	4
goes	4		analyzing interpreting and utilizing	2	4
interpreting	4		basic familiarity with ms	2	4
make	4		beyond the qualitative side	2	4
organization	4		chance to add value	2	4
address	3		conflicting and confusing designed	2	4
analytical	3		constant pressure to make	2	4
analyze	3		control flood of data	2	4

FIGURE 5.10 Word frequency result in JMP for the course description

Word Frequency Analysis Using Voyant

1. Access the *Case Data* files' repository and in the folder *Dataset A: Training Survey*, and open the file *Attendee PreSurvey Results Data.csv* with Excel.

2. Copy the contents of the attendee's comments on what they want to see in the course (cells B2-B18) to your computer.

3. Open the Voyant tool, either using the web-based version (*https://voyant-tools.org/*) or running the Voyant server, as explained in Chapter 17.

4. Paste the attendees' comments into the data entry box in Voyant and press *Reveal*.

5. In the upper left-hand corner panel, click on *Terms* to switch from the word cloud mode to the table mode.

6. The resulting word frequency list sorted by most frequent words should look something like that in Figure 5.11.

			Term	Count	Trend
⊕	☐	1	data	27	
⊕	☐	2	analysis	9	
⊕	☐	3	excel	6	
⊕	☐	4	learn	5	
⊕	☐	5	looking	5	
⊕	☐	6	tools	5	
⊕	☐	7	better	4	
⊕	☐	8	interpreting	4	
⊕	☐	9	like	4	
⊕	☐	10	quantitative	4	
⊕	☐	11	use	4	

Cirrus · *Terms* · *Links* · ?

FIGURE 5.11 Word frequency result in Voyant for attendees' survey responses

7. We can do the same thing for the course description and compare the two results.

8. In the *Case Data* repository, in the *Dataset A Training Survey* folder, find the course description text file *Data Analysis Fundamentals.docx*. First, we convert it into a text file using the techniques in Chapter 3. Save it as *Data Analysis Fundamentals.txt*.

9. Open the text file in a text editor and copy it to your computer.

10. Open Voyant and paste it into the data entry box, or upload the file. Then click *Reveal*.

11. Switch the word cloud into a table. Figure 5.12 shows the word frequency for the course description, which can be compared to the attendees' list in Figure 5.11.

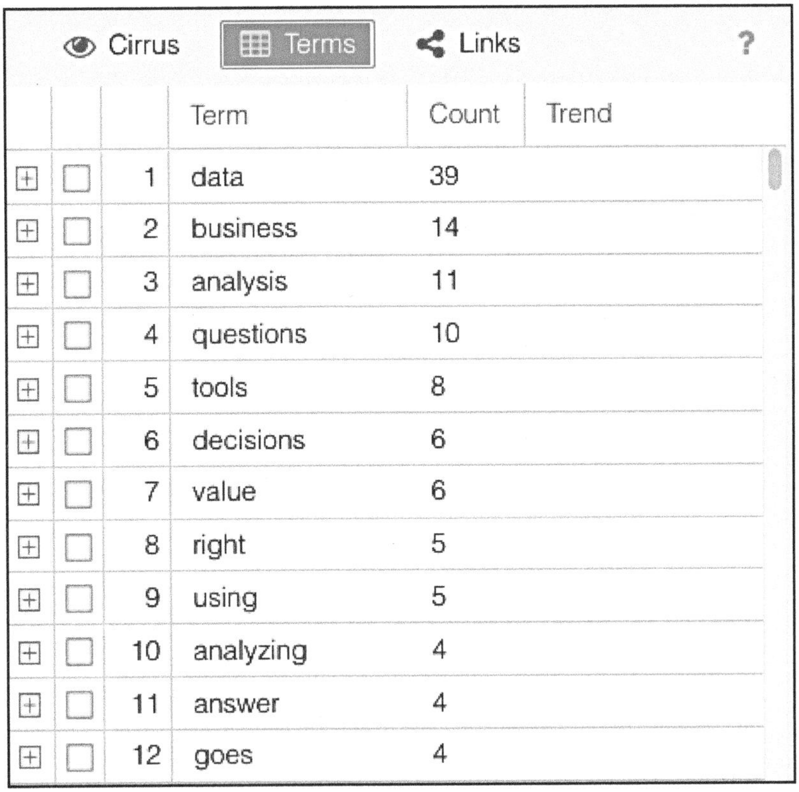
Cirrus
Terms
Links
?

	Term	Count	Trend
1	data	39	
2	business	14	
3	analysis	11	
4	questions	10	
5	tools	8	
6	decisions	6	
7	value	6	
8	right	5	
9	using	5	
10	analyzing	4	
11	answer	4	
12	goes	4	

FIGURE 5.12 Word frequency result in Voyant for the course description

Word Frequency Analysis Using R

1. In the *Case Data* file folder under *Dataset A: Training Survey*, copy and rename the *Attendee PreSurvey Result data.csv* as *casea.csv*.

2. Install the packages we need using Repository(CRAN):
```
dplyr, tidytext
```

3. Import the library and read the data:
```
> library(dplyr)
> library(tidytext)

> casea <- read.csv(file.path("casea.csv"),
  stringsAsFactors = F)
```

4. Tokenize the contents of the dataset and remove the stop words:
```
> tidy_a <- casea %>%
        unnest_tokens(word, text) %>%
        anti_join(stop_words)
```

5. Get the results of the word frequency analysis (shown in Figure 5.13):
```
> tidy_a %>%
  count(word, sort = TRUE)
```

word <chr>	n <int>
data	27
analysis	9
excel	6
learn	5
tools	5
interpreting	4
quantitative	4
analyze	3
decisions	3
understanding	3
1–10 of 109 rows	

FIGURE 5.13 Word frequency data frame of the training survey text field

Exercise 5.2 - Case Study Using Dataset D: Job Descriptions

If you had several jobs you were applying for, you might want to find out what skills the employers are looking for. We can do a word frequency analysis of the text of the job postings. In subsequent chapters, we will do a keyword analysis of your resume against the job descriptions as an additional analysis. For now, we just want to extract the most frequent words and create a sorted word frequency list.

This exercise works with generic job descriptions that we obtained from the US Bureau of Labor Statistics. They have a detailed occupation description file that we can use in place of job descriptions. We look at some related occupational descriptions (software developers, database administrators, and architects). We then combine the descriptions appearing in the occupations as one text file to extract the most frequent words there.

Let's use word frequency analysis to answer the following question:

What are the most frequent words in the descriptions of the related occupations?

1. Access the repository of case files, and in the folder *Dataset D: Job Description*, open file *O*NET Jobs.csv* in Excel. Create a *Selected Jobs.xlxs* spreadsheet and transfer a copy of the *Software Developers, Applications; Software Developers, Systems Software; Database Administrators; Database Architects;* and *Data Warehousing Specialists* occupational descriptions (see Figure 5.14) to this new spreadsheet.

A	B	C	D
Job	Description		
Software Developers, Applications	Software Developers, Applicatic		
Software Developers, Systems Software	Software Developers, Systems S		
Database Administrators	Database Administrators Admin		
Database Architects	Database Architects Design stra		
Data Warehousing Specialists	Data Warehousing Specialists D		

FIGURE 5.14 *Selected Jobs* worksheet

2. Create a new column called *job&description*. Using the CONCATENATE formula in Excel, create a combination of the job title (column A) and the job description (column B) and enter it in column C. Label the column *job&description*. Save the file.

Word Frequency Analysis using Excel

Using the techniques shown in Exercise 5.1, take the following steps:

1. Open the *Selected Jobs.xlxs* spreadsheet in Excel.

2. Concatenate all the *job&description* text data into one cell.

3. Paste the contents of the concatenated text into a separate worksheet.

4. Separate all the words into individual cells by using the *Data -> Text to Columns* function. Copy the entire row.

5. In a separate worksheet, paste the row as a column by transposing. Label the column *TEXT*.

6. Paste the stop words in a column to the left of the *TEXT* column just created.

7. Using COUNTIF formulas, create a *COUNT* and *STOP* columns as in Exercise 5.1.

8. Create a pivot table of the *TEXT*, *COUNT*, and *STOP* columns. Select *TEXT* for rows, *STOP* for the filter, and *COUNT* for results.

9. Filter out the stop words by selecting "0" as the only *STOP* value.

10. Sort the results by count of *COUNT* from largest to smallest.

11. Figure 5.15 shows the word frequency table for the five occupations and the pivot table's analysis parameters.

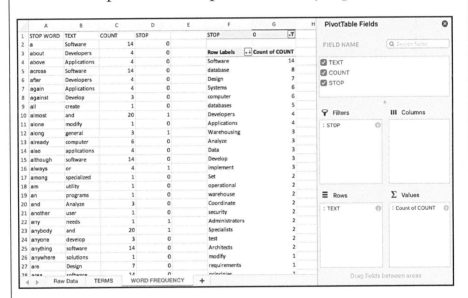

FIGURE 5.15 Selected jobs' word frequency in Excel

Word Frequency Analysis Using SAS JMP

1. Import the *Selected Jobs.xlxs* spreadsheet to JMP.

2. Click *Analyze*, select *Text Explorer*. Drag *job&description* to *Text Columns* and select *OK*.

3. Figure 5.16 shows the resulting selected job word frequency.

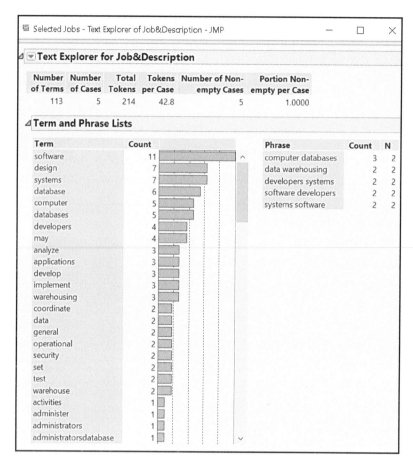

FIGURE 5.16 Selected jobs' word frequency in JMP

Word Frequency Analysis Using Voyant

1. Open the *Selected Jobs.xlxs* file with Excel.

2. Copy the contents of the column *job&description* (cells C2-C6) to your computer.

3. Open the Voyant tool either using the Web-based version (*https://voyant-tools.org/*) or running the Voyant server, as explained in Chapter 17.

4. Paste the attendees' saved data in the data entry box in Voyant and press *Reveal*.

5. In the upper left-hand corner panel, click on *Terms* to switch from the word cloud mode to the table mode.

6. The resulting word frequency list sorted by most frequent words should look something like that in Figure 5.17.

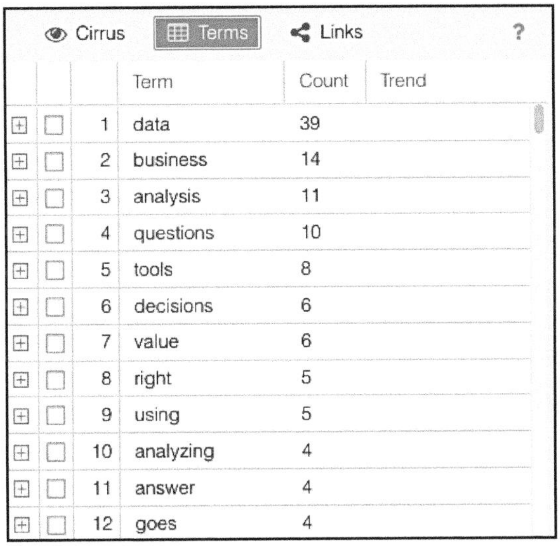

			Term	Count	Trend
⊞	☐	1	data	39	
⊞	☐	2	business	14	
⊞	☐	3	analysis	11	
⊞	☐	4	questions	10	
⊞	☐	5	tools	8	
⊞	☐	6	decisions	6	
⊞	☐	7	value	6	
⊞	☐	8	right	5	
⊞	☐	9	using	5	
⊞	☐	10	analyzing	4	
⊞	☐	11	answer	4	
⊞	☐	12	goes	4	

Cirrus / **Terms** / **Links**

FIGURE 5.17 Word frequency result in Voyant for the software and database jobs descriptions

Word Frequency Analysis Using R

1. In the *Case Data* file folder under *Dataset D: Job Descriptions*, copy and rename the copy of *O*NET JOBS.csv* as *cased.csv*.

2. Install the packages we need using Repository(CRAN):

```
dplyr, tidytext, ggplot2
```

3. Import the library and read the data:

```
> library(dplyr)
> library(tidytext)

> cased <- read.csv(file.path("cased.csv"),
  stringsAsFactors = F)
```

4. Select the jobs we are interested in:

```
> target_d <- cased %>% filter_at(vars(job), any_
vars(. %in% c('Software Developers, Applications',
        'Software Developers, Systems Software',
        'Database Administrators',
        'Database Architects',
        'Data Warehousing Specialists')))
# concatenate the job title and job description

> target_d <- target_d %>%
    unite(txt, job, description, sep =" ", remove
    = FALSE)
```

5. Tokenize the contents of the dataset and remove the stop words:

```
> tidy_d <- target_d %>%
    unnest_tokens(word, txt) %>%
    anti_join(stop_words)
```

6. Get the results of the word frequency analysis (shown in Figure 5.18):

```
> tidy_d %>%
    count(word, sort = TRUE)
```

word <chr>	n <int>
software	14
database	8
design	7
systems	7
computer	6
databases	5
applications	4
developers	4
analyze	3
data	3

1–10 of 97 rows

FIGURE 5.18 Word frequency data frame of the selected job descriptions

Exercise 5.3 - Case Study Using Dataset C: Product Reviews

You work for a product manufacturer and have received a file with customer feedback on your product. You want to learn what your customers are saying about the product and decide to do a word frequency analysis on the text of their comments.

Let's use the word frequency analysis to answer the following question:

What are the most frequent words that best represent what customers are saying about the product?

Word Frequency Analysis Using Excel

1. Access the repository of *Case Data* files, and in the folder *Dataset C: Product Reviews*, open the file *Product Reviews. xlsx* in Excel. Save the file as *Product Review Solutions.xlsx.*

2. For the brand Windex, select all the data in the *reviews.text* column.

3. In the same file, select a new worksheet. Paste the data.

4. In another column, concatenate all the text to create a Bag of Words. In this case, you will run into a problem: any given Excel cell has a maximum limit of 32,750 characters. By row 154, you run out of room, and you get the error message #VALUE! for subsequent rows. There is a solution: You need to make three passes.

5. At row 155, copy the value directly from the adjacent cell, not using the formula. The formula you entered previously will continue to work until row 311. Repeat this process. You now have all the words in three cells: B154, B310, and the last cell, B348.

6. Copy the content of these three cells into a new worksheet into the first three rows.

7. Separate all the words into individual cells by using the *Data -> Text to Columns* function. Do this for all three rows.

8. In a separate worksheet, paste the first row of data from the previous stop. Paste it as a column by transposing. Label the column *TEXT*.

9. Repeat for the other two rows of parsed words, but paste each at the bottom of the column as you transfer them in. You should end up with a column of 13,594 rows of individual words.

10. Paste the stop words in a column to the left of the *TEXT* column just created.

11. Using *COUNTIF* formulas, create a *COUNT* and *STOP* columns as in Exercise 5.1.

12. Create a pivot table of the *TEXT*, *COUNT*, and *STOP* columns. Select *TEXT* for rows, *STOP* for *Filter*, and *COUNT* for *Values*. Make sure to Count, not Sum the *COUNT* variable.

13. Filter out the stop words by selecting "0" as the only *STOP* value.

14. Sort the results by count of *COUNT* from largest to smallest.

15. Figure 5.19 shows the word frequency table for the five occupations, together with the analysis parameters for the pivot table.

STOP	0	⊽
Row Labels ⊽↓	**Count of COUNT**	
Windex	296	
review	147	
promotion	145	
collected	145	
product	139	
windows	101	
glass	96	
clean	94	
streaks	69	
cleaning	69	
mirrors	54	
cleaner	53	
bottle	52	
using	48	
surfaces	45	
leaves	42	
free	41	
cleans	40	
It's	39	
streak	37	
window	37	
love	36	

FIGURE 5.19 Word frequency analysis in Excel for the Windex customer comments

Word Frequency Analysis Using SAS JMP

1. Access the repository of *Case Data* files, and in the folder *Dataset C: Product Reviews*, open the file *Product Reviews. csv* with JMP.

2. Use the *Data Filter* to select only the rows where *brand = Windex*.

3. Click *Analyze*, select *Text Explorer*. Drag the reviews.text variable into the *Text Column* box and press *OK*. Figure 5.20 shows the proper choices.

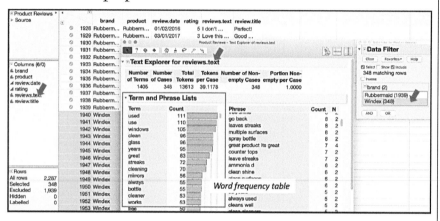

FIGURE 5.20 Setting up the term frequency analysis and the results in SAS JMP

Word Frequency Analysis Using Voyant

1. Access the repository of case files, and in the folder *Dataset C: Product Reviews*, open the file *Product Reviews.csv* with Excel.

2. Copy the contents of the column *reviews.text* (cells E1941-E2288) to your computer.

3. Open the Voyant tool either by using the Web-based version (*https://voyant-tools.org/*) or running the Voyant server, as explained in Chapter 17.

4. Paste the attendees' saved data into the data entry box in Voyant and press *Reveal*.

5. In the upper left-hand corner panel, click on *Terms* to switch from the word cloud mode to the table mode.

6. The resulting word frequency list sorted by most frequent words should look something like that in Figure 5.21.

			Term	Count	Trend
⊞	☐	1	windex	307	
⊞	☐	2	product	149	
⊞	☐	3	review	147	
⊞	☐	4	collected	145	
⊞	☐	5	promotion	145	
⊞	☐	6	used	111	
⊞	☐	7	use	110	
⊞	☐	8	windows	105	
⊞	☐	9	clean	96	
⊞	☐	10	glass	96	
⊞	☐	11	years	94	
⊞	☐	12	great	82	
⊞	☐	13	streaks	71	
⊞	☐	14	cleaning	69	
⊞	☐	15	mirrors	56	

Cirrus | Terms | Links | ?

FIGURE 5.21 Word frequency result using Voyant for the Windex customer reviews

Word Frequency Analysis Using R

1. In the *Case Data* file folder under *Dataset C: Product Reviews*, copy and rename the *Product Reviews.csv* as *casec.csv*.

2. Install the packages we need using Repository (CRAN):
```
dplyr, tidytext
```

3. Import the library and read the data:

```
> library(dplyr)
> library(tidytext)

> casec <- read.csv(file.path("casec.csv"),
stringsAsFactors = F)

# concatenate reviews text and reviews title
> casec <- casec %>%
    unite(review_combined, reviews.text, review.
    title, sep =" ", remove = FALSE)
```

4. Tokenize the contents of the dataset and remove the stop word:

```
> tidy_c <- casec %>%
      unnest_tokens(word, text) %>%
      anti_join(stop_words)
```

5. Get the results of the word frequency analysis (shown in Figure 5.22):

```
> tidy_c %>%
    count(word, sort = TRUE)
```

word <chr>	n <int>
mop	3103
spray	1201
product	990
love	935
bottle	880
bought	671
cleaning	646
reveal	640
trigger	582
handle	565
1-10 of 11 rows	

FIGURE 5.22 Word frequency data frame of the product reviews

Additional Exercise 5.4 - Case Study Using Dataset B: Consumer Complaints

We work for a major bank. They were able to acquire a file with complaints made to a government regulatory agency. As a data analyst, you have been assigned the task of summarizing the complaints. You decide to start your analysis by doing a word frequency analysis of the text of their complaints. Use the techniques for word frequency analysis to answer the following question:

What are the most frequent words in the bank complaints for Bank of America?

Use the file *BankComplaints.csv* found in the *Case Data* repository under the *Dataset B: Consumer Complaints* directory. Find the word frequency table using JMP, Voyant, or the R tools.

## CHAPTER 6

KEYWORD ANALYSIS

Keyword analysis is also known as keyword extraction or keyword detection. *Keyword analysis* is a text analysis technique that extracts the most frequent and most important words and expressions from text data. It helps summarize the content of texts and recognize the main topics discussed. It is most powerfully used to optimize how search engines find and index webpages from your company's website. It is an integral part of Search Engine Optimization (SEO).

With keyword analysis, you can find keywords from all types of text data: documents, business reports, social media postings, online reviews, and news reports. Suppose you want to analyze your product's many online reviews on your favorite e-commerce site, like Amazon. Keyword extraction helps you sift through all the text data comprising the reviews and obtain the most important and frequent words that best describe the reviews very quickly. Then you can see what your customers are mentioning most often, saving you the work of examining all the reviews manually.

We can use the techniques we studied in Chapter 5 to compute the word frequencies in a document to find keywords. It is just a matter of determining how many of the most frequent words are deemed to be enough to fully characterize a document by its keywords. That decision is made by the analyst. The top five? The top 10? The top 25? You determine that by inspection.

You can start with keywords and look for their occurrence in a target document. Let's say you want to know what percentage of your customers are price sensitive. Looking at social media postings or product feedback data, you can do a keyword search across all postings and determine how frequent "price" as a keyword is.

Once you compute the keywords (the top most frequently used words), you can compare two documents. Look for the frequency of occurrence in a target document of the keywords extracted from a source document. We can make it the basis for document comparison, as well. This technique has many uses in the business world. We explore a few such uses through the exercises in this chapter.

The Excel techniques we present here are based on single word searches. Other tools we use, JMP, Voyant, and even R, can also analyze two- or three-word keyword phrases, which can also be very useful. If Excel is your tool of choice and you don't venture further, there are relatively inexpensive add-ons to Excel that do word frequency analysis, including two- and three-word sequences.

Exercise 6.1 – Case Study Using Dataset D: Resume and Job Description

In this exercise, we try to match a resume to a set of job descriptions. Suppose you are looking for work and select a small number of jobs that seem interesting. Can you narrow the search and prioritize the assignments using keyword analysis? Essentially, you want to answer the question

Which jobs am I interested in applying to match my resume most closely?

We extract the most frequent words from a resume and use the most appropriate ones for a keyword search through the list of jobs. We use a generic engineer's resume and select the definitions of a few software development occupations from the O*NET database of occupations in place of real jobs. We perform a word frequency analysis of the resume to get the list of the most frequent words (using techniques in Chapter 5). We also do a word frequency analysis of the selected occupations and call these the keywords to be used against the resume. Then we use COUNTIF to see how many of these keywords appear in the resume for each occupation to rank the frequency of appearance of the keywords in the resume.

Keyword Analysis in Excel

1. Access the repository of case files and in the folder *Dataset D: Occupation Description* open file *O*NET JOBS Plus Resume. csv* in Excel.

2. Extract the occupation description and enter it into another spreadsheet and label it *Selected Occupations* for the following occupations:

   - Software Developers, Applications

   - Software Developers, Systems Software

   - Database Administrators

   - Database Architects

   - Data Warehousing Specialists

3. Copy the first row of the occupation file (the resume row) and paste it after the *Selected Occupations* file's last data row.

4. Using the techniques from Chapter 5, perform a word frequency analysis for each selected occupation and the resume. Make sure to use the stop word list. You should generate the same results as in Exercise 5.4 (shown in Figure 6.1).

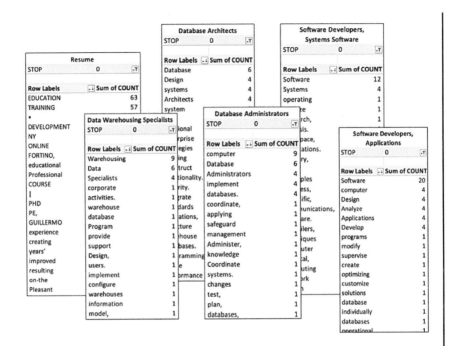

FIGURE 6.1 The term frequencies for the occupations and the resume

5. After saving the resulting term frequency tables, scrape each term frequency table's first column (list of terms) and paste them into the opened spreadsheet in separate columns; label each column with the occupation name.

6. Once the Excel spreadsheet is populated with the resume terms and the keywords terms from each occupation, use the Excel COUNTIF function to find all the occupation keyword occurrences in the resume.

7. Add all the occurrences by occupation to find the occupation with the highest number of hits against the resume. Figure 6.2 shows the resulting computations. It appears that the resume is more similar to the *Systems Development* jobs than the *Database* jobs.

Resume	Database Administrators		Database Architects		Data Warehousing Specialists		Software Developers, Applications		Software Developers, Systems Software	
EDUCATION		5		3		3		5		9
TRAINING	computer	1	Database	0	Warehousing	0	Software	0	Software	0
.	Database	0	Design	0	Data	1	computer	1	Systems	1
DEVELOPMENT	Administrators	0	systems	1	Specialists	0	Design	0	operating	0
NY	implement	0	Architects	0	corporate	0	Analyze	0	analyze	0
ONLINE	databases	0	system	0	activities	0	Applications	0	Research	0
FORTINO,	coordinate	0	set	0	warehouse	0	Develop	1	analysis	1
educational	applying	0	relational	0	database	0	programs	1	aerospace	0
Professional	safeguard	0	enterprise	0	Program	0	modify	1	applications	0
COURSE	management	1	strategies	0	provide	0	supervise	0	military	0
I	Administer	0	existing	0	support	0	create	0	Apply	0
PHD	knowledge	1	construct	0	Design	0	optimizing	0	principles	0
PE,	Coordinate	0	functionality	0	users	0	customize	0	business	1
GUILLERMO	systems	1	security	1	implement	1	solutions	0	scientific	0
experience	changes	0	Integrate	0	configure	0	database	0	communications	1
creating	test	0	standards	0	warehouses	0	individually	0	software	0
years'	plan	0	operations	0	information	1	databases	1	compilers	0
improved	databases	0	structure	0	model	0	operational	0	techniques	1
resulting	measures	0	warehouse	0			client	0	computer	1
on-the	security	1	databases	1			programmers	0	medical	0
Pleasant			programming	0			team	0	computing	0
vastly			refine	0			application	1	network	0
Mill			performance	1			user	0	design	0

FIGURE 6.2 Completed comparison analysis to determine which job had the highest keyword hits against the resume's most frequent terms (partial view)

Keyword Analysis in JMP

1. Access the repository of case files and in the folder *Dataset D: Occupation Description* open file *O*NET JOBS Plus Resume. csv* in JMP.

2. Using the JMP *Data Filter* function, select only AFORTINO from the *Job* column.

3. Using the *Text Explorer* function under the *Analyze* function, drag the *description* into the *Text Columns* box. Click OK (see Figure 6.3.)

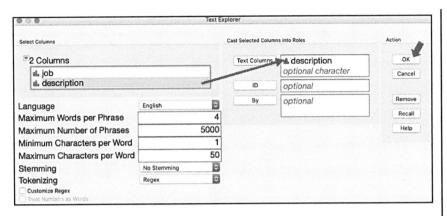

FIGURE 6.3 Finding the term frequency for the resume

4. Save the *Term Table* (pull down the red triangle in the upper left-hand corner of the term table). Figure 6.4 shows the resulting term frequency analysis.

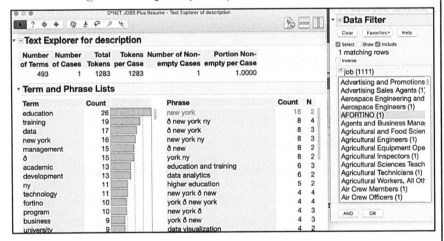

FIGURE 6.4 The term frequency table for the resume

5. Scrape the first column and paste it into a new Excel spreadsheet. Label the column *Resume*.

6. Repeat steps 3, 4, and 5 for *Software Developers, Application; Software Developers, Systems; Database Administrators; Database Architects;* and *Data Warehousing Specialists.*

7. The resulting term frequency tables should look something like Figure 6.5. These are the keywords we will look for in our resume.

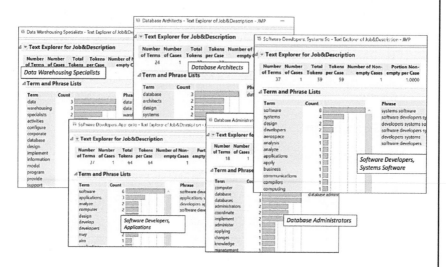

FIGURE 6.5 The term frequencies for the occupations

8. After saving the resulting term tables, scrape each term frequency table's first column (list of terms) and paste them into the opened spreadsheet in separate columns; label each column with the occupation name.

9. Once the Excel spreadsheet is populated with the resume terms and the keywords terms from each occupation, use the Excel COUNTIF function to find all the occupation keyword occurrences in the resume.

10. Add all the occurrences by occupation to find the occupation with the highest number of hits against the resume. Figure 6.6 shows the resulting computations. It appears that the resume is more similar to the two *Database* jobs than to the others, but not by much.

Resume	Database Administrators		Database Architects		Data Warehousing Specialists		Software Developers, Applications		Software Developers, Systems Software	
education		5		5		3		4		3
training	computer	1	database	0	data	1	client	0	embedded	0
data	databases	0	design	0	warehousing	0	coordinating	0	engineering	1
new york	coordinate	0	systems	1	activities	0	create	0	formulate	0
managemen	database	0	architects	0	configure	0	customize	0	general	0
ð	implement	0	construct	0	corporate	0	database	0	industrial	0
academic	administer	0	databases	0	database	0	databases	0	level	0
developmen	administrators	0	enterprise	0	design	0	developers	0	mathematical	0
ny	applying	0	existing	0	implement	0	development	1	may	0
technology	changes	0	functionality	0	information	1	efficiency	0	medical	0
fortino	knowledge	1	integrate	0	model	0	general	0	military	0
program	management	1	large	0	program	0	individually	1	network	0
business	may	0	new	1	provide	0	modify	0	operating	0
university	measures	0	operations	0	specialists	0	needs	0	operational	1
analytics	plan	0	performance	1	support	0	operational	0	principles	0
courses	safeguard	0	programming	0	users	0	optimizing	0	requirements	0
faculty	security	1	refine	0	warehouse	0	programmers	0	research	0
graduate	systems	1	relational	0	warehouses	0	programs	0	scientific	0
programs	test	0	security	1			solutions	0	set	0
developed			set	0			specialized	0	specifications	0
engineering			standards	0			supervise	0	techniques	1
innovation			strategies	1			team	0	test	0
associate			structure	0			use	0	computer science	1
college			system	0			user	0		
visualization			warehouse	0			utility	0		
course							within	1		
curriculum							working	0		

FIGURE 6.6 Completed comparison analysis to determine which job had the highest keyword hits against the resume's most frequent terms (partial view)

Keyword Analysis in Voyant

1. Access the repository of case files and in the folder *Dataset D: Occupation Description* open file *O*NET JOBS Plus Resume. csv* in Excel.

2. Open the Voyant tool, either using the Web-based version *(https://voyant-tools.org/)* or running the Voyant server, as explained in Chapter 15.

3. From the *O*NET JOBS Plus Resume.csv* file, scrape the resume from the first row in the *description* cell.

4. Paste the text of the resume into the Voyant data entry screen and press *Reveal*. You will see the familiar analysis screen.

5. In the upper left-hand panel, select *Table* instead of *Cirrus* (word cloud). This gives the word frequencies as a table rather than as a picture, as shown in Figure 6.7.

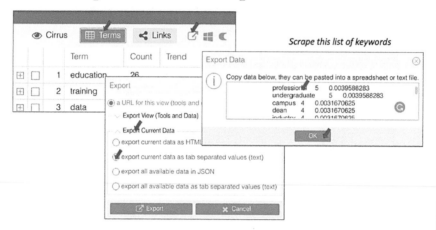

FIGURE 6.7 Finding the term frequency for the resume using Voyant

6. Scrape the keywords and paste the data into a new Excel spreadsheet. Label the column *Resume*.

7. Repeat steps 3, 4, and 5 for *Software Developers, Application; Software Developers, Systems; Database Administrators; Database Architects; and Data Warehousing Specialists.*

8. After saving the resulting frequent term tables, scrape each term frequency and paste them into the opened spreadsheet in separate columns; label each column with the occupation name.

9. Once the Excel spreadsheet is populated with the resume terms and the keywords terms from each occupation, use the Excel COUNTIF function to find all the occupation keyword occurrences in the resume.

10. Add all the occurrences by occupation to find the occupation with the highest number of hits against the resume. Figure 6.8 shows the resulting computations. It appears that the resume is more similar to the two *System Development* jobs than to the others, but not by much.

Resume	Database Administrators		Database Architects		Data Warehousing Specialists		Software Developers, Applications		Software Developers, Systems Software	
education		5		4		5		7		7
training	computer	1	database	0	computer	1	software	0	software	0
data	databases	0	design	0	databases	0	analyze	0	systems	1
new	coordinate	0	systems	1	coordinate	0	applications	0	design	0
york	database	0	architects	0	database	0	computer	1	aerospace	0
managemen	implement	0	construct	0	implement	0	design	0	analysis	1
academic	administer	0	databases	0	administer	0	develop	1	analyze	0
developmen	administrators	0	enterprise	0	administrators	0	aim	0	applications	0
ny	applying	0	existing	0	applying	0	application	1	apply	0
technology	changes	0	functionality	0	changes	0	area	1	business	1
fortino	knowledge	1	integrate	0	knowledge	1	client	0	communications	1
program	management	1	large	0	management	1	coordinating	0	compilers	0
business	measures	0	new	1	measures	0	create	0	computer	1
university	plan	0	operations	0	plan	0	customize	0	computing	0
analytics	safeguard	0	performance	1	safeguard	0	database	0	develop	1
courses	security	1	programming	0	security	1	databases	0	developers	0
faculty	systems	1	refine	0	systems	1	developers	0	distribution	0
graduate	test	0	relational	0	test	0	development	1	embedded	0

FIGURE 6.8 Completed comparison analysis to determine which job had the highest keyword hits against the resume (partial view)

Keyword Analysis in R

1. In the *Case Data* file folder under *Dataset D: Job Descriptions*, copy *O*NET JOBS.csv* and name the copy *cased.csv*.

2. Install the packages we need using Repository(CRAN):

```
dplyr, tidytext, textstem, readr
```

3. Import the library and read the case data (Figure 6.1 shows the example resume data):

```
> library(dplyr)
> library(tidytext)
> library(textstem)
> library(readr)
> cased <- read.csv(file.path("cased.csv"),
stringsAsFactors = F)
> resume <- read_file("fortino_resume.txt")
# make resume content a dataframe
> resume_df <- tibble(text= resume)
> resume_df
```

	text
1	ANDRÉS GUILLERMO FORTINO, PE, PHD 75 Grist Mill L...

FIGURE 6.9 Data frame object of resume_df

4. Select the jobs (occupations) we are interested in:

```
> target_d <- cased %>% filter_at(vars(job), any_
vars(. %in% c('Software Developers, Applications',
  'Software Developers, Systems Software',
  'Database Administrators',
  'Database Architects',
  'Data Warehousing Specialists')))
# concatenate the job title and job description
> target_d <- target_d %>%
    unite(txt, job, description, sep =" ",
    remove = FALSE)
```

	txt	job	description
1	Software Developers, Applications Software Developer...	Software Developers, Applications	Software Developers, Applications Develop, create, an...
2	Software Developers, Systems Software Software Deve...	Software Developers, Systems Software	Software Developers, Systems Software Research, des...
3	Database Administrators Database Administrators Ad...	Database Administrators	Database Administrators Administer, test, and imple...
4	Database Architects Database Architects Design strat...	Database Architects	Database Architects Design strategies for enterprise d...
5	Data Warehousing Specialists Data Warehousing Speci...	Data Warehousing Specialists	Data Warehousing Specialists Design, model, or imple...

FIGURE 6.10 Data frame object of *target_d*

5. Add additional stop words for the resume content, if needed (optional):

```
> my_stop_words <- tibble(
  word = c("ny","york","fortino"),lexicon =
  "resume")
> all_stop_words <- stop_words %>%
    bind_rows(my_stop_words)
```

6. Tokenize the contents of the dataset, lemmatize the words, and remove the stop words:

```
# for 'Software Developers, Applications'
> t1 <- target_d[1,] %>%
    unnest_tokens(word, txt) %>%
    mutate(word = lemmatize_words
    (word)) %>%
    anti_join(stop_words)

# for 'Software Developers, Systems Software'
> t2 <- target_d[2,] %>%
    unnest_tokens(word, txt) %>%
    mutate(word = lemmatize_words
    (word)) %>%
    anti_join(stop_words)

# for 'Database Administrators'
> t3 <- target_d[3,] %>%
    unnest_tokens(word, txt) %>%
    mutate(word = lemmatize_words
    (word)) %>%
    anti_join(stop_words)
```

```r
# for 'Database Architects'
> t4 <- target_d[4,] %>%
    unnest_tokens(word, txt) %>%
    mutate(word = lemmatize_words
    (word)) %>%
    anti_join(stop_words)

# for 'Data Warehousing Specialists'
> t5 <- target_d[5,] %>%
    unnest_tokens(word, txt) %>%
    mutate(word = lemmatize_words
    (word)) %>%
    anti_join(stop_words)

> tidy_resume <- resume_df %>%
    unnest_tokens(word, text) %>%
    mutate(word = lemmatize_words
    (word)) %>%
    anti_join(all_stop_words)
```

7. Find the top 10 most frequently used keywords in the resume:

```r
> kwtop10 <- tidy_resume %>%
    count(word, sort = TRUE) %>%
    filter(n>3) %>%
    slice(1:10)

> kwtop10["word"]
```

	word	n
1	education	26
2	train	20
3	program	18
4	datum	17
5	management	15
6	academic	13
7	development	13
8	develop	11
9	technology	11
10	business	9

FIGURE 6.11 Top 10 keywords in the resume and number counts

8. We now use these frequent words in the resume as keywords for our analysis. Using these top ten words as keywords, do a frequency search for them in the job file to match the resume to the jobs. Find which jobs have the most keywords corresponding to the keywords of the resume (Figure 6.12 gives an example of this matching):

```
> kwt1 <- t1 %>%
    count(word, sort = TRUE) #%>% filter(n>1)
> kwt2 <- t2 %>%
    count(word, sort = TRUE) #%>% filter(n>1)
> kwt3 <- t3 %>%
    count(word, sort = TRUE) #%>% filter(n>1)
```

```
> kwt4 <- t4 %>%
    count(word, sort = TRUE) #%>% filter(n>1)
> kwt5 <- t5 %>%
    count(word, sort = TRUE) #%>% filter(n>1)
# find out which keywords appear both in the job
(Software Developers, Applications) and resume
> intersect(kwt1["word"], kwtop10["word"])
```

| word |
| <chr> |
| develop |
| development |
| program |

FIGURE 6.12 Words that appear both in the resume and the job description for Software Developers (Applications)

```
# get the total number of keywords
> length(intersect(kwt1["word"],
kwtop10["word"])$word)

# find out which keywords appear both in the job
(Software Developers, Systems Software) and resume
> intersect(kwt2["word"], kwtop10["word"])
# get the total number of keywords
> length(intersect(kwt2["word"],
kwtop10["word"])$word)

# find out which keywords appear both in the job
(Database Administrators) and resume
> intersect(kwt3["word"], kwtop10["word"])

# get the total number of keywords
> length(intersect(kwt3["word"],
kwtop10["word"])$word)

# find out which keywords appear both in the job
(Database Architects) and resume
> intersect(kwt4["word"], kwtop10["word"])
```

```
# get the total number of keywords
> length(intersect(kwt4["word"],
kwtop10["word"])$word)

# find out which keywords appear both in the job
(Data Warehousing Specialists) and resume
> intersect(kwt5["word"], kwtop10["word"])

# get the total number of keywords
> length(intersect(kwt5["word"],
kwtop10["word"])$word)
```

Exercise 6.2 - Case Study Using Dataset G: University Curriculum

In this exercise, we try to match a job description to a university curriculum. Suppose you are a graduate student enrolled in a master's degree program. You want to know which curriculum courses will benefit you most in preparing for a specific job you are interested in. Essentially you want to answer the question

Which courses in my master's program will prepare me best for the job I am interested in?

We extract the most frequent words from the job description and use the most appropriate ones for a keyword search through the curriculum.

For this analysis, we focus on the six core classes in the exemplar graduate program. We are interested in ranking the six classes to see which one prepares the students for the Information Technology Manager occupation, as defined by the Bureau of Labor Statistics O*NET database of occupations:

Information Technology Project Managers - Plan, initiate, and manage information technology (IT) projects. Lead and guide the work of technical staff. Serve as liaison between business and technical aspects of projects. Plan project stages and assess business implications for each stage. Monitor progress to assure deadlines, standards, and cost targets are met.

Our analysis question then is

Which of the core classes best prepares me for this occupation?

For the Excel, JMP, and Voyant exercises, we extract keywords from the six core classes and compare them to the most frequent terms for the occupation in question.

Keyword Analysis in Excel

1. Access the repository of case files, and in the folder *Dataset G: University Curriculum*, open the file *Graduate Course Descriptions.xlsx* in Excel.

2. Copy the *title, description*, and *description plus title* columns to a new spreadsheet. Label the worksheet tab as *All Graduate Course Data*.

3. Extract the rows of data for the six core classes form the *Graduate Course Descriptions.xlsx*:

   • Financial Management

   • Information Technology & Data Analytics

   • Managing in a Global Economy

   • Project Management in the Information Age

   • Quantitative Models for Decision-Makers

   • Research Process & Methodology

4. Paste them into another tab in the opened spreadsheet and label it *Extracted Course Plus Job*.

5. Access the repository of case files and in the folder *Dataset D: Occupation Description* open file *O*NET JOBS Plus Resume. csv* in Excel.

6. Extract the occupation description for the Information Technology Project Managers occupation and paste into the *All Graduate Course Data* tab.

7. You are now ready to do the word frequency analysis and keyword extraction. Follow the same process as in Chapter 5.

8. Create seven additional tabs for the analysis worksheet, one for the occupation, and one for the courses.

9. Copy a job description into the appropriate worksheet.

10. Copy the description and parse it into individual terms using the *Data -> Text to Columns* function in Excel.

11. Select the terms row and paste into another section of the worksheet transposed as a column and label as *TEXT*.

12. Count how many times each word in the *TEXT* column is found in the description and add it to the column next to the *TEXT* column. Label it at as COUNT.

13. Add the STOP word list as another column next to the *TEXT* column, as you did in Chapter 5. Label it as STOP WORDS.

14. Use COUNTIF in a column called STOP next to the COUNT column to find out if the *TEXT* word is one of the STOP words.

15. Create a Pivot Table of the *TEXT*, COUNT, and STOP columns.

16. Select *TEXT* as the Rows STOP and the filter and do a count of the COUNT variables.

17. Filter out the *STOP* = 1 instances, leaving behind only those words, not on the STOP list (the uncommon words).

18. Sort the *TEXT* word from the most frequent to the least frequent using Sum of COUNT.

19. You now have a list of the most frequent terms for the course.

20. Repeat for all core classes in the list of courses and for the job description. You should generate the same results as in Exercise 5.4, as shown in Figure 6.13.

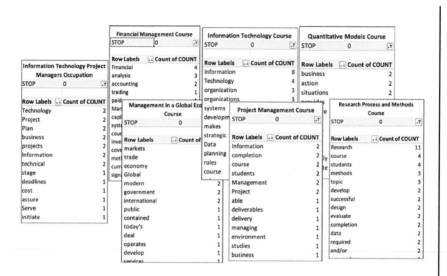

FIGURE 6.13 The term frequencies for the courses in the curriculum

21. After saving the resulting term frequency tables, scrape each term frequency table's first column (list of terms) and paste them into the opened spreadsheet in separate columns; label each column with the occupation name.

22. Once the Excel spreadsheet is populated with the resume terms and the keywords terms from each occupation, use the Excel COUNTIF function to find all the occurrences of each occupation keyword in the resume.

23. Add all the occurrences by occupation to find the occupation with the highest number of hits against the resume. Figure 6.14 shows the resulting computations. It appears that the Project Management course (7), followed by the Information Technology (3) courses, have the most similarity to the occupation, which makes sense.

Occupation	Financial Management Course		Information Technology Course		Management in a Global Economy Course		Project Management Course		Quantitative Models Course		Research Process and Methods Course	
Technology		1		3		1		7		3		2
Project	Financial	0	Information	1	markets	0	information	1	business	1	Research	0
Plan	analysis	0	Technology	1	trade	0	completion	0	action	0	course	0
business	accounting	0	organization	0	economy	0	course	0	situations	0	students	0
projects	trading	0	organizations	0	Global	0	students	0	provides	0	methods	0
Information	paid	0	systems	0	modern	0	Management	0	executive	0	topic	0
technical	Management	0	development	0	government	0	Project	1	choose	0	develop	0
stage	capital	0	makes	0	international	0	able	0	decision	0	successful	0
deadlines	system	0	strategic	0	public	0	deliverables	0	initiate	1	evaluate	0
cost	course	0	Data	0	contained	0	delivery	0	course	0	completion	0
assure	investment	0	planning	0	today's	0	managing	0	efficiently	0	and/or	0
Serve	covers	0	roles	0	deal	0	environment	0	corporate	0	data	0
initiate	methods	0	course	0	operates	0	studies	0	courses	0	required	0
standards	current	0	role	0	develop	0	business	1	Quantitative	1	and/or	0
Lead	signatures	0	issues	0	services	0	addition	0	sound	0	proposal	0
progress	decision	0	contribution	0	economies	0	manage	1	Models	1	formal	0
liaison	theory	0	expected	0	market-based	0	tools	1	creative	0	collection	0
guide	decision-making	0	studies	0	boundaries	0	techniques	0	Decision-Makers	0	infringing	0
targets	Internet	0	students	0	national	0	simulation	0	expected	0	survey	0

FIGURE 6.14 Completed comparison analysis to determine which course had the highest keyword hits against the occupation's most frequent terms (partial view) using Excel

Keyword Analysis in JMP

1. Access the repository of case files, and in the folder *Dataset G: University Curriculum* open the file *Graduate Course Descriptions.xlsx* in JMP.

2. We obtain the word frequencies for these six core courses:

- Financial Management

- Information Technology & Data Analytics

- Managing in a Global Economy

- Project Management in the Information Age

- Quantitative Models for Decision-Makers

- Research Process & Methodology

3. Using the JMP *Data Filter* function, select only the *Financial Management* from the *description plus title* column.

4. Using the *Text Explorer* function under the *Analyze* function, drag *description* into the *Text Columns* box. Click OK (see Figure 6.15.)

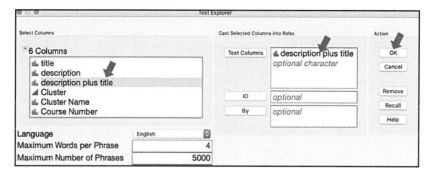

FIGURE 6.15 Finding the term frequency for the Financial Management course

5. Save the *Term Table* (pull down the red triangle in the upper left-hand corner of the term table.) Figure 6.16 shows the resulting term frequency analysis.

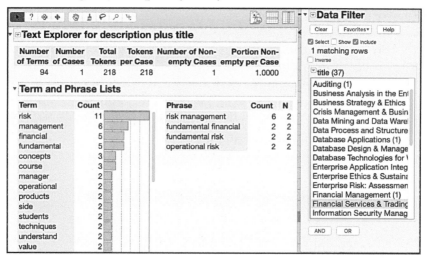

FIGURE 6.16 The term frequency table for the resume

6. Scrape the first column and paste it into a new Excel spreadsheet. Label the column with the name of the course.

7. Repeat steps 3, 4, 5, and 6 for all the other courses.

8. Access the repository of case files, and in the folder *Dataset D: Occupation Description*, open file *O*NET JOBS Plus Resume. csv* in JMP.

9. Filter out all but the *Information Technology Project Management* occupation.

10. Using the *Text Explorer* function under the *Analyze* function, drag *description* into the *Text Columns* box. Click OK.

11. Save the *Term Table* (pull down the red triangle in the upper left-hand corner of the term table).

12. Add the frequent terms to the spreadsheet where we are accumulating the keywords extracted for the courses. Put the occupation frequent terms into the first column, and use COUNTIF to generate a count of how many keywords are found in the occupation for each course.

13. The resulting analysis should look something like that in Figure 6.17. You can see that, as expected, the core class in project management has the most significant number of hits, followed by the information technology course.

Occupation	Financial Management Course		Information Technology Course		Management in a Global Economy Course		Project Management Course		Quantitative Models Course		Research Process and Methods Course	
Technology		3		4		1		8		3		2
business	risk	0	information	1	markets	0	completion	0	action	0	research	0
information	management	0	development	0	economy	0	course	0	business	1	course	0
plan	financial	0	organization	0	trade	0	problem	0	situations	0	students	0
project	fundamental	0	organizations	0	global	0	students	0	ability	0	methods	0
projects	concepts	0	systems	0	government	0	able	0	analyze	0	topic	0
technical	course	0	technology	2	international	0	addition	0	appropriate	0	upon	0
technology	manager	0	course	0	modern	0	business	0	choose	1	also	0
aspects	operational	0	decision	0	one	0	case	0	continuously	0	collection	0
assess	products	0	issues	0	among	0	concurrently	0	corporate	0	completion	0
assure	side	0	makes	0	another	0	define	0	course	0	data	0
cost	students	0	planning	0	arise	0	deliverables	0	courses	0	design	0
deadlines	techniques	0	role	0	based	0	delivery	0	creative	0	develop	0
guide	understand	0	roles	0	boundaries	0	environment	0	critical	0	evaluate	0
implications	value	0	strategic	0	business	0	explores	1	decision	0	formal	0
initiate	world	0	achieve	0	completion	0	first	0	decisions	0	proposal	0
lead	ability	0	addresses	0	connections	0	information	1	effectively	0	required	0
liaison	accounting	0	advances	0	contained	0	manage	0	efficiently	1	successful	0
manage	asset	0	advantage	0	countries	0	management	0	environment	0	able	0
managers	assignments	0	age	0	course	0	managing	0	executive	0	acceptable	0

FIGURE 6.17 Completed comparison analysis to determine which course had the highest keyword hits against the occupation's most frequent terms (partial view)

Keyword Analysis in Voyant

1. Access the repository of case files, and in the folder *Dataset G: University Curriculum* open the file *Graduate Course Descriptions.xlsx* in Excel.

2. We obtain the word frequencies for these six core courses:

   - Financial Management

   - Information Technology & Data Analytics

   - Managing in a Global Economy

   - Project Management in the Information Age

   - Quantitative Models for Decision-Makers

   - Research Process & Methodology

1. Open the Voyant tool, either using the Web-based version (*https://voyant-tools.org/*) or running the Voyant server, as explained in Chapter 15.

2. From the open file *Graduate Course Descriptions.xlsx* scrape the course description from the Financial Management course *description* cell.

3. Paste the text of the course description into the Voyant data entry screen and press *Reveal*. You will see the familiar analysis screen.

4. In the upper left-hand panel, select *Table* instead of *Cirrus* (word cloud). This gives the word frequencies as a table rather than as a picture, as shown in Figure 6.18.

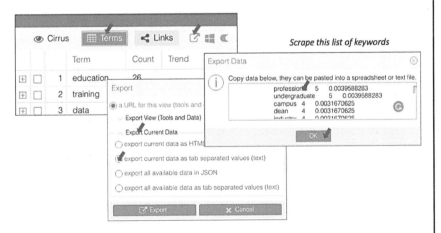

FIGURE 6.18 Finding the term frequency for the resume using Voyant

5. Scrape the keywords and paste the data into a new Excel spreadsheet. Label the column *Financial Management Course*.

6. Repeat steps 3, 4, and 5 for all the other courses.

7. After saving the resulting frequent term tables, scrape and enter each of the term frequency tables into a new spreadsheet in separate columns; label each column with the course names.

8. Lastly, repeat the process for the *Information Technology Project Manager* occupation description found in the folder *Dataset D: Occupation Description*, in the file *O*NET JOBS Plus Resume.csv*. Open the file in Excel and scrape the description and paste it into Voyant to generate its word frequency table. Insert the data into the opened worksheet and label the column *Occupation*.

9. Once the Excel spreadsheet is populated with the occupation and the keywords terms from each occupation, use the Excel COUNTIF function to find all the occurrences of each occupation keyword in the resume.

10. Add all the occurrences by course to find the course with the highest number of hits against the occupation. Figure 6.19 shows the resulting computations. It appears that the occupation is most similar to the Project Management course, as expected, with the Information Technology course a distant second place.

Occupation	Financial Management Course		Information Technology Course		Management in a Global Economy Course		Project Management Course		Quantitative Models Course		Research Process and Methods Course	
Technology		3		4		4		8		3		2
business	risk	0	information	1	change	0	completion	0	action	0	research	0
information	management	0	technology	2	practices	0	course	0	business	1	course	0
plan	financial	0	development	0	course	0	information	1	decision	0	students	0
project	fundamental	0	organization	0	expected	0	management	0	situations	0	methods	0
projects	concepts	0	organizations	0	organizational	0	problem	0	ability	0	topic	0
technical	course	0	systems	0	professionals	0	project	1	analyze	0	collection	0
technology	manager	0	course	0	progress	0	students	1	appropriate	0	completion	0
aspects	operational	0	data	0	teams	0	able	0	choose	0	data	0
assess	products	0	decision	0	theories	0	addition	0	continuously	0	design	0
assure	side	0	issues	0	workplace	0	age	0	corporate	0	develop	0
cost	students	0	makes	0	actions	0	business	1	course	0	evaluate	0
deadlines	techniques	0	planning	0	activities	0	case	0	courses	0	formal	0
guide	understand	0	role	0	best	0	concurrently	0	creative	0	proposal	0
implications	value	0	roles	0	complacency	0	define	0	critical	0	required	0
initiate	world	0	strategic	0	complex	0	deliverables	0	decisions	0	successful	0
lead	ability	0	achieve	0	initiatives	0	delivery	0	effectively	0	able	0
liaison	accounting	0	addresses	0	interactive	0	environment	0	efficiently	0	acceptable	0
manage	asset	0	advances	0	manage	1	explores	0	environment	0	affords	0

FIGURE 6.19 Completed comparison analysis to determine which course had the highest keyword hits against the occupation or job (partial view) using the Voyant tool

Keyword Analysis in R

1. In the *Case Data* file folder under *Dataset G: University Curriculum*, copy *Graduate Course Description.csv* and name the copy *caseg.csv*.

2. Install the packages we need using Repository(CRAN):

   ```
   dplyr, tidytext, textstem, readr
   ```

   1. Import the library and read the case data (Figure 6.5):

   ```r
   > library(dplyr)
   > library(tidytext)
   > library(textstem)
   > library(readr)

   # read the case data and specify the course we are
   interested in.

   > caseg <- read.csv(file.path("caseg.csv"),
   stringsAsFactors = F, strip.white=TRUE)

   > target_g <- caseg %>% filter_at(vars(title),
   any_vars(. %in% c('Business Analysis in the
   Enterprise', 'Data Mining and Data Warehousing',
   'Data Process and Structure', 'Information
   Technology & Data Analytics', 'Object-Oriented
   Systems Design')))
   ```

	title	description	description.plus.title	Cluster	Cluster.Name	Course.Number
1	Business Analysis in the Enterprise	Business Analysis in the Enterprise This course investi...	This course investigates the concepts and techniques ...	6	Systems Development	GC3255
2	Data Mining and Data Warehousing	Data Mining and Data Warehousing In the competitiv...	In the competitive information age, data mining and ...	5	Operations Management	GC3510
3	Data Process and Structure	Data Process and Structure This course examines dat...	This course examines database models from a manag...	7	Database	GC3505
4	Information Technology & Data Analytics	Information Technology & Data Analytics The organi...	The organization is examined as a system, and the ro...	5	Operations Management	GC1240
5	Object-Oriented Systems Design	Object-Oriented Systems Design This course address...	This course addresses the concepts, skills, methodolo...	6	Systems Development	GC3530

FIGURE 6.20 Data frame object of *target_g*

```r
# Specify the job we are interested in. Here we are
interested in "Business Intelligence Analyst"

> job_target <- cased[which(cased$job == "Business
Intelligence Analysts"),]

> job_target <- job_target %>%
  unite(text, job, description, sep =" ", remove =
  FALSE)
```

2. Tokenize the contents of the dataset, lemmatize the words, and remove the stop words:

```
# for job, "Business Intelligence Analyst"
> tidy_job <- job_target %>%
    unnest_tokens(word, text) %>%
    mutate(word = lemmatize_words(word)) %>%
    anti_join(all_stop_words)
# for course, "Business Analysis in the Enterprise"
> c1 <- target_g[1,] %>%
    unnest_tokens(word, description.plus.title) %>%
    mutate(word = lemmatize_words(word)) %>%
    anti_join(stop_words)
# for course, "Data Mining and Data Warehousing"
> c2 <- target_g[2,] %>%
    unnest_tokens(word, description.plus.title) %>%
    mutate(word = lemmatize_words(word)) %>%
    anti_join(stop_words)
# for course, "Data Process and Structure"
> c3 <- target_g[3,] %>%
    unnest_tokens(word, description.plus.title) %>%
    mutate(word = lemmatize_words(word)) %>%
    anti_join(stop_words)
# for course, "Information Technology & Data
Analytics"
> c4 <- target_g[4,] %>%
    unnest_tokens(word, description.plus.title) %>%
    mutate(word = lemmatize_words(word)) %>%
    anti_join(stop_words)
```

```
# for course, "Object-Oriented Systems Design"
> c5 <- target_g[5,] %>%
    unnest_tokens(word, description.plus.title) %>%
    mutate(word = lemmatize_words(word)) %>%
    anti_join(stop_words)
```

3. Find the frequently used keywords in the job description (Figure 6.6):

```
> kw_bia <- tidy_job %>%
count(word, sort = TRUE)
```

	word	n
1	intelligence	3
2	analyst	2
3	business	2
4	datum	2
5	devise	1
6	financial	1
7	generate	1
8	identify	1
9	information	1
10	market	1
11	method	1
12	pattern	1
13	periodic	1
14	produce	1
15	query	1
16	report	1
17	repository	1
18	source	1
19	trend	1

FIGURE 6.21 Keywords for the Business Intelligence Analyst job

4. Find which courses have the most keywords corresponding to the keywords of the selected job description (Figure 6.7):

```
> kwc1 <- c1 %>%
  count(word, sort = TRUE) #%>% filter(n>1)
> kwc2 <- c2 %>%
  count(word, sort = TRUE) #%>% filter(n>1)
```

```
> kwc3 <- c3 %>%
  count(word, sort = TRUE) #%>% filter(n>1)

> kwc4 <- c4 %>%
  count(word, sort = TRUE) #%>% filter(n>1)

> kwc5 <- c5 %>%
  count(word, sort = TRUE) #%>% filter(n>1)
```

```
# find out which keywords appear both in the course
(Business Analysis in the Enterprise) and job
descriptions
```

```
> intersect(kwc1["word"],kw_bia["word"])
```

word <chr>
business
datum
information

FIGURE 6.22 Keywords appear both in the job description and course, Business Analysis in the Enterprise

```
# get the total number of shared keywords
> length(intersect(kwc1["word"],kw_bia["word"]))
```

```
# find out which keywords appear both in the
course (Data Mining and Data Warehousing) and job
descriptions
> intersect(kwc2["word"],kw_bia["word"])
```

```
# get the total number of shared keywords
> length(intersect(kwc2["word"],kw_bia["word"]))
```

```
# find out which keywords appear both in the course
(Data Process and Structure) and job descriptions
> intersect(kwc3["word"],kw_bia["word"])
```

```
# get the total number of shared keywords
> length(intersect(kwc3["word"],kw_bia["word"]))
```

```
# find out which keywords appear both in the course
(Information Technology & Data Analytics) and job
descriptions
> intersect(kwc4["word"],kw_bia["word"])

# get the total number of shared keywords
> length(intersect(kwc4["word"],kw_bia["word"]))

# find out which keywords appear both in the
course (Object-Oriented Systems Design) and job
descriptions
> intersect(kwc5["word"],kw_bia["word"])

# get the total number of shared keywords
> length(intersect(kwc5["word"],kw_bia["word"]))
```

Exercise 6.3 - Case Study Using Dataset C: Product Reviews

In this exercise, we try to get our customers' level of concern with a particular issue based on their product reviews. We have product review data for a window cleaning product. The keyword we use for our analysis is "clean." We want to answer the question

What percentage of customers have a concern with the cleaning effectiveness of our product?

We will look for the frequency of the appearance of the keyword "clean."

Keyword Analysis in Excel

1. Access the case files' repository and in the folder *Dataset C: Product Reviews*, open the file *Product Reviews.xlxs*. There are two different brands: *Rubbermaid* and *Windex*. Filter out the *brand=Rubbermaid* rows and save the remaining rows in a separate worksheet. Save the file as a separate Excel file labeled *Product Reviews Windex Keyword Analysis.xlxs*.

2. Create a column to the right of the table and label it *COUNT*. Enter the COUNTIF formula for every row to discover the number of times the word "clean" is used, as well as any of its derivatives, such as "cleans" or "cleaning." Use the following formula:

```
=COUNTIF(E2,"*clean*")
```

=COUNTIF(E2,"*clean*")				
D	E	F	G	H
ting	reviews.text	review.title	COUNT	
4	I love the product and it cleans, shines and leaves a ref	Refreshing Clean	=COUNTIF(E2,"*clean*")	
5	I have always gone back to Windex after trying new pro	Great Product, Can't Go	0	
5	Windex has always been the best product for windows	great product	0	
2	Windex doesn't clean mirrors, glass like it used to. Leav	Did You Change Ingredie	1	
5	Big bottle, great bargain. Best window glass cleaner on	Windex is the Best!	1	
4	Cleans a variety of surfaces and shines!! Quick and eas	Great Product!	1	

FIGURE 6.23 Formula to count the occurrence of "clean" in each product review

3. Count how many non-zero rows there are. You will see that there 188 mentions of some form of the keyword "clean" and its derivatives out of 348 reviews, which indicates that over 50% of our customers had "clean" on their minds when they wrote the review.

4. Now let's repeat the process by seeing how many noticed the product has ammonia. Create another analysis column and look for the percentage of customers mentioning the word "ammonia." You will see it is only 3%. If you wanted this brand element to be noticed, you need to change the marketing approach to get customers to mention it more frequently.

5. Now extract the *brand=Rubbermaid* rows, and paste them into a new worksheet. Label it *Rubbermaid Keyword Analysis.* Repeat steps 2 through 4 to count the appearance of the word "mop" in each product review. It appears in 73% of the reviews.

6. Now let's do a competitive analysis. Repeat the steps and look for how often the customers mention a competitive product, "Swiffer." This occurs 8% of the time.

E	F	G	H	I	J	K
reviews.text	review.title	COUNT "mop"	COUNT "Swiffer"			
I really love the mop. Only concern is the r	Used Many I	1	0			
I am a handicapped man, with limited use	The Perfect I	1	0		COUNT "mop"	
I would give it 0 star if I could. This is my s	Rubbermaid	0	0		Row Labels ⬇	Count of COUNT "mop"
This mop is perfect! It's thin so it gets und	You Must Bu	1	0		0	27%
I really like this mop. It does a great job in	I Like It But...	1	0		1	73%
I purchased the Reveal Spray Mop about y	Very disappc				Grand Total	100%
I came across the warning that this mop h	Defective Sp	=COUNTIF(E8,"*mop*")				
I hate this mop! I bought it to replace a Sv	does not get	1	1		COUNT "Swiffer"	
A great idea and worked well for about 6 r	reveal spray	1	1		Row Labels ⬇	Count of COUNT "Swiffer"
This is my second Rubbermaid spray mop	the bottle le:	1	0		0	92%
I saw this at someone's house and loved it	Reveal Spray	1	0		1	8%
Oddly enough I wrote Rubbermaid on line	Reveal Spray	1	0		Grand Total	100.00%
I've had my Reveal mop for a couple of ye:	Years Of Goc	1	0			

FIGURE 6.24 Formulas and pivot table analysis for the occurrence of the words "mop" and "Swiffer" in the Rubbermaid reviews

Additional Exercise 6.4 - Case Study Using Dataset B: Customer Complaints

The dataset available in *Dataset B: Customer Complaints* has an extensive set of bank service complaints (tens of thousands). It was compiled by the United States federal agency that regulates banks. Analyze first the complaints about one particular bank, Bank of America. Analyze the matter of "late fees," using this term as a keyword. Compute its frequency.

What percentage of Bank of America customers have a concern with late fees?

You can repeat the analysis, but now consider all banks. Answer the question

Which banks seem to have a significant problem with late fees?

The complaints have been characterized and tracked with the categorical variable *Issues*. It is a good source of keywords. Using a data dictionary (if available) or a pivot table to summarize the variable *Issues*, determine what other keywords may be used for the keyword analysis. Select different keywords that seem essential and perform the text analysis of the complaints texts to find their prevalence. Compare the frequency of the selected category in the *Issues* variable (use a pivot table) and compare it to the frequency of that as a keyword in the text of the complaints. How do they compare?

## CHAPTER 7

SENTIMENT ANALYSIS

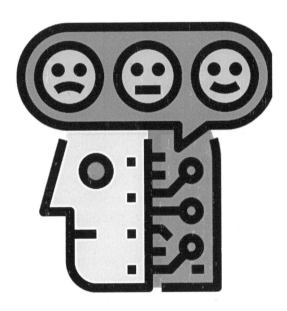

This chapter presents some basic techniques to gauge the positive or negative aspects of what someone wrote. It is generally applied to customer feedback, customer reviews, and similar opinion-based data. Essentially, we want to generate a set of positive opinion words (such as "good," "love," "high," and "excellent") and their opposites (such as "bad," "hate," "low," and "poor"). We will use each one as a keyword and count the frequency of each word's appearance in the target text, as we did in Chapter 6. Once we tabulate the frequencies and compare the ratios of positive to negative words, we can obtain a general indication of the writers' opinions, whether it is positive or negative. We do this first in Excel and then proceed to analyze it with our other tools. Understanding how to do it with Excel gives the beginner a good idea of what is behind the computation of more sophisticated programs.

There are many commercial products that provide excellent sentiment analysis, but we will still use the same tools as before. Although one can perform a much more fine-grained analysis and even analyze real-time text streams (such as tweets) with commercial products, we only use static text files here and the basic tools introduced so far.

What is Sentiment Analysis?

Text data mining is used in sentiment analysis to determine whether what someone wrote is positive, negative, or neutral. Sentiment analysis helps business data analysts gauge public opinion, conduct market research, monitor brand, and product reputation, and understand customer experiences.

A basic task in sentiment analysis is classifying a given text's polarity at the document, sentence, or feature/aspect level—whether the expressed opinion in a document, a sentence, or an entity feature/aspect is positive, negative, or neutral.

Sentiment analysis (also known as opinion mining or emotion AI) refers to natural language processing, text analysis, computational linguistics, and biometrics to systematically identify, extract, quantify, and study affective states and subjective information. Sentiment analysis is often applied to "voice of the customer" materials (in the language of marketing) such as product reviews and customer survey responses, social media postings, and healthcare materials. There are many applications of sentiment analysis; they range from marketing to customer service to clinical medicine.

Although sentiment analysis can be very fine-grained (levels of satisfaction or dissatisfaction by each customer), we only perform a rough "polarity" type of analysis in this chapter – a generally positive or negative level of satisfaction. Sentiment analysis may yield compelling results when applied to real-time social media data and in tweets. Once familiar with these concepts, you may want to explore more sophisticated applications.

We use the Excel COUNTIF function to generate an analysis of text fields to perform the customer sentiment analysis. We answer this question:

Do customers feel positively or negatively about a product?

Exercise 7.1 - Case Study Using Dataset C: Product Reviews – Rubbermaid

Analysis in Excel

1. Access the case files' repository, and in the folder *Dataset C: Product Reviews*, open file *Product Reviews.xlxs*. There are two different brands: *Rubbermaid* and *Windex*. Let's first filter for the *Rubbermaid* brand by selecting only those rows and save them in a separate excel file, *rubbermaid_sentiment.xlxs* (Figure 7.1).

	A	B	C
1	Rubbermaid	reviews.text	review.title
2		1 I really love the mo	Used Many Mops This Is Quite Awesome
3		2 I am a handicapped	The Perfect Mop
4		3 I would give it 0 sta	Rubbermaid reveal mop
5		4 This mop is perfect!	You Must Buy This Mop!
6		5 I really like this mor	I Like It But...
7		6 I purchased the Rev	Very disappointed!
8		7 I came across the w	Defective Spray Trigger
9		8 I hate this mop! I bo	does not get floors clean
10		9 A great idea and wo	reveal spray mop
11		10 This is my second R	the bottle leaks
12		11 I saw this at someo	Reveal Spray Mop
13		12 Oddly enough I wro	Reveal Spray Mop
14		13 I've had my Reveal	Years Of Good Service
15		14 I bought this mop a	Very green
16		15 I have purchased 3	Poor Quality
17		16 I loved my reveal bi	spray trigger
18		17 I bought this mop a	Loved It When It Worked.
19		18 I love this mop. I tea	Reveal Spray Mop
20		19 I have purched 3 of	Ro
21		20 I bought this mop a	Great Idea But Problems With Trigger (And Smell)
22		21 I have had a reveal	Frustrating And Disappointing.

Rubbermaid | Sentiment Analysis | ⊕

FIGURE 7.1 Rubbermaid sentiment rows extracted from the *Product Reviews.xls* file

2. Create a list of the negative and positive word lists in a new tab, *Sentiment Analysis*, as shown in Figure 7.2.

positive_words	negative_words
good	bad
positive	negative
best	worst
easy	hard
great	poor
love	hate
always	never

FIGURE 7.2 Positive and negative word lists used to estimate sentiment analysis

3. Now use each one as a keyword, and with the COUNTIF function, find out how many times each keyword appears in all the customer reviews. Summarize the results for the *review.text* field and *review.title* field. Now create a summary table for positive and negative keywords, as shown in Figure 7.3. Add the counts from both variables to get an overall sentiment.

	A	B	C	D	E	F
1				Sentiment Analysis		
2				Title	Review	All
3		Positive	Word	Count	Count	Count
4			good	92	205	297
5			positive	0	8	8
6			best	67	116	183
7			easy	44	41	85
8			great	229	484	713
9			love	209	711	920
10			always	4	102	106
11				645	1667	2312
12		Negative	Word	Count	Count	Count
13			bad	23	66	89
14			negative	0	20	20
15			worst	7	4	11
16			hard	5	191	196
17			poor	90	67	157
18			hate	11	68	79
19			never	3	98	101
20				139	514	653

FIGURE 7.3 Count of the occurrence of positive and negative keywords in the *reviews.txt* and *reviews.title* fields for the Rubbermaid data rows

4. After repeating the analysis for all the positive and negative words, sum their occurrence for totals by positive and negative words.

5. Subtract the negative occurrences from the positive occurrences and divide by the total number of comments to get an overall sentiment. You should obtain a number between (-1) and (+1), which can be expressed as a positive or negative percentage. Use a formula such as (see Figure 7.3 for cell references)

```
=(F11-F20)/(F11+F20)
```

6. Analyze the percentage of positive and negative word occurrences and gauge whether customers feel positively or negatively about the product. The results can be seen in Figure 7.4. It seems customers are quite happy with the product, giving it a +56% overall rating (a positive result).

	A	B	C	D	E	F
1				Sentiment Analysis		
2				Title	Review	All
3		Positive	Word	Count	Count	Count
4			good	92	205	297
5			positive	0	8	8
6			best	67	116	183
7			easy	44	41	85
8			great	229	484	713
9			love	209	711	920
10			always	4	102	106
11				645	1667	2312
12		Negative	Word	Count	Count	Count
13			bad	23	66	89
14			negativ(	0	20	20
15			worst	7	4	11
16			hard	5	191	196
17			poor	90	67	157
18			hate	11	68	79
19			never	3	98	101
20				139	514	653
21						
22					Sentiment	56%
23						

FIGURE 7.4 Overall customer sentiment for the Rubbermaid product

Analysis Using JMP

1. Access the case files' repository and in the folder *Dataset C: Product Reviews*, open file *Product Reviews.xlxs*. There are two different brands: *Rubbermaid* and *Windex*. Let's first filter for the *Rubbermaid* brand by selecting only those rows and save them in a separate Excel file *rubbermaid_sentiment.xlxs*. Import it to JMP.

2. Click *Analyze*, and select *Text Explorer*. Drag *reviews.text* to *Text Columns* and choose *OK* (see Figure 7.5).

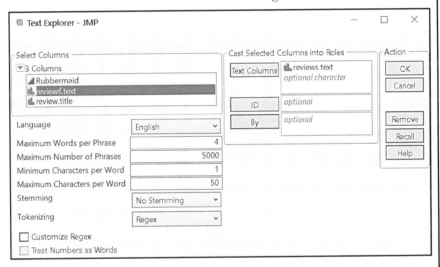

FIGURE 7.5 Using the *Text Explorer* JMP function to analyze the *reviews.text* text variable

3. Select the red triangular drop-down button, choose *Display Options*, and click *Show Filters for All Tables*, as in Figure 7.6.

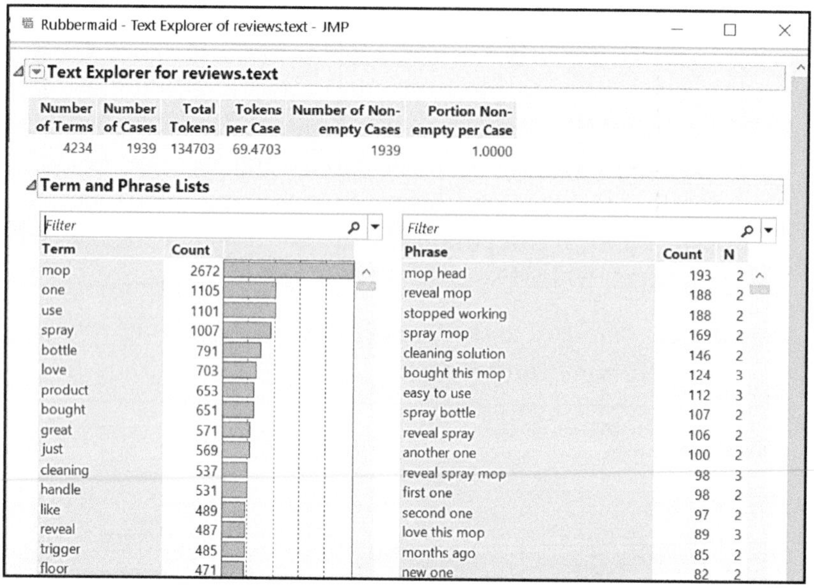

FIGURE 7.6 Result of using the *Text Explorer* JMP function to analyze the *reviews.text* text variable

4. User the filter to detect the occurrence of each positive word in the positive keyword list. Figure 7.7 shows the words "good," "positive," "best," "easy," "great," "love," and "always."

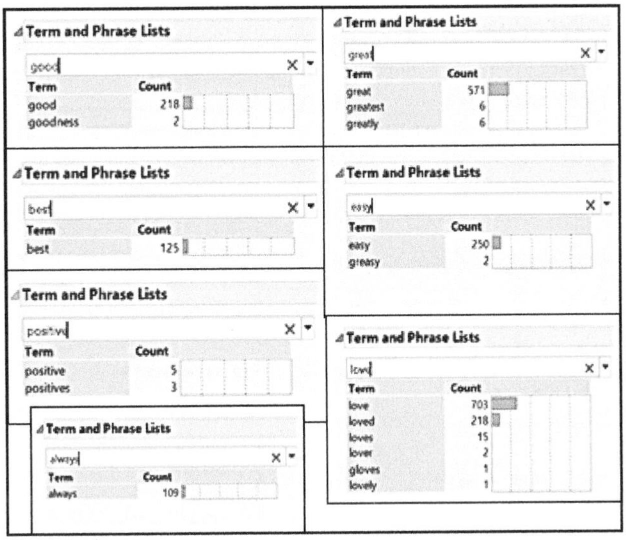

FIGURE 7.7 Text Explorer *reviews.text* filter for "good," "positive," "best," "easy," "great," "love," and "always"

5. User the filter to detect the occurrence of each negative word in the negative keyword list. Figure 7.8 shows the results for "bad," "negative," "worst," "hard," "poor," "hate," and "never."

◢ Term and Phrase Lists			◢ Term and Phrase Lists	
hard	X ▾		negative	X ▾
Term	**Count**		**Term**	**Count**
hardwood	115		negative	19
hard	92		negatives	2
hardware	9			

◢ Term and Phrase Lists

hardly	6		bad	X ▾
harder	4		**Term**	**Count**
hardwoods	3		bad	64
hardcore	1		badly	3
hardened	1			
hardness	1			

◢ Term and Phrase Lists

poor	X ▾		hate	X ▾
Term	**Count**		**Term**	**Count**
poor	54		whatever	30
poorly	15		hate	26
poorer	2		hated	17

◢ Term and Phrase Lists

worst	X ▾		never	X ▾
Term	**Count**		**Term**	**Count**
worst	4		never	106
			nevertheless	2

FIGURE 7.8 Text Explorer *reviews.text* filter for "bad," "negative," "worst," "hard," "poor," "hate," and "never"

Sentiment on the Title of the Review					Sentiment on the Text of the Review			
Postive word	**Postive word count**	**Negative word**	**Negative word count**		**Postive word**	**Postive word count**	**Negative word**	**Negative word count**
good	93	bad	25		good	220	bad	67
positive	0	negative	0		positive	8	negative	21
best	67	worst	7		best	125	worst	4
easy	45	hard	3		easy	250	hard	92
great	231	poor	83		great	583	poor	71
love	173	hate	9		love	937	hate	43
always	4	never	3		always	109	never	106
Total	613	Total	130		Total	2232	Total	404
	Sentiment	+	0.65			Sentiment	+	0.69

FIGURE 7.9 Compilation of the sentiment analysis from the JMP text analysis of the review titles and texts

6. As you can see from Figure 7.9, the JMP results show overwhelmingly positive customer reviews.

7. Repeat the same process for the *review.title* variable to see if the customer-supplied titles yield a similar result. Similar results for the analysis of the title variable are also shown in Figure 7.9.

Exercise 7.2 - Case Study Using Dataset C: Product Reviews-Windex

We are now going to do this analysis again, but for another product in the table. We will analyze customer sentiment towards a Windex product. We do it here in Excel and SAS JMP, and then in the next exercise, we will do it in R for both brands.

1. Access the case files' repository and in the folder *Dataset C: Product Reviews*, open file *Product Reviews.xlxs*. There are two different brands: *Rubbermaid* and *Windex*. Keep only the Windex rows and save the data in a separate Excel file called *windex_sentiment.xlxs*. The resulting table is shown in Figure 7.10.

	A	B	C
1	review	reviews.text	review.title
2	1	I love the product and it cleans, sl	Refreshing Clean
3	2	I have always gone back to Winde	Great Product, Can't Go Wrong With Windex!!
4	3	Windex has always been the best	great product
5	4	Windex doesn't clean mirrors, gla	Did You Change Ingredients
6	5	Big bottle, great bargain. Best win	Windex is the Best!
7	6	Cleans a variety of surfaces and s	Great Product!
8	7	26 FlOz Original BarCode 19800 7	Product Good, Spray Mechanism Terrible
9	8	Excellent! Works great on many d	Windex Is Excellence!
10	9	best overall cleaner on window, r	Excellent cleaner on mirrors, windows and a lot more!
11	10	Works in every room and on ever	Best all round
12	11	I have now purchased two differe	Would Love To Use It But I Can't... Bottle Keeps Breaking
13	12	I have used Windex for over 35 y	Instead of Streak Free, it should read Streaks Freely
14	13	I confess I once tried a different b	No Other Product Beats Windex
15	14	Perfect for washing windows.	Great Product.
16	15	It's handy and quickly clean up th	It's handy to keep it on hand to clean windshield and mirror
17	16	I use windex for many applicatior	I Use Windex For Many Applications. Love The Product.
18	17	I use Windex on my countertops	Windex has all I need for cleaning
19	18	This is the most useless product t	Windex Advanced

FIGURE 7.10 A portion of the product reviews showing only Windex customer reviews

2. Create a list of the negative and positive word lists in a new worksheet called *Sentiment Analysis*. Use the same word lists that are used in *Exercise 7.1*.

3. Now use each one as a keyword, and with the COUNTIF function, determine many times each keyword appears in all the customer reviews. Summarize the results for the *review.text* field and the *review.title* field. Create a summary table for positive and negative keywords, as shown in Figure 7.11. Add the counts from both variables to get an overall sentiment.

	A	B	C	D	E	F
10			Sentiment Analysis			
11				Title	Review	All
12		Positive	Word	Count	Count	Sum
13			good	21	36	57
14			positive	0	0	0
15			best	22	29	51
16			easy	6	14	20
17			great	53	68	121
18			love	21	37	58
19			always	17	50	67
20			sum	140	234	374
21		Negative	Word	Count	Count	Sum
22			bad	3	4	7
23			negative	0	0	0
24			worst	0	2	2
25			hard	0	7	7
26			poor	1	3	4
27			hate	1	3	4
28			never	2	18	20
29			sum	7	37	44

FIGURE 7.11 Count of the occurrence of positive and negative keywords in the *reviews.txt* and *reviews.title* fields for the Windex data rows

4. Repeat the same process for the rest of the negative and positive words.

5. Sum the occurrence of all positive and negative words. Remember to subtract the negative occurrences from the positive occurrences and divide by the total number of comments. You should obtain a number between (-1) and (+1), which can be expressed as a positive or negative percentage. Use a formula such as (see Figure 7.8 for cell references)

```
=(F11-F20)/(F11+F20)
```

6. Analyze the percentage of positive and negative word occurrences and gauge whether customers feel positively or negatively about the product. The results can be seen in Figure 7.12. It seems customers are quite happy with the product, giving it a +79% overall rating.

	A	B	C	D	E	F
10				Sentiment Analysis		
11				Title	Review	All
12		Positive	Word	Count	Count	Sum
13			good	21	36	57
14			positive	0	0	0
15			best	22	29	51
16			easy	6	14	20
17			great	53	68	121
18			love	21	37	58
19			always	17	50	67
20			sum	140	234	374
21		Negative	Word	Count	Count	Sum
22			bad	3	4	7
23			negative	0	0	0
24			worst	0	2	2
25			hard	0	7	7
26			poor	1	3	4
27			hate	1	3	4
28			never	2	18	20
29			sum	7	37	44
30						
31					Sentiment	79%

FIGURE 7.12 Overall customer sentiment for the Windex product

1. Access the case files' repository and in the folder *Dataset C: Product Reviews*, open file *Product Reviews.xlxs*. There are two different brands: *Rubbermaid* and *Windex*. Let's keep only the Windex rows and save the data in a separate Excel file named *windex_sentiment.xlxs*. Import this file to JMP.

2. Click *Analyze*, and select *Text Explorer*. Drag *review.title* to *Text Columns* and select *OK* (see Figure 7.13).

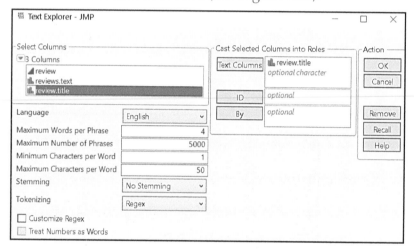

FIGURE 7.13 Text Explorer for the *review.title* variable

3. Select the red drop-down button, choose *Display Options*, and click *Show Filters for All Tables* (see Figure 7.14).

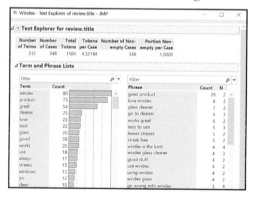

FIGURE 7.14 The Text Explorer *review.title* results

4. Use the filter to detect the occurrence of each positive word in the positive word list. Figure 7.15 shows a sample of the results for "good." Repeat the same process for "positive," "best," "easy," "great," "love," and "always."

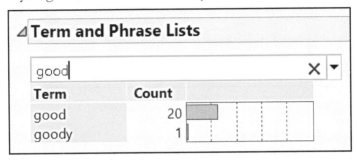

FIGURE 7.15 The Text Explorer *review.title* with a filter for "good"

5. Continue to use the filter to detect the occurrence of each negative word in the negative word list. Figure 7.16 shows a sample of "bad." Repeat the same process for "negative," "worst," "hard," "poor," "hate," and "never."

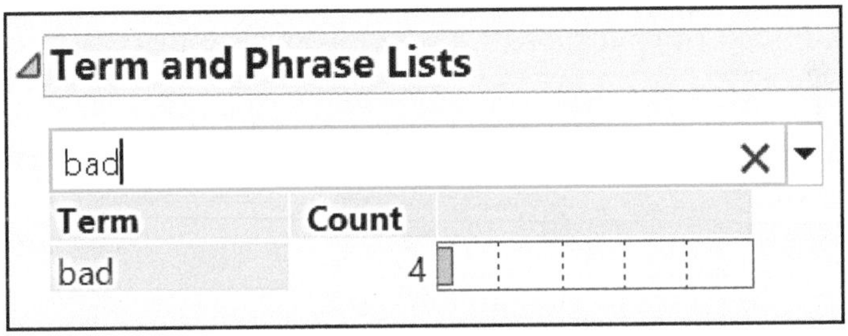

FIGURE 7.16 The Text Explorer for *review.title* with a filter for "bad"

6. Repeat the same process on *reviews.text*.

7. Copy the results for each positive and negative keyword and their occurrence to an Excel workbook, as shown in Figure 7.17. We see overwhelming positive sentiment for this product.

Sentiment on the Title of the Review				Sentiment on the Text of the Review			
Postive word	Postive word count	Negative word	Negative word count	Postive word	Postive word count	Negative word	Negative word count
good	20	bad	4	good	40	bad	4
positive	0	negative	0	positive	0	negative	0
best	22	worst	0	best	31	worst	2
easy	6	hard	0	easy	15	hard	8
great	54	poor	1	great	83	poor	3
love	23	hate	1	love	36	hate	1
always	17	never	2	always	55	never	21
Total	142	Total	8	Total	260	Total	39
	Sentiment	+	0.89		Sentiment	+	0.74

FIGURE 7.17 Excel result of Windex generated from JMP

Exercise 7.3 – Case Study Using Dataset C: Product Reviews-Both Brands

Analysis in R

1. In the *Case Data* file folder under *Dataset C Product Reviews*, make a copy of *Product Reviews.csv*. Name this new file *casec. csv*.

2. Install the packages we need using Repository(CRAN):

   dplyr, tidytext, textstem, ggplot2

3. Import the library and read the case data:

```
> library(dplyr)

> library(tidytext)

> library(textstem)

> casec <- read.csv(file.path("casec.csv"),
stringsAsFactors = F, strip.white=TRUE)

> casec <- casec %>%

    unite(review_combined, reviews.text, review.
    title, sep =" ", remove = FALSE)
```

4. Tokenize the contents of the dataset, lemmatize the words, and remove the stopwords:

```
> tidy_c <- casec %>%
    unnest_tokens(word, review_combined) %>%
    mutate(word = lemmatize_words(word)) %>%
    anti_join(stop_words)
```

5. Use built-in lexicon "AFINN" to conduct sentiment analysis for each date (as shown in Figure 7.18):

```
> afinn_c <- tidy_c %>%
#pair tokenized words with AFINN lexicon
    inner_join(get_sentiments
    ("afinn")) %>%
    group_by(review.date,brand) %>%
#calculate the sentiment score of the date
    summarize(sentiment = sum(value)) %>%
    mutate(method = "AFINN") %>%
#convert date format
mutate(review.date = as.Date(review.date, "%Y-%m-
%d")) %>%
    arrange(review.date) %>%
#specify time period
filter(review.date >="2014-01-01" & review.
date<="2017-01-01")
> afinn_c
```

	review.date	brand	sentiment	method
1	2014-01-01	Rubbermaid	-2	AFINN
2	2014-01-05	Rubbermaid	20	AFINN
3	2014-01-07	Rubbermaid	10	AFINN
4	2014-01-08	Rubbermaid	4	AFINN
5	2014-01-09	Rubbermaid	-2	AFINN
6	2014-01-09	Windex	-8	AFINN
7	2014-01-10	Rubbermaid	-5	AFINN
8	2014-01-10	Windex	11	AFINN
9	2014-01-12	Rubbermaid	8	AFINN
10	2014-01-14	Rubbermaid	4	AFINN
11	2014-01-14	Windex	11	AFINN
12	2014-01-15	Rubbermaid	2	AFINN
13	2014-01-16	Rubbermaid	-19	AFINN
14	2014-01-19	Rubbermaid	-16	AFINN
15	2014-01-20	Rubbermaid	2	AFINN
16	2014-01-21	Rubbermaid	6	AFINN
17	2014-01-21	Windex	1	AFINN
18	2014-01-23	Rubbermaid	-4	AFINN
19	2014-01-25	Windex	-4	AFINN
20	2014-01-27	Rubbermaid	2	AFINN

Showing 1 to 20 of 504 entries, 4 total columns

FIGURE 7.18 Sentiment analysis score by review date and brand

6. Visualize the result (as seen in Figure 7.19):

```
> library(ggplot2)

> myplot <- ggplot(afinn_c, aes(review.date,
sentiment, fill = brand))
+ geom_col(show.legend = F) + facet_wrap
(~brand, ncol = 1, scales = "free_x")

> myplot
```

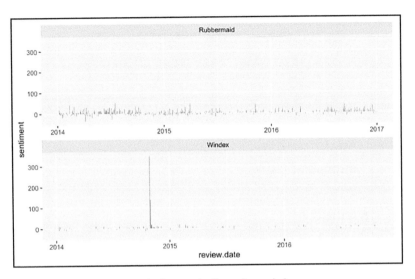

FIGURE 7.19 Sentiment analysis trend of two brands by year

7. Use built-in lexicon "bing" to conduct the sentiment analysis (the results are shown in Figure 7.20):

```
# get negative lexicon
> bing_negative <- get_sentiments
("bing") %>%

    filter(sentiment == "negative")

# get positive lexicon
> bing_positive <- get_sentiments
("bing") %>%

    filter(sentiment == "positive")

> tidy_c %>%
# specify the brand, here we can put
either "Rubbermaid" or "Windex"

    filter(brand == "Rubbermaid") %>%
```

```
# specify whether we would like to look at the
negative or positive words in reviews
    inner_join(bing_negative) %>%
    count(word, sort = TRUE)
```

word <chr>	n <int>
break	860
disappoint	272
leak	221
issue	142
poor	139
waste	136
bad	109
hard	99
fail	76
frustrate	74

1-10 of 352 rows

FIGURE 7.20 Sentiment analysis (negative) of the selected brand (Rubbermaid)

## CHAPTER 8

VISUALIZING TEXT DATA

New tools have been developed to easily extract meaning from unstructured text data. That text data may come from open-ended responses in surveys, tweets, emails, or Facebook postings. It could be a database of contracts or a collection of books in electronic form. Some of the tools we will use are functions in Excel. We use the COUNTIF function to estimate the sentiment analysis in product reviews. We then use open-source Web-based text analytic tools to create word clouds and perform simple word frequency analysis to extract the underlying meaning from text. To exemplify these techniques, we will use the text files of five travel books, amounting to over one million words of text, and perform some fundamental analysis to illustrate the visualization of text data. (This scenario is analogous to extracting meaning from a corpus of Facebook postings, email logs, or Twitter feeds.) This technique answers the business question "What are they saying?" by visualizing a summary of the analysis.

What Is Data Visualization Used For?

An analyst typically creates visuals of the analysis results as the analysis progresses. These are graphs of data for analysis; they are rough graphs with no thought given to making them compelling at this point in the analysis. It is likely that no one other than the analyst will ever see most of those rough analysis charts. These graphs may even accumulate in an electronic research notebook (typically a PowerPoint document) with slides as containers for the analysis charts. At the end of the analysis, these graphs and numerical summaries of results accumulated in such a notebook are used to draw conclusions and answer questions. We call this charting process *data visualization for analysis*. The tools and techniques shown in this chapter help with creating those preliminary charts to make sense of the textual data and start the detailed analysis process. The last step is to create compelling visuals that tell the story. This last step in creating a story with data is *data visualization for communication*.

The process of creating a few well-crafted visuals from the many used for analysis is described in the book *Data Visualization for Business Decisions* [Fortino20]. Often, analysts are not given much time to present their findings. If you look at the work of neurobiologist John Medina [Medina08], he exhorts us to use no more than ten minutes to make our case, lest we bore our audience. In any event, we must present our findings with as few slides as possible. The analyst looks over the rough graphs produced in analysis, looks at the conclusions, and then asks: "Which of these are the most powerful visuals to make the point and underscore conclusions most compellingly?" There are probably no more than three or four such visuals that have to be recreated or enhanced to make them more readable to new eyes.

In this chapter, we will concentrate on producing visuals of our text to understand the import of all those words. We have four exercises: (1) the results of a pre-training survey, (2) consumer complaints about a bank, (3) two product reviews; and (4) visualizing over 1,000,000 words from five full-length books.

Exercise 8.1 – Case Study Using Dataset A: Training Survey

We polled employees in our company who were about to undergo training in data analysis. You want to inform the instructor what the students wish to learn in the class. We have already analyzed this information using other quantitative techniques. Here, we want to quickly understand what the employees are telling us they want from the class, so we also create a word cloud of their input. The question we want to answer is

Can we create a picture of the most frequent words of their open-ended requests?

Visualizing the Text Using Excel

1. The first place to start is to do a word frequency analysis, like that shown in Chapter 5. Return to Chapter 5 and look at the word frequency analysis solution, primarily the pivot table results.

2. Use the Chapter 5 *Dataset A: Training Survey* Excel spreadsheet results.

3. Open the *Pivot* worksheet, and select all the words with occurrence greater than and equal to 3, as shown in Figure 8.1.

Row Labels	Count of COUNT
Data	39
business	14
Analysis	11
questions	10
tools	8
value	6
decisions	5
using	5
goes	4
analyzing	4
interpreting	4
Answer	4
organization	4
basic	3
Identify	3
Create	3
Issues	3
information	3

FIGURE 8.1 Word frequency table from the training survey file

4. From the main Excel ribbon, select *Insert*, then select *Treemap*. The resulting visual of the word frequencies appears in Figure 8.2.

5. It does not yield an actual word cloud but a very reasonable facsimile. It is a suitable pictorial representation of the most important words.

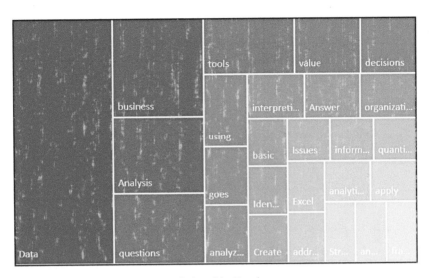

FIGURE 8.2 Training survey word cloud in Excel

Visualizing the Text Using JMP

1. Access the case files' repository and in the folder *Dataset A: Training Survey*, and open the file *Data Analysis Fundamentals*. Import it to JMP.

2. Click *Analyze*, and select *Text Explorer*. Drag *TEXT* to *Text Columns* and select *OK*, as shown in Figure 8.3.

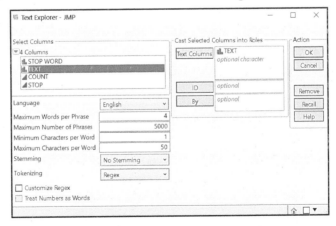

FIGURE 8.3 The Text Explorer showing *TEXT* being selected

3. Next to *Text Explorer*, select the red drop-down button, choose *Display Options*, and click *Show Word Cloud*. You can change the colors and shapes here. The resulting word cloud should look something similar to Figure 8.4.

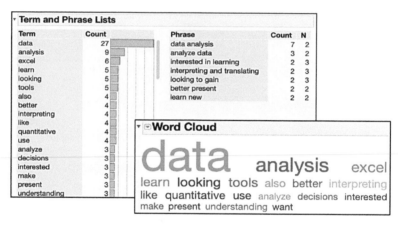

FIGURE 8.4 *Data Analysis Fundamentals* word cloud in JMP

Visualizing the Text Using Voyant

1. Using the Case Dataset provided, open the *Dataset A: Training Survey* folder, and find the *Attendee PreSurvey Results Data Comments Only.xlsx* spreadsheet file.

2. Use a Web browser with access to the Internet.

3. Load the Voyant text analysis program found at *https://voyant-tools.org/* (Figure 8.5). Alternatively, use the version of Voyant you downloaded and installed on your computer, as done in Chapter 17. You should see a screen similar to that in Figure 8.5.

FIGURE 8.5 Training Survey word cloud using Voyant

Visualizing the Text Using R

1. In the Case Data file folder under *Dataset A: Training Survey*, copy the file *Attendee PreSurvey Result data.csv*. Name the copy *casea.csv*.

2. Install the packages we need using Repository(CRAN):

```
dplyr, tidytext, wordcloud
```

3. Import the library and read the data:

```
> library(dplyr)
> library(tidytext)

> casea <- read.csv(file.path("casea.csv"),
stringsAsFactors = F)
```

4. Tokenize the contents of the dataset and remove the stop words:

```
> tidy_a <- casea %>%
    unnest_tokens(word, text) %>%
    anti_join(stop_words)
```

5. Get the results of the word frequency analysis (shown in Figure 8.6):

```
> tidy_a %>%
  count(word, sort = TRUE)
```

word <chr>	n <int>
data	27
analysis	9
excel	6
learn	5
tools	5
interpreting	4
quantitative	4
analyze	3
decisions	3
understanding	3

1-10 of 109 rows

FIGURE 8.6 Word frequency data frame of the training survey

6. Visualize the word frequency by word cloud (similar to that in Figure 8.7):

```
> library(wordcloud)
> pal = brewer.pal(8,"Dark2") # set up color
parameter
> tidy_a %>%
  count(word) %>%
  with(wordcloud(word, n, max.words = 20,
  random.order = F, random.color = T,
  color = pal))
```

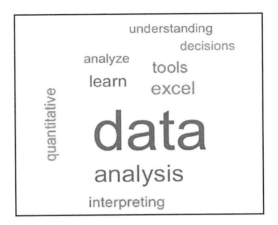

FIGURE 8.7 Word cloud of the training survey results

Exercise 8.2 – Case Study Using Dataset B: Consumer Complaints

Here, we use JMP, Voyant, and R to generate word cloud visual text analysis of text fields to perform customer sentiment analysis. We don't use Excel in this example because the number of rows of data makes the word frequency analysis techniques in Excel too cumbersome and time-consuming to execute effectively. (This example proves there are some limitations to Excel for certain kinds of large data files.) In this example, we answer the question

Can we determine some of the recurring customer complaint themes by analyzing a word cloud of the complaints?

Visualizing the Text Using JMP

1. Access the repository of case files and in the folder *Dataset B: Consumer Complaints*, open the file *BankComplaints.xlxs*. Import it to JMP.

2. Click *Rows*, and select *Data Filter*. Select the column *Company*, and add *Bank of America* in the filter. The selections are shown in Figure 8.8.

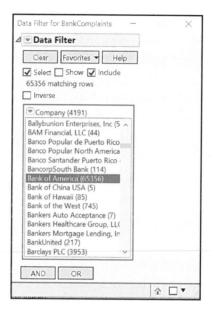

FIGURE 8.8 Filtering all bank complaints and retaining only those for Bank of America

3. Click *Analyze*, and select *Text Explorer*. Drag the *Consumer complaint narrative* variable to the *Text Columns*, and select *OK*.

FIGURE 8.9 Invoking the *Text Explorer* to analyze the consumer complaint narratives

4. Select the red drop-down button next to *Text Explorer,* choose *Term Options,* and click *Manage Stop Words.* We need to manage unwanted words, such as *XXX, bank,* and *America.* We want to remove these, which we can do by accessing the stop word list. Enter them into the *User* list and click *OK.* They have now been removed from the word cloud and frequency list.

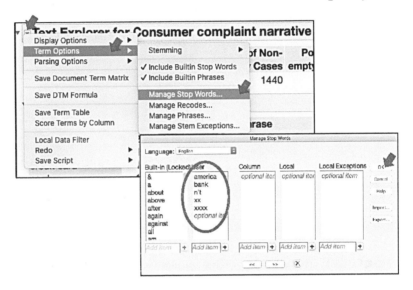

FIGURE 8.10 Removing unwanted words using the stop word list

5. Select the red drop-down button next to *Text Explorer*, choose *Display Options,* and click *Word Cloud.* You should see a display, as shown in Figure 8.11, of the desired word cloud.

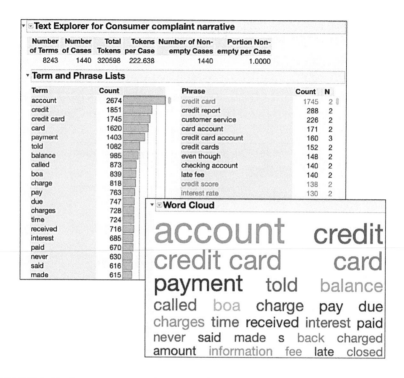

FIGURE 8.11 Consumer complaint word cloud in JMP

Visualizing the Text Using Voyant

1. Access the repository of case files and in the folder *Dataset B: Consumer Complaints*, open the file *Subset of Bank Complaints. xls* using Excel.

2. Select the entire column F: *Consumer complaint narrative.*

3. Launch Voyant and paste the contents for column F into the data entry box in Voyant. Press *Reveal.* You should see the word cloud for the complaints.

4. To remove the unwanted words (such as *XXX, bank,* and *America*), press the button in the right-hand corner of the word cloud panel. Follow the steps shown in Figure 8.12 and enter the unwanted words into the stop word list.

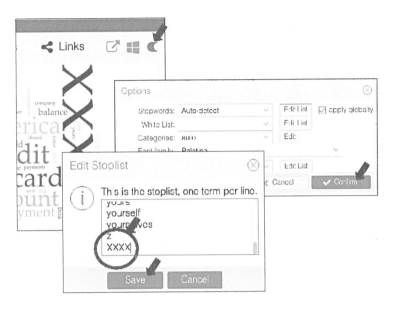

FIGURE 8.12 Editing the stop word list in Voyant

5. You should see a word cloud like that shown in Figure 8.13.

FIGURE 8.13 Consumer complaints word cloud in Voyant

Visualizing the Text Using R

1. In the *Case Data* file folder under *Dataset B: Consumer Complaints*, copy the file *BankComplaints.xlsv* and name the copy *caseb.csv*.

2. Install the packages we need using Repository(CRAN):

   ```
   dplyr, tidytext
   ```

3. Import the library and read the data:

   ```
   > library(dplyr)
   > library(tidytext)
   > caseb <- read.csv(file.path("caseb.csv"),
   stringsAsFactors = F)
   > colnames(caseb)[4] <- "text"
   ```

4. Tokenize the contents of the dataset and remove the stop words:

   ```
   > tidy_b <- caseb %>%
       unnest_tokens(word, text) %>%
       anti_join(stop_words)
   ```

5. Get the results of the word frequency analysis (see the results in Figure 8.14):

   ```
   > tidy_b %>%
       count(word, sort = TRUE)
   ```

word <chr>	n <int>
billing	285
disputes	237
account	213
credit	151
cancelling	145
closing	145
customer	134
fee	132
embezzlement	122
fraud	122
1–10 of 52 rows	

FIGURE 8.14 Word frequency data frame of the bank complaints

6. Visualize the word frequency using a word cloud (as shown in Figure 8.15):

```
> library(wordcloud)
> pal = brewer.pal(8,"Dark2") # set up color
parameter
> tidy_b %>%
    count(word) %>%
    with(wordcloud(word, n, max.words = 20,
    random.order = F, random.color = T,
    color = pal))
```

FIGURE 8.15 The word cloud of bank complaints for Bank of America

Exercise 8.3 – Case Study Using Dataset C: Product Reviews

We collected comments from our customers for some products and now want to understand what they are saying. Let's create a word cloud of their comments. The question we want to answer is

Can we create a picture of the most frequent words of their comments about a product?

Visualizing the Text Using Excel

1. The first place to start is to do a word frequency analysis, as shown in Chapter 5. Return to Chapter 5 and look at the word frequency analysis solution, primarily the pivot table result.

2. Continue with Chapter 5 *Dataset C: Product Reviews.* We will continue with the analysis of the Rubbermaid product.

3. Open *Pivot worksheet,* and select all the words with an occurrence greater than and equal to 7. You should see a table such as in Figure 8.16.

Row Labels	Count of COUN
Windex	369
product	199
review	147
promotion	145
collected	145
Glass	116
windows	114
clean	103
streaks	83
cleaning	77
cleaner	76
mirrors	60
love	59
bottle	57
using	54
surfaces	52
leaves	49

FIGURE 8.16 Windex consumer feedback word frequency analysis from the exercise in Chapter 5

4. From the main Excel ribbon, select *Insert*, then select *Treemap*. It will not yield a word cloud, but a very good picture of the data. It should be a good picture of the most important words from the customer comments. The resulting Treemap is shown in Figure 8.17.

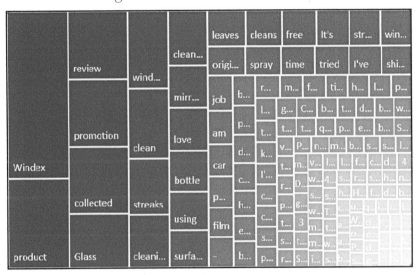

FIGURE 8.17 Treemap of the Windex product reviews

Visualizing the Text Using JMP

1. Access the case files' repository and in the folder *Dataset C: Product Reviews*, and open the file *Product Reviews.xlxs*. Import it to JMP, as shown in Figure 8.18.

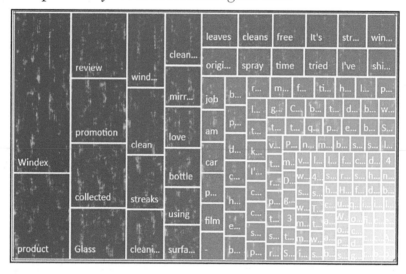

FIGURE 8.18 The product review data loaded into JMP

2. Click *Rows*. Select *Data Filter*, and choose the column brand. This time, we only include Windex, as shown in Figure 8.19.

FIGURE 8.19 Filtering for the Windex records only

3. Click *Analyze*, and select *Text Explorer*. Drag *reviews.text* to *Text Columns* and select *OK*. Remove the unwanted stop words, as shown in the previous exercise, and display a word cloud. You should see results similar to those shown in Figure 8.20.

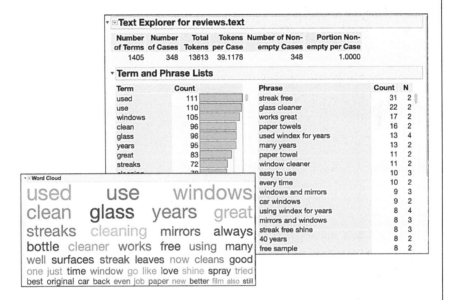

FIGURE 8.20 Word frequency results and word cloud for Windex customer feedback after some unwanted words were removed via the stop word list

Visualizing the Text Using Voyant

1. Access the repository of case files, and in the folder *Dataset C: Product Reviews*, load the file *Product Reviews.xlxs* using Excel.

2. Select the cells in column E: *reviews.text* for the *Windex* rows only. Copy the data onto your computer.

3. Launch Voyant and paste the contents for selected rows in column E into the data entry box in Voyant. Press *Reveal*. You should see the word cloud for the Windex reviews.

4. Remove the unwanted words (such as "Windex," "product," and "reviews") as was done in the previous exercise.

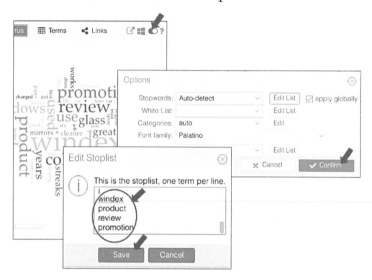

FIGURE 8.21 Editing the stop word list in Voyant

5. You should then see a word cloud like that shown in Figure 8.22.

FIGURE 8.22 Windex customer review word cloud in Voyant

Visualizing the Text Using R

1. In the *Case Data* file folder under *Dataset C: Product Reviews*, rename the file *Product Reviews.csv* as *casec.csv*.

2. Install the packages we need using Repository(CRAN):

```
dplyr, tidytext, wordcloud
```

3. Import the library and read the data:

```
> library(dplyr)
> library(tidytext)
> casec <- read.csv(file.path("casec.csv"),
stringsAsFactors = F)
# concatenate reviews text and reviews title
> casec <- casec %>%
    unite(review_combined, reviews.text,
    review.title, sep =" ", remove = FALSE)
```

4. Tokenize the contents of the dataset and remove the stop words:

```
> tidy_c <- casec %>%
    unnest_tokens(word, text) %>%
    anti_join(stop_words)
```

5. Get the results of the word frequency analysis (shown in Figure 8.23):

```
> tidy_c %>%
    count(word, sort = TRUE)
```

word <chr>	n <int>
mop	3103
spray	1201
product	990
love	935
bottle	880
bought	671
cleaning	646
reveal	640
trigger	582
handle	565
1-10 of 11 rows	

FIGURE 8.23 Word frequency data frame of the Rubbermaid product reviews

6. Visualize the word frequency using a word cloud (as shown in Figure 8.24):

```
> library(wordcloud)
> pal = brewer.pal(8,"Dark2") # set up color
parameter
> tidy_c %>%
   count(word) %>%
   with(wordcloud(word, n, max.words = 20,
   random.order = F, random.color = T,
   color = pal))
```

FIGURE 8.24 Word frequency data frame of the product reviews

Exercise 8.4 – Case Study Using Dataset E: Large Text Files

Let's now do a word cloud of a large number of words. We will load five complete travel books that contain nearly 1,000,000 words between them and create a word cloud of their combined texts. The question we are interested in answering with this word cloud is

What are the main themes derived from these five travel books by looking at the most frequent words in their combined texts?

Visualizing the Text Using Voyant

1. Using the Case Dataset provided, open the *Dataset E: Large Text Files* folder and find these text files:

   InnocentsAbroadMarkTwain.txt

   MagellanVoyagesAnthonyPiagafetta.txt

   TheAlhambraWashingtonIrving.txt

   TravelsOfMarcoPolo.txt

   VoyageOfTheBeagleDarwin.txt

2. Use a Web browser with access to the Internet.

3. Load the Voyant text analysis program found at *https:// voyant-tools.org/*. Alternatively, use the version of Voyant you downloaded and installed in your computer, as shown in Chapter 17. You should see a screen similar to that in Figure 8.25.

FIGURE 8.25 Web-based text analytic tool data entry screen

4. Load all five texts into the corpus for analysis (Figure 8.26). The word cloud is shown in the upper left hand panel. You can us the rest of the resulting analysis to explore the texts.

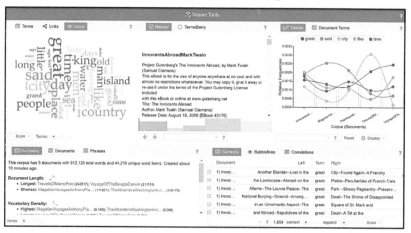

FIGURE 8.26 Results of analyzing one million words of text in a corpus of five travel books

References

1. [Medina08] Medina, John. *Brain Rules: 12 Principles for Surviving and Thriving at Work, Home, and School.* Seattle, WA, Pear Press, 2008.

2. [Fortino20] Fortino, Andres. *Data Visualization for Business Decisions: A Laboratory Notebook.* Mercury Learning & Information, 2020.

## CHAPTER 9

CODING TEXT DATA

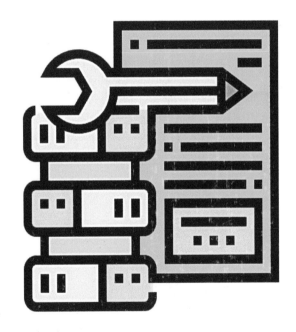

In this chapter, we analyze text data using a traditional approach. Text data is called *qualitative data*, as opposed to the *quantitative data* that we collect as numerical or categorical data. Researchers have developed a sophisticated technique to analyze qualitative data, which is referred to as *coding*. It is a way of translating text that is difficult to enumerate and characterizing it using an analyst-based scheme, the coding, into something that can be tabulated by quantizing the text data.

There are two kinds of coding. One is *inductive*, where the analyst extracts basic categories using a close reading of the text. For example, consider reading many social media postings, like tweets, that have not been categorized by adding hashtags. Inductive coding is essentially the process of adding those hashtags, which in your opinion, categorize each tweet. The other form of coding is *deductive* coding. In that case, we start with a preconceived notion of what the codes are and use them to classify each text.

We provide plenty of practice to do both types of coding. We use survey responses and ask you to inductively create codes, categorize each survey response, and tabulate the responses. We do the same thing for customer feedback of products. For the deductive coding practice, we employ a well-known code system for categorizing books, the Dewey decimal system, and ask you to categorize books according to that scheme.

What is a Code?

In qualitative inquiry, a code is most often a word or short phrase that symbolically assigns a summative, salient, essence-capturing, or evocative attribute for a portion of language-based data. The data can consist of social media postings, interview transcripts, participant observation field notes, journals, documents, open-ended survey responses, or e-mail correspondence. The process often occurs in two passes or *cycles*. The portion of data coded during the first cycle of the coding processes can range in magnitude from a single word to a full paragraph or an entire page of text. In the second cycle of the coding process, the portions coded can be the same units, longer passages of text, analytic memos about the data, and even a reconfiguration of the codes themselves developed thus far. Analysis coding is the critical link between data collection and an explanation of meaning.

In qualitative text data analysis, a code is a construct generated by the researcher that symbolizes or translates data into the analysis space. It is an attribute that, through interpretation, ascribes meaning to each individual data element. The process categorizes the text, essentially quantizing the data space, so it may more readily be analyzed for pattern detection and categorization. For example, a newspaper article's headline is the coding for the article, or the title of a non-fiction book is a code for the book itself. The placement of a book on a shelf in a library organized with the Dewey Decimal system is also just such a categorization. The placement of a newspaper or magazine article into the labeled section of that publication is also coding. This coding of text by its content represents and captures the text's primary content and essence. Chapter titles of a book are a coding scheme for the book. Mendelyan explains the process very well in his article on qualitative coding [Mendelyan19].

What are the Common Approaches to Coding Text Data?

A fundamental division of coding approaches is they are either (1) *concept-driven coding* (deductive) or (2) *data-driven coding* (inductive or open coding). You may approach the data with a developed system of codes and look for concepts/ideas in the text (deductive, concept-driven approach). You can look for ideas/concepts in the text without a preceding conceptualization and let the text speak for itself (inductive, data-driven coding). Analysts can either use a pre-determined coding scheme or review the initial responses or observations to construct a coding scheme based on the major categories that emerge.

Both methods require initial and thorough readings of the text data to find patterns or themes. An analyst identifies several passages of the text that share the same code, i.e., an expression for a shared concept, in other words, *affinities*.

What is Inductive Coding?

Inductive coding, also called *open coding*, starts from scratch and creates codes by analyzing the text data itself. There is not a preconceived set of codes to start; all codes arise directly from the survey responses. We perform mostly inductive coding here. But we will also consider externally provided codes to discover their prevalence in the text. We did that in the section about keyword analysis.

How does inductive coding work?

1. Break your qualitative dataset into smaller samples (randomly select a few of the survey responses). This works well if you have thousands of survey responses.

2. Read the samples of the data.

3. Create codes for the sample data.

4. Reread the sample and apply the codes.

5. Read a new sample of data, applying the codes you created for the first sample.

6. Note where codes don't match or where you need additional codes.

7. Create new codes based on the second sample.

8. Go back and recode all responses again. This is the step where you can use the codes as keywords and do a preliminary classification of the responses by keyword analysis. A human-based classification can interpolate close matches by affinity coding.

9. Repeat the process from step 5 until you have coded all of your text data.

If you add a new code, split an existing code into two, or change the description of a code, make sure to review how this change will affect the coding of all responses. Otherwise, the same responses at different points in the survey could end up with different codes.

Do not look for this algorithm to provide accurate results. There may be some human error and bias that intrudes in the process. But with a bit of introspection, the analyst can take care to keep bias out of the analysis. The results will be good enough, but not perfect or rigorously accurate.

Exercise 9.1 – Case Study Using Dataset A: Training

The training department of a company wants to arrange a course for its employees to improve their skills in data analysis. They conduct a survey with employees who wish to attend the training to ask them about the most important concepts they want to learn from the course. The HR manager intends to share the survey results with the training vendor and the instructor of the course. This will help focus the course on the immediate needs of the attendees. The business question to be answered by coding is

What are the most significant concepts that the instructor should stress in the data analysis training class?

The training department of a company wants to arrange a course for its employees to improve their skills in data analysis. They conduct a survey with employees who wish to attend the training to ask them about the most important concepts they want to learn from the course. The HR manager intends to share the survey results with the training vendor and the instructor of the course. This will help focus the course on the immediate needs of the attendees. The business question to be answered by coding is

What are the most significant concepts that the instructor should stress in the data analysis training class?

The survey asked: *"What do you want to learn in the Data Analysis Essentials class?"* The dataset contains answers to two additional questions: *"How would you rate your Microsoft Excel skill level?"* and *"What is your position title?"* The responses are documented in the spreadsheet *Attendee PreSurvey Results.xlsx*. Figure 9.1 shows some of the responses. Your task is to use inductive coding to discover the attendees' expectations.

Record	What are you looking to learn in the Data Analysis Essentials class?	How would you rate your Microsoft Excel skill level?	What is your position title?
1	I'm looking to learn how to better present grants and budget data so that interpreting and translating them into decisions will be easier. I'm also hoping to learn new ways of manipulating data.	Intermediate	Program Coordinator
2	To better understand quantitative analysis and how to translate data into easily readable formats	Intermediate	Program Analyst
3	Skills in Quantitative and Qualitative Data Analysis would enable me to make recommendations within project management, for example, being able to look at budgets in a meaningful way and/or make comparisons between sets of data. Having empirical data to back up an idea is often necessary, but just having the data isn't always enough...	Intermediate	Exec Assistant/Project Coordinator
4	I am looking to gain tools and information to allow for proficient data analysis in the future	Intermediate	Program Oifficer
5	I am interested in learning different approaches to organizing, summarizing and interpreting quantitative data using Excel.	Intermediate	Program Specialist/Executive Assistant
6	As an aspiring Budget Analyst, I want tools that I can use to organize, summarize and interpret data. Specifically, I want to learn more about regression, trend lines, and other scenarios in Excel; Interpreting and translating data into decisions is key to adding value on rotation and in my future conversion positions. Hopefully, we'll use charts to visually display data. Overall, I want more information on how to analyze data that my stakeholders use to make decisions.	Intermediate	Management Intern
7	I am seeking a refresher on data analysis tools within Microsoft Excel. I am interested in pivot tables and any other tools that help with analyzing large batches of data. I am also interested in learning recommended methods for displaying data so that others can understand more easily. Any info on these areas would be great, but overall I am open to any other areas that the course focuses on also.	Intermediate	Budget Analyst

FIGURE 9.1 Some of the 17 survey responses for the data analysis course attendees

1. Open the spreadsheet *Attendee PreSurvey Results.xlsx* found in the folder *Dataset A: Training*.

2. Copy columns A and B onto another tab in the spreadsheet.

3. Read the attendees' comments in the first five rows of the data in column B.

4. Create some codes (data analysis concepts the attendees seem to want to learn).

5. Write those codes as column headers starting in column E.

6. Reread the sample and apply the codes (enter a "1" under the appropriate column).

7. Read the rest of the rows of data, applying the codes you created for the first sample.

8. Note where codes don't match or where you need additional codes.

9. Create new codes based on the second sample.

10. Go back and recode all responses again, adding a "1" in the appropriate column. Note that some survey responses may match several codes. Be sure to enter a "1" for every code that matches.

11. Generate the totals at the bottom of each column.

12. In another tab, post the list for codes in a column and add the corresponding frequencies of appearance in the responses. Sort the list and plot a bar graph to show the most desired topics. Figure 9.2 shows the resulting frequency analysis and identification of the most desired topical coverage.

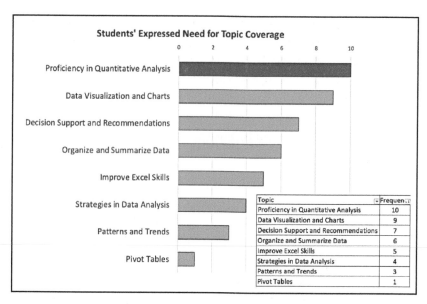

Topic	Frequency
Proficiency in Quantitative Analysis	10
Data Visualization and Charts	9
Decision Support and Recommendations	7
Organize and Summarize Data	6
Improve Excel Skills	5
Strategies in Data Analysis	4
Patterns and Trends	3
Pivot Tables	1

FIGURE 9.2 Resulting frequency analysis and identification of the most desired topical coverage

Exercise 9.2 - Case Study Using Dataset J: Remote Learning

During the Spring of 2020, many universities worldwide abruptly shut down their classrooms and turned to remote learning. Although online education had been going on for many years before the event, there was a concern that now that students were forced to take all classes remotely, there would be some dissatisfaction. As an attempt to keep students engaged and thriving under the new regime, one professor examined the issues of remote vs. in-class learning. He conducted a survey of students using the following statements: *"Compare and contrast learning in a physical classroom vs. learning remotely, as a substitute, during this time of crisis. Tell us what you like and what you don't like, what works, and what does not work."*

As you can see, this approach will yield an open-ended response. The professor was not expecting short, concise answers, but gave students the opportunity to express themselves. This was not meant to be a comprehensive study, but to produce imperfect indicators of students' concerns that perhaps could be quickly addressed during the crisis to complete the semester successfully. The professor wanted to know

What were the students' most significant concerns in switching from in-person to all-remote classes?

The data is documented in the spreadsheet *Remote Education Student Survey.xlsx*. Figure 9.3 shows some of the 32 responses. Your task is to use inductive coding to discover what the most crucial student concerns are.

Timestamp	Compare and contrast learning in a physical classroom versus learning remotely, as a substitute, during this time of crisis. Tells us what you like, and what you don't like. What works, and what does not work.
2020/04/15 6:47:50 PM AST	the remote learning save lots of time and let us safe at home in the situation. however, it's hard to concentrate and the interactive is not as good as physical classroom
2020/04/15 6:48:12 PM AST	I like the convinient time flexibility but i dont think i can concentrate.
2020/04/15 6:48:21 PM AST	I like that we save the traveling time between school and home. However, I don't like that professor doesn't know that we cannot catch up sometimes
2020/04/15 6:48:21 PM AST	I don't like that online classes create a sense of isolation and sometimes is hard for me to stay on focus. However, online classes offer flexibility and teach you to be self-disciplined.
2020/04/15 6:48:30 PM AST	Having class remotely can save a lot of time on the way to school, and can stay safe from the virus. But, it is easy to lose the concentration, can not learn much.
2020/04/15 6:48:35 PM AST	I prefer in physical classroom cause it give me no chance to loose my mind
2020/04/15 6:48:51 PM AST	The learning efficiency in remote class will be lower than the physical class due to the technology issue. However, the remote class might be more interesting because this new format of lecture and this could be safer.
2020/04/15 6:48:51 PM AST	It's convenient but i can't concentrated on class well, and staying at home makes work inefficient
2020/04/15 6:48:52 PM AST	I like the physical classroom since I can communicate with professors and classmates without the technology issues. Sometimes I may be distracted by other things if learning remotely.
2020/04/15 6:48:59 PM AST	Like: no need to spend half an hour to go to the classroom Dislike: group discussion is ineffective; hard to focus

FIGURE 9.3 Some of the 32 survey responses used to discover students' concerns with an abrupt change of modality in their class from in-person to all-remote

1. Open the spreadsheet *Remote Education Student Survey.xlsx* found in the folder *Dataset J: Remote Learning.*

2. Copy column B onto another tab in the spreadsheet.

3. Read the attendees' comments in the first five rows of the data in column A.

4. Create some codes (data analysis concepts the attendees want to learn).

5. Write those codes as column headers starting in column B.

6. Reread the sample and apply the codes (enter a "1" under the appropriate column).

7. Read the rest of the rows of data, applying the codes you created for the first sample.

8. Note where codes don't match or where you need additional codes.

9. Create new codes based on the second sample.

10. Go back and recode all responses again, adding a "1" in the appropriate column. Note that some survey responses may match several codes. Be sure to enter a "1" for every code that matches.

11. Generate the totals at the bottom of each column, as shown in Figure 9.4.

Compare and contrast learning in a physical classroom versus learning remotely, as a substitute, during this time of crisis. Tells us what you like, and what you don't like. What works, and what does not work.	Remote Save Time	Remote Hard to Concentrate	Remote Convinient	Remoteley Professor not know	Remote makes you more Isolated	Remote Need self-discipline
the remote learning saves lots of time and let us safe at home in the situation. however, it's hard to concentrate and the interactive is not as good as physical classroom	1	1				
I like the convinient time flexibility but i dont think i can concentrate.		1	1			
I like that we save the traveling time between school and home. However, I don't like that professor doesn't know that we cannot catch up sometimes	1			1		
I don't like that online classes create a sense of isolation and sometimes is hard for me to stay on focus. However, online classes offer flexibility and teach you to be self-disciplined.		1			1	1
Having class remotely can save a lot of time on the way to school, and can stay safe from the virus. But, it is easy to lose the concentration, can not learn much.	1	1	1			
I prefer in physical classroom cause it give me no chance to loose my mind		1				
The learning efficiency in remote class will be lower than the physical class due to the technology issue. However, the remote class might be more interesting because this new format of lecture and this could be safer.						
It's convenient but i can't concentrated on class well, and staying at home makes work inefficient		1	1			

FIGURE 9.4 Sample coding of some of the survey responses

12. In another tab, post the list for codes in a column and add the corresponding frequencies of appearance in the responses. Sort the list and plot a bar graph to show the most sought-after topics of concern. Figure 9.5 shows the resulting frequency analysis and identification of the most frequent issues. We see that out of 14 identified issues, and four stand out as recurring themes for over 50% of all students. The rest barely registered in the single digits. We can safely assume these four are their primary concerns.

Code	Count	Frequency	REMOTE
Physical classoorm Discussion more engaging	16	50%	Worse
Remote Save Time	13	41%	Better
Remote Convinient	13	41%	Better
Remote Hard to Concentrate	12	38%	Worse
There are Tech issues with Remote	2	6%	Worse
Remote is Safer	2	6%	Better
No interactions with others as much with Remote	2	6%	Worse
With Remote Recorded content	2	6%	Better
Remoteley Professor not know	1	3%	Worse
Remote makes you more Isolated	1	3%	Worse
Remote Need self-discipline	1	3%	Worse
Easy to ask questions Face to Face	1	3%	Worse

FIGURE 9.5 Resulting frequency analysis and identification of the most crucial student concerns

13. We can further categorize each code as to whether it implies a positive or a negative in switching from in-person to all-remote (coded as better or worse). Figure 9.6 summarizes the results of this extra coding using a pivot table on the frequency table. We can deduce that the positive and the negatives balance each other out. The students have concerns, but they are happy to be safe and completing their studies.

Is remote learning better or worse than face to face?		
Row Labels ▼	Sum of Count	Sum of Count2
Better	30	45%
Worse	36	55%
Grand Total	66	100%

FIGURE 9.6 Resulting frequency analysis and identification of the most crucial student concerns

What is Deductive Coding?

Deductive coding means you start with a predefined set of codes, then assign those codes to new qualitative data. These codes might come from previous research, or you might already know what themes you're interested in analyzing. Deductive coding is also called *concept-driven* coding.

For example, let's say you're conducting a survey on customer experience. You want to understand the problems that arise from long call wait times, so you choose to make "wait time" one of your codes before you start examining the data.

Our dataset of bank complaints has two variables of interest in trying to understand customer complaints. One of them, the *Consumer complaint narrative*, had the free text customer narrative of the nature of their complaint. That's the text data we want to analyze by coding. Implicit coding in the last section would have us study their complaints and implicitly look for what codes we might use. There is another variable in the dataset, the *Issue* variable. It contains the customer categorizing the primary issue in the complaint. They check the box on over two dozen possible complaints the survey maker thought the complaint could be about. We could use these two dozen categories as codes to code the *Consumer complaint narrative* data, looking for additional patterns beyond the simplistic top-level categorization by the customer. These per-supplied codes become the basis for our deductive analysis.

The deductive approach can save time and help guarantee that your areas of interest are coded. But care needs to be taken so as not to introduce bias; when you start with predefined codes, you have a bias as to what the answers may be.

In one case, there was an employee exit interview survey conducted by a major computer manufacturer. The company owners were proud of taking good care of their employees, so they were always amazed that anyone would leave their employ. The exit interview survey was created with the collaboration of the first-line managers. The survey included myriad questions on why someone would leave the company. Fortunately, a good survey designer thoughtfully added a final a text field question that asked "Is there anything else you wish to tell us?" When they finally analyzed these text responses using coding, they found that the overwhelming reason these employees were leaving was something that was left out in the survey: they were dissatisfied with their interactions with the first-line managers. This important idea would have been missed if preconceived codes had been the only source of feedback. This anecdotal story shows why text analysis can help us make sense of what our customers or employees are saying that sometimes the rest of the data does not cover. Make sure you don't miss other important patterns by focusing too hard on proving your own hypothesis.

Exercise 9.3 - Case Study Using Dataset E: Large Text Files

The Dewey Decimal System is an important classification scheme for books used by libraries. Using its pre-determined codes, we will classify some classic texts as an exercise in coding. Assume you are the librarian and have received several manuscripts that need to be classified using the system. You read some of the first pages of each book, and you need to decide how to code the text according to the Dewy Decimal System. Figure 9.7 shows the ten major Dewey Decimal System classifications and topical coverage of each significant area.

Dewey #	10 Main Classes	Kinds of Books
000-099	General Works	encyclopedias, almanacs, record books, such as Guinness
100-199	Philosophy and Psychology	paranormal phenomena, such as ghosts, ethics, how we think
200-299	Religion	mythology, religions
300-399	Social Science	government, holidays, folklore, fairy tales, education, community
400-499	Language	English and foreign languages, sign language, dictionaries
500-599	Natural Science	math, chemistry, biology, weather, rocks, plants, animals in nature
600-699	Applied Science	inventions, health, drugs, transportation, cooking, pets
700-799	Fine Arts and Recreation	crafts, art, drawing, painting, music, games, TV, movies, sports
800-899	Literature	short stories, poetry, plays, jokes, riddles (fiction could be here)
900-999	History and Geography	countries, flags, historical events, biographies (92 or 920)

FIGURE 9.7 The Dewey Decimal System's book classification coding scheme

1. Open the spreadsheet *Text Excerpts For Classification.xlsx* found in the folder *Dataset E: Large Text Files*.

2. Using the scheme above, classify each text by reading the book's first page found in column B.

3. The results (including book title and author) can be found in the second tab in the worksheet.

Documenting Your Codes

The meaning of codes should be documented in a separate file or in another worksheet within the same spreadsheet containing the data. Make short descriptions of the meaning of each code. It is helpful to you and also to other researchers who will have access to your data/analysis.

Here is what you should document about your codes (after Gibbs [Gibbs07]):

1. The label or name of the code

2. Who coded it (name of the researcher/coder)

3. The date when the coding was done/changed

4. Definition of the code; a description of the concept it refers to

5. Information about the relationship of the code to other codes you are working with during the analysis.

The authoritative reference for coding textual data is the book by Saldaña: *The Coding Manual for Qualitative Researchers* [Saldaña15]. We explored some simple techniques here, we refer you to the more detailed text for larger, more complex projects.

Affinity Analysis

What is Affinity Analysis?

The affinity diagram process organizes a large number of ideas into their natural relationships. It is the organized output from a brainstorming session. You can use it to generate, organize, and consolidate information related to a product, process, complex issue, or problem. After generating ideas, group them according to their affinity or similarity. This idea creation method taps a team's creativity and intuition. It was created in the 1960s by Japanese anthropologist Jiro Kawakita (see his 1975 book *The KJ Method–A Scientific Approach to Problem-Solving* [Kawakita75].)

The Affinity Diagram is a method that can help you gather large amounts of data and organize them into groups or themes based on their relationships. The Affinity Diagram is excellent for grouping data collected during research or for ideas generated during brainstorming. Dam explains it in detail in his article on affinity diagrams [Dam18].

The Affinity Diagram lets a group move beyond its current way of thinking and preconceived categories. This technique accesses the knowledge and understanding residing untapped in our intuition. Affinity Diagrams tend to have 40 to 60 categories.

How Does it Apply to Business Data Analysis?

We can use this technique in several ways. Say we surveyed what customers wanted in a product. Besides asking quantitative questions (such as "on a scale of 1 to 5…"), we also ask open-ended questions (such as "Is there anything else you want us to know…"). Doing a word frequency analysis of the text responses to the open-ended questions and comparing it to the word frequency analysis of the product description tells us if we are meeting expectations. The more the two-word frequency tables match, the more we are speaking the customers' language.

As another example, consider a company that launched a campaign to make employees more aware of the new company mission. After a while, an employee survey asks the open-ended question: "Can you tell us what you think the company mission statement is?" By doing a word frequency analysis of the mission statement and comparing it to the frequency analysis of the employee's responses, we can gauge how successful our education awareness campaign has been.

Affinity Diagram Coding

Exercise 9.4 - Case Study Using Dataset M: Onboarding Brainstorming

The ACME company wants to understand the difficulties around the excessive time needed for onboarding new employees. A select team of hiring managers, new employees, human resource managers, and peer employees conducted a brainstorming session and identified 15 problems. All of the ideas were documented on the spreadsheet *Onboarding.xlxs*. Figure 9.8 shows the initial table of observations. Your task is to find the most recurring issue is so it can be addressed immediately. We do this by coding the observations to the identified affinity codes. We also set up categories of problems that can be used to monitor performance and new issues as they arise in the future.

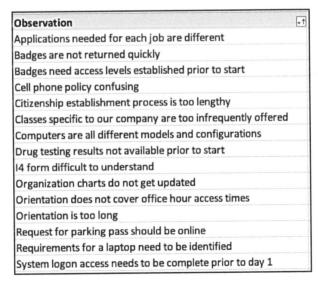

Observation
Applications needed for each job are different
Badges are not returned quickly
Badges need access levels established prior to start
Cell phone policy confusing
Citizenship establishment process is too lengthy
Classes specific to our company are too infrequently offered
Computers are all different models and configurations
Drug testing results not available prior to start
I4 form difficult to understand
Organization charts do not get updated
Orientation does not cover office hour access times
Orientation is too long
Request for parking pass should be online
Requirements for a laptop need to be identified
System logon access needs to be complete prior to day 1

FIGURE 9.8 The 15 observations from the onboarding problem identification brainstorming session

1. Open the spreadsheet *Onboarding.xlxs* found in the folder *Dataset M: Onboarding Brainstorming*.

2. Take the first observation and label it as belonging to group A. Enter "A" in the second column next to the observation.

3. Take the second observation and ask *"Is this similar to the first one, or is it different?"* Then, you label it "A" if it belongs in a similar group or in a new group, "B."

4. You continue observation by observation, and you label similar ideas as belonging to the same group and create new groups when ideas do not fit into an existing cluster. Try not to have too many groups. See similarities between ideas so they can be placed in the same group.

5. You should now have 3-10 groups. In our case, you probably found four groups, as in Figure 9.9.

Observation	Group
Applications needed for each job are different	A
Badges are not returned quickly	D
Badges need access levels established prior to start	A
Cell phone policy confusing	A
Citizenship establishment process is too lengthy	C
Classes specific to our company are too infrequently offered	A
Computers are all different models and configurations	C
Drug testing results not available prior to start	C
I4 form difficult to understand	B
Organization charts do not get updated	B
Orientation does not cover office hour access times	A
Orientation is too long	A
Request for parking pass should be online	B
Requirements for a laptop need to be identified	A
System logon access needs to be complete prior to day 1	D
Clusters for Coding	
Training	A
Paperwork	B
Regulatory	C
Technology	D

FIGURE 9.9 Grouping the 15 observations by their affinity to each other, creating four major affinity groups, and subsequently naming the groups to identify the codes

6. Now we decide on the best names for those clusters. Read through the observations in each set or group and see if you can discover a theme. Assign names to the clusters to help you create an information structure and to discover themes.

7. Rank the most important clusters over the less important clusters. Be aware of which values, motives, and priorities you use as foundation ideas before you start ranking: Is this your user's priority, your company's, the market's, the stakeholder's, or your own? Which ones should you put the most emphasis on?

8. After reading through the observations, you realize they fall into one of four broad categories: training issues, paperwork issues, regulatory issues, and technology issues. You are managing the onboarding process needed to identify any commonalities or relationships between the ideas.

9. Create a new worksheet distributing the codes across the identified groups. Categorize each observation by the group it belongs to. ACME can now track these four areas and assign them to the appropriate groups for resolution. The process also highlights areas of deficiency.

10. Figure 9.10 shows the resulting affinity coding of the observations and the most frequent issues.

Observation	Coding			
	Training	Paperwork	Regulatory	Technology
Applications needed for each job are different	1			
Badges are not returned quickly				1
Badges need access levels established prior to start	1			
Cell phone policy confusing	1			
Citizenship establishment process is too lengthy			1	
Classes specific to our company are too infrequently offered	1			
Computers are all different models and configurations			1	
Drug testing results not available prior to start			1	
I4 form difficult to understand		1		
Organization charts do not get updated		1		
Orientation does not cover office hour access times	1			
Orientation is too long	1			
Request for parking pass should be online		1		
Requirements for a laptop need to be identified	1			
System logon access needs to be complete prior to day 1				1
Frequency	7	3	3	2

FIGURE 9.10 The 15 observations categorized by affinity code and identification of the most frequent category of problems

References

1. [Kawakita75] Kawakita, Jiro. *The KJ Method–A Scientific Approach to Problem Solving*. Kawakita Research Institute 2 (1975).

2. [Dam18] Dam, R., and T. Siang. "Affinity Diagrams–Learn How to Cluster and Bundle Ideas and Facts"[online]. The Interaction Design Foundation (2018).

3. [Mendelyan19] Mendelyan, A. "Coding qualitative data: How to code qualitative research." *URL: https://getthematic.com/insights/coding-qualitative-data* (2019).

4. [Saldaña15] Saldaña, Johnny. *The Coding Manual for Qualitative Researchers*. Sage, 2015.

5. [Gibbs07] Gibbs, G. R. Thematic coding and categorizing. *Analyzing Qualitative Data*, 703, 38-59. (2007).

## CHAPTER 10

NAMED ENTITY RECOGNITION

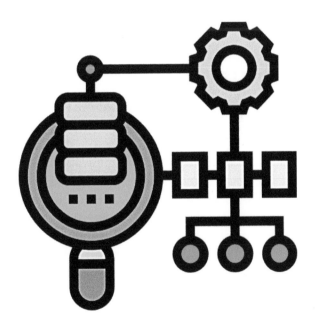

In this chapter, we continue our work on text data mining. Here, we use a more sophisticated algorithm from a rapidly emerging field: information extraction. In previous chapters, we used information extraction to acquire business knowledge from text, but it was a relatively simple and basic approach. This chapter expands the work to the use of algorithms classified as machine learning. Another name for this area is Natural language Processing (NLP), and the Stanford University people who do this work are the best in their field. We make use of their algorithm, which they are graciously allowing us to employ.

We will extract named entities (person, places, dates) from several document types. After installing and practicing with simple datasets (short paragraphs, a fictional story, and a Wikipedia page), we will work with business documents (i.e., financial reports). We conclude with extracting, classifying, and tabulating named entities in large datasets using books.

Named Entity Recognition

Named Entity Recognition, NER, is a standard NLP problem dealing with information extraction. The primary objective is to locate and classify named entities in a text into predefined categories such as the names of persons, organizations, locations, events, expressions of times, quantities, monetary values, and percentages. NER systems extract real-world entities from the text, such as a person's name, an organization, or an event. NER is also known as entity identification, entity chunking, or entity extraction. Extracting the leading entities in a text helps sort unstructured data and detect important information, which is crucial to deal with large datasets.

Most NER systems are programmed to take an unannotated block of text, such as

"Mary bought 300 acres of Blueberry Hill Farm in 2020"

and produce an annotated block of text that highlights the names of entities:

"[Mary]$_{\text{Person}}$ bought 300 acres of [Blueberry Hill Farm]$_{\text{Organization}}$ in [2020]$_{\text{Time}}$."

In this example, a person's name consisting of one token, a three-token company name, and a temporal expression were detected and classified.

NER is part of the emerging field of information extraction, a critical area in our current information-driven world. Rather than indicating which documents need to be read by a user, it extracts pieces of information that are important to the user's needs. Links between the extracted information and the original documents are maintained to allow the user to reference context. The kinds of information that these systems extract vary in detail and reliability. For example, named entities such as persons and organizations can be extracted with a high reliability but do not provide attributes, facts, or events that those entities have or participated in. In our case, we concentrate on named entity extraction.

What is a Named Entity?

In information extraction, a *named entity* is a real-world object, such as people, locations, organizations, or products, that can be denoted with a proper name. It can be abstract (company) or have a physical existence (person). It may also include time data, such as dates. As an example, consider the sentence, "Washington was a president of the United States." Both "Washington" and the "United States" are named entities since they refer to specific objects (George Washington and the United States). However, "president" is not a named entity since it can refer to many different items in different worlds (in different presidential periods referring to different persons, or even in different countries or organizations referring to different people). Rigid designators usually include proper names as well as certain natural terms, like biological species and substances.

Common Approaches to Extracting Named Entities

The Stanford Named Entity Recognizer is an excellent example of a NER. The Stanford NER is implemented in Java. It provides a default trained model for recognizing entities like organizations, people, and locations. It also makes available models trained for different languages and circumstances.

The Stanford NER is referred to as a CRF (Conditional Random Field) classifier. Conditional Random Field sequence models have been implemented in the software. Your own custom models can be trained with a Stanford NER labeled dataset for various applications with proper instruction.

Classifiers – The Core NER Process

A core function of a NER is to classify parts of the text. The algorithms that perform this function are *classifiers*. Some are trained to recognize elements of the text, like parts of speech (POS) such as sentences, nouns, and punctuation. Other classifiers identify named entities, names, dates, and locations. The classifiers can be applied to raw text one classifier at a time or together. Since we are not linguists but wish to process text for business information, the type of classifier we will employ is called an entity classifier. This is important because we will be directed to load and run the proper classifier to get the intended results when we use the Stanford NER. Jenny Finkel created the CFR codes used in our exercises [Finkel05]. The feature extractors were created by Dan Klein, Christopher Manning, and Jenny Finkel. Much of the documentation and usability testing was done by Anna Rafferty [Manning14].

What Does This Mean for Business?

A NER may add semantic understanding to any large body of the text. It has multiple business use-cases, such as classifying and prioritizing news content for newspapers. It can also generate candidate short-lists from a large number of CVs for recruiters, for example. When integrated into email and chat systems, the use of NER technology could enable a business to extract and collate information from large amounts of documentation across multiple communication channels in a much more streamlined, efficient manner. Using a NER allows you to instantly view trending topics, companies, or stock tickers, and provides you with a full overview of all your information channels containing relevant content, such as meeting notes shared via email or daily discussions over chat systems. In a world where business managers can send and receive thousands of emails per day, removing the noise and discovering the true value in relevant content may be the difference between success and failure. There are a number of popular NER libraries and very mature products available today.

We demonstrate a few capabilities using one such NER based on the Stanford NLP set of tools. A NER algorithm's precision and accuracy rely on whether it has been trained using pre-labeled texts that are similar in context to its end use-case. Since a NER algorithm forms an understanding of entities through grammar, word positioning, and context, this final element is of crucial importance. If omitted, it can result in low accuracy scores.

Exercise 10.1 - Using the Stanford NER

The Stanford NER may be downloaded from *https://nlp.stanford. edu/software/stanford-ner-4.0.0.zip*. Follow the instructions given in Chapter 15 for further information. It may also be invoked directly from the set of files provided with this book under the *Tools* directory. The Standard NER is a Java application. If you have the latest Java program installed on your computer, it should open immediately upon being invoked. Otherwise, you may have to load or update Java.

Open the directory *Tools* and open the *Stanford-ner-4.0.0* directory. You will see various versions of the Java program there. It is suggested you start by invoking the *Stanford-ner.jar* program. You will see a simple input screen that looks like what is shown in Figure 10.1.

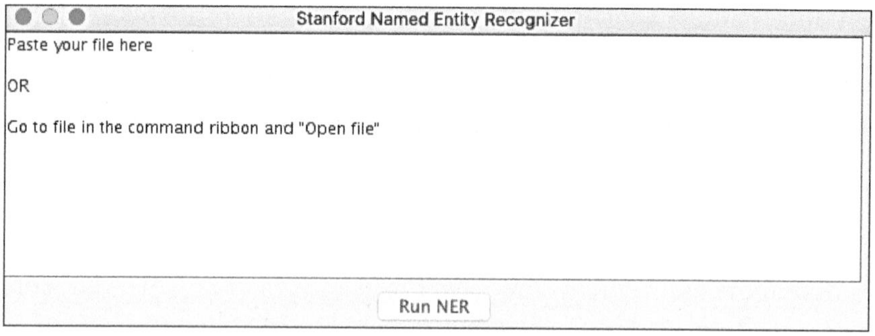

FIGURE 10.1 The Stanford NER text entry screen without a classifier

The program is not ready to run until you load a classifier. Go to the program command ribbon on the top of the screen click on the *classifier* menu choice. In the pull-down menu, select *Load CRF from File*. Navigate the file menu window to locate the file folder classifiers under the *Stanford -ner-4.0.0 folder*. There you will find and load the named entity classifier *english.all.3class.distsim.crf. ser.gz*. The text interface panel has the added named entities legend showing the highlight colors for identified entities.

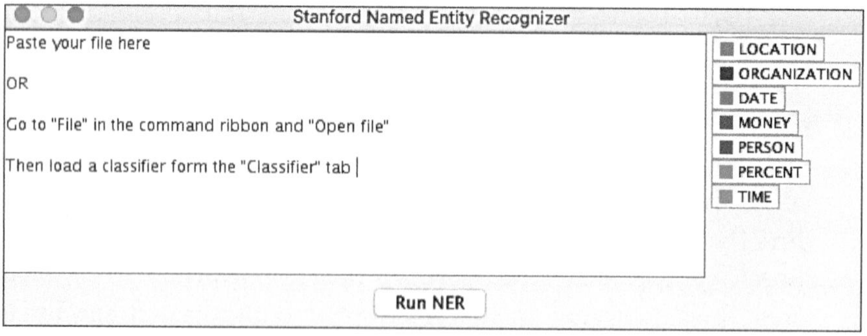

FIGURE 10.2 The Stanford NER text entry screen after loading a classifier ready to be used by loading a text file

Exercise 10.2 – Example Cases

Let's start simple. Copy the following sentence into the buffer:

Barack Obama was born on August 4, 1961, in Honolulu, Hawaii, which was 4 days ago.

Paste it into the NER's text entry screen. Press *Run NER*. You should see the text with named entities tagged, as in Figure 10.3

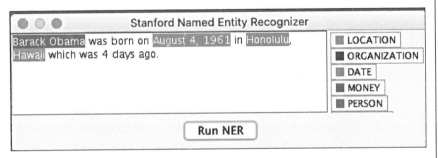

FIGURE 10.3 Simple text with named entities tagged by the NER

1. Let's load the text from a file. In the program command ribbon, use the *File* tab and select *Open File*, as shown in Figure 10.4.

FIGURE 10.4 The *File* management tab in the NER command ribbon

2. Navigate to the *stanford-ner-4.0.0* directory open the file *sample.txt*. Press *Run NER* to extract the entities, as shown in Figure 10.5.

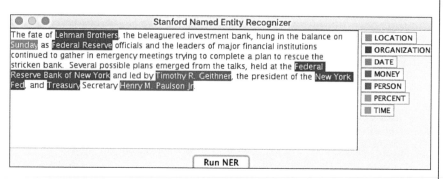

FIGURE 10.5 The extraction of named entities from a file loaded from the command ribbon

3. The Stanford NER can also load HTML documents directly from the Internet. Navigate to the Wikipedia page on George Washington. Copy the URL. Using the *File* function of the NER, load the webpage by pasting the URL link into the offered window. The webpage for George Washington will be loaded into the text window.

4. Press *Run NER* and see the resulting tagged text. Your results should look something like what you see in Figure 10.6 (the figure shows a similar text with the facts of in the Wikipedia page, not an exact replica).

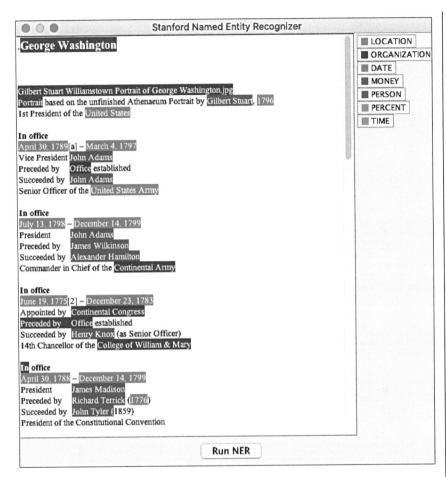

FIGURE 10.6 Loading and extracting entities from a webpage. This is a simulation of the retrieved page on George Washington showing dates, locations, organizations, and names correctly identified as *named entities*.

5. Let's examine a case where there are few entities of interest, and this technique does not yield interesting results. Using the *File* command in the NER, load the *Little Red Riding Hood. txt* fable file. After running the NER, we see that there is but one named entity at best, the name of the editor of this version of the fable. Figure 10.7 shows the resulting extraction. This is not a good technique to extract meaning from such a file.

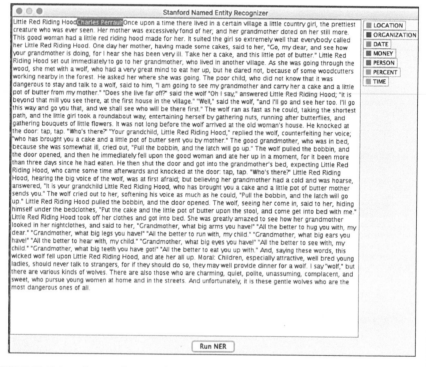

FIGURE 10.7 Loading and extracting entities for a web page

Application of Entity Extraction to Business Cases

Here, we download the extracted list of entities to a text file, which is a function of the NER, and then post-process that file to extract further information. The program and function we use to tabulate the entity list are Excel and pivot tables.

Suppose we wanted a list of all named entities in a corporate financial report. We use the Apple 2019 10K annual financial report publicly filed with the United States Securities and Exchange Commission (found in the Edgar public database). Our business question is

What are the most frequent names, locations, and dates in the 2019 Apple 10K financial report?

The financial report is large (over 300 pages), which should not be a problem for the NER to process. To exemplify the technique, we limit the file to the first 23 pages. We leave the reader to process the full file as an additional exercise. Be mindful that a large text file can take up to a full minute to be processed by the NER.

Exercise 10.2 - Case Study Using Dataset H: Corporate Financial Reports

1. Load the file *Apple 2019 10K Part 1.txt* found in the folder *Dataset H: Corporate Financial Reports* into the Stanford NER.

2. Load the *english.all.3class.distsim.crf.ser.gz* classifier and run the NER. Be patient; it may take some time to return results.

3. The results should look like those shown in Figure 10.8.

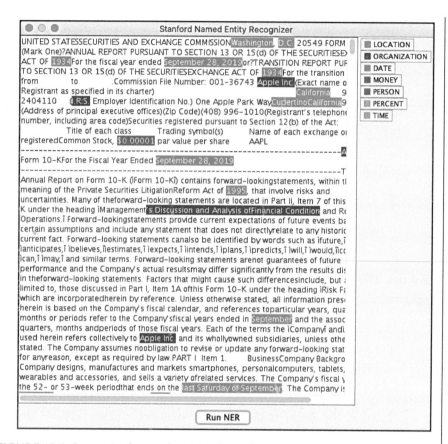

FIGURE 10.8 Recognized named entities from the 2019 Apple 10K financial filing with the SEC

4. From the *File* menu on the NER, run the *Saved Tagged File As…* function. The file may be saved wherever you wish (typically, while working on a project, it is suggested to save it on the desktop to be filed away later). Save it as *NER Apple 2019 10K Part 1.txt*. Open it in a text editor and assure yourself that the named entity tags are indeed present.

5. We now do some postprocessing to create the needed list. We use Microsoft Word to create the file to be loaded and further cleaned in Excel before running a pivot table.

6. Open *Apple 2019 10K Part 1.txt* in Word. Search and replace the character "<" with it preceded with a carriage return ("^p<"). This places each tagged named entity at the start of a new line and separates it from the rest of the text. The processed file with the final list in Word should look like what is shown in Figure 10.9.

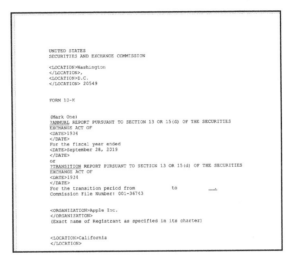

UNITED STATES
SECURITIES AND EXCHANGE COMMISSION

<LOCATION>Washington
</LOCATION>,
<LOCATION>D.C.
</LOCATION> 20549

FORM 10-K

(Mark One)
?ANNUAL REPORT PURSUANT TO SECTION 13 OR 15(d) OF THE SECURITIES
EXCHANGE ACT OF
<DATE>1934
</DATE>
For the fiscal year ended
<DATE>September 28, 2019
</DATE>
or
?TRANSITION REPORT PURSUANT TO SECTION 13 OR 15(d) OF THE SECURITIES
EXCHANGE ACT OF
<DATE>1934
</DATE>
For the transition period from   to   ___.
Commission File Number: 001-36743

<ORGANIZATION>Apple Inc.
</ORGANIZATION>
(Exact name of Registrant as specified in its charter)

<LOCATION>California
</LOCATION>

FIGURE 10.9 Post-processing of the 2019 Apple 10K financial filing NER analysis in Word

7. Select the entire text and copy it into the buffer (or save it as a UTF-8 text file).

8. Open a blank Excel spreadsheet and paste or load the list. Label the column Tagged Data. Sort the data by that column in descending order. Delete any rows that do not have "<" in them as the first character (also delete any rows that have "</" as the first and second character). That should leave a list of the tagged entities that looks like that shown in Figure 10.10.

	A
1	**Tagged Entities**
2	<DATE>1934
3	<DATE>1934
4	<DATE>1934
5	<DATE>1977
6	<DATE>1995
7	<DATE>2017
8	<DATE>2019
9	<DATE>2019
10	<DATE>2019
11	<DATE>2019
12	<DATE>2019
13	<DATE>2019
14	<DATE>2019
15	<DATE>2019
16	<DATE>2019
17	<DATE>2019
18	<DATE>2019
19	<DATE>2019
20	<DATE>2019
21	<DATE>2019
22	<DATE>2019
23	<DATE>2019
24	<DATE>2019
25	<DATE>2019
26	<DATE>fall of 2019
27	<DATE>last Saturday of September

FIGURE 10.10 Recognized named entities from the 2019 Apple 10K financial filing with the SEC

9. Using the *Text to Columns* function in the *Data ribbon*, split the *Tagged Entities* column by the ">" character. Replace the "<" character in the first column and rename the first column *Entity Type* and the second column *Value*. Select the data in both columns and create a named table called *Entities*.

10. Create a pivot table with the *Entities* table data and enumerate by entity type. Add a subfield of *Value* to count multiple entries. The results should look similar to those shown in Figure 10.11.

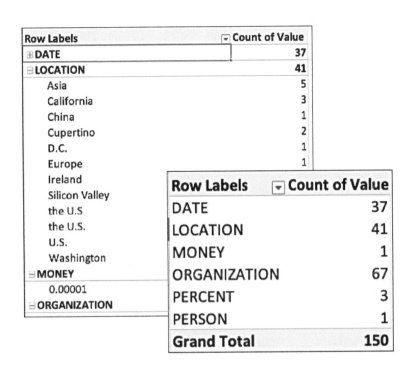

Row Labels	Count of Value
⊞ DATE	37
⊟ LOCATION	41
Asia	5
California	3
China	1
Cupertino	2
D.C.	1
Europe	1
Ireland	
Silicon Valley	
the U.S	
the U.S.	
U.S.	
Washington	
⊟ MONEY	
0.00001	
⊟ ORGANIZATION	

Row Labels	Count of Value
DATE	37
LOCATION	41
MONEY	1
ORGANIZATION	67
PERCENT	3
PERSON	1
Grand Total	**150**

FIGURE 10.11 Recognized named entities from the 2019 Apple 10K financial filing with the SEC

Additional Exercise 10.3 - Case Study Using Dataset L: Corporate Financial Reports

Perform the same analysis as in Exercise 10.2, but for the IBM and the Amazon financial reports found in the folder *Dataset H: Corporate Financial Reports*.

Application of Entity Extraction to Large Text Files

Let's now try to apply these tools to large text files. We use the book-length travel accounts by Charles Darwin (*The Voyage of the Beagle*) and Mark Twain (*Innocents Abroad*). As before, we download the extracted list of entities to a text file, and then post-process that file to extract further information.

Our business question is

What are the most frequent names and locations in the travel diary (essentially blog postings) of these two authors?

These books are large (almost 200,000 words each), which should not be a problem for the NER to process. We use one file (*Voyages*) below and leave the other (*Travels*) to the reader to do as an additional exercise. Be mindful that these large text files can take up to several minutes to be processed by the NER.

Exercise 10.4 – Case Study Using Dataset E: Large Text Files

1. Load the file *VoyageOfTheBeagleDarwin.txt* found in the folder *Dataset E: Large Text Files*, and subfolder *Travel Books*, into the Stanford NER.

2. Load the *english.all.3class.distsim.crf.ser.gz* classifier and run the NER. Be patient; it may take some time to return the results.

3. The results should look like those shown in Figure 10.12. The NER program identified over 4,200 named entities.

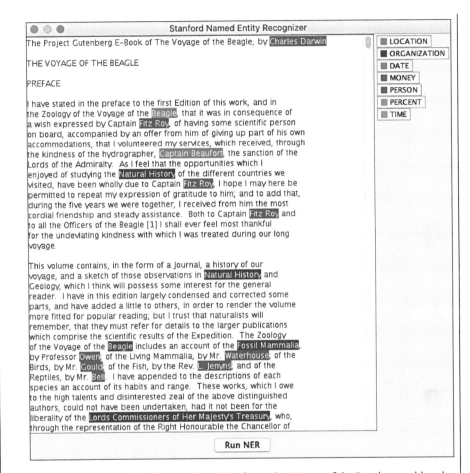

FIGURE 10.12 Recognized named entities from the *Voyage of the Beagle* travel book by Darwin

4. Using the same process as Exercise 10.3, extract the 4,300 named entities in Excel and tabulate by entity type. Use a pivot table obtain a list of the people Darwin mentions most frequently in the book. The resulting sorted tabulation of names in the book should look like what is shown in Figure 10.13. Notice that the name "Gutenberg" is an anomaly because it refers to the publisher of the e-text, but is not mentioned in the book by Darwin.

Row Labels	Count of Value
⊞ DATE	457
⊞ LOCATION	2240
⊞ MONEY	12
⊞ ORGANIZATION	666
⊞ PERCENT	1
⊟ PERSON	892
Fitz Roy	54
Buenos Ayres	46
Rosas	23
Portillo	17
Gutenberg	15
Waterhouse	14
Bushby	14
Sulivan	13
Ehrenberg	13
Owen	11
Lyell	11
Richardson	10

FIGURE 10.13 Recognized named entities from the *Voyage of the Beagle* book by Darwin showing the top people named in the book

Additional Exercise 10.5 – Case Study Using Dataset E: Large Text Files

Perform the same analysis as in Exercise 10.4, but for the *Innocents Abroad* travel book by Mark Twain found in the folder *Dataset E: Large Text Files*.

References

1. [Finkel05] Jenny Rose Finkel, Trond Grenager, and Christopher Manning. 2005. Incorporating Non-local Information into Information Extraction Systems by Gibbs Sampling. *Proceedings of the 43nd Annual Meeting of the Association for Computational Linguistics (ACL 2005)*, pp. 363-370. *http://nlp.stanford.edu/~manning/papers/gibbscrf3.pdf*

2. [Manning14] Manning, Christopher D., Mihai Surdeanu, John Bauer, Jenny Rose Finkel, Steven Bethard, and David McClosky. "The Stanford CoreNLP natural language processing toolkit." In *Proceedings of 52nd annual meeting of the association for computational linguistics: system demonstrations*, pp. 55-60. 2014.

## CHAPTER 11

TOPIC RECOGNITION IN DOCUMENTS

This chapter continues the work begun in Chapter 10 with information extraction. Rather than extract only proper names, locations, and temporal elements, we also want to recognize whole topics in the texts. We simplistically did this work by word frequency analysis (Chapter 5) and keyword analysis (Chapter 6). We extended it using qualitative data coding (Chapter 8). We now analyze the text with sophisticated machine learning algorithms to extract meaning through latent keywords and then relating those words to topics. It helps us classify texts by comparing them to each other and grouping them by emerging topics.

In the first set of exercises, we apply topic modeling to a simple dataset: university curricula. Can we identify the topics in graduate courses in a program to classify by topic? Does the topic classification make sense? Then we move onto a set of travel books and see if we can extract topics from each, with sufficient definition to classify them. Lastly, we apply the topic extraction tool to a set of books, each belonging to a different Dewey Decimal System's class, and extract topics sufficiently to identify similar books. Then we create a crude librarian robot. Once trained, we can use these orthogonal topics to recognize the topics in an unknown book, classify it, and put it on the proper library shelf.

Information Retrieval

Information retrieval (IR) is a field of study dealing with the representation, storage, organization of, and access to documents. The documents may be books, reports, pictures, videos, or webpages. The point of an IR system is to provide the analysis with easy access to documents containing the desired information. An excellent example of an information retrieval system is the Google search engine.

The difference between an information retrieval system and a data retrieval system like an RDBMS is that the IR system input is unstructured. In contrast, data retrieval (a database management system or DBMS) deals with structured data with well-defined data constructs. For data extraction, or querying, extracting data from an RDBMS produces precise results or no results when there is no match, whereas querying an IR system produces multiple ranked results with partial matching.

Document Characterization

We identify and extract topics from unstructured text in this chapter—the unstructured text parts of documents that are written in prose. Most textual documents are characterized by three kinds of information about the document: (1) its metadata, (2) its formatting, and (3) its content. The second characterization (formatting) is not too interesting to us, so we will not discuss it here. The first (metadata) is very interesting, but the metadata elements may be collected as traditional numerical, categorical, and time variables, which can be analyzed with traditional means. It is the third characterization (content) that is of interest here and will be pursued.

Metadata characterization refers to the ownership, authorship, and other items of information about a document. The Library of Congress subject coding is an example of metadata. Another example of metadata is the category headings used for the Yahoo search engine. Many disciplines use specific *ontologies*, which are hierarchical taxonomies of terms describing certain knowledge topics, to standardize category headings. The Dewey Decimal System, encountered in Chapter 6, and the Library of Congress document subject coding are examples of metadata.

Content characterization is interesting and challenging. It refers to attributes that denote the semantic content of a document. Content characterization is of primary interest in this chapter. We wish to extract information about the content of the document. A common practice in information retrieval is to represent a textual document by a set of keywords called index terms (or simply, *terms*). We did that in Chapter 6 and Chapter 7. An *index term* is a word or a phrase in a document whose semantics give an indication of the document's theme. The index terms, in general, are mainly nouns because nouns have meaning by themselves.

Topic Recognition

A topic model is a simplified representation of a collection of documents. Topic modeling software identifies words with topic labels, such that words that often show up in the same document are more likely to receive the same label. It can identify common subjects in a collection of documents – clusters of words that have similar meanings and associations – and discourse trends over time and across geographical boundaries.

Topic modeling is a method for finding and tracing clusters of words (called *topics*) in large bodies of texts. Topic modeling is very popular with digital humanities scholars, partly because it offers some meaningful improvements to simple word-frequency counts and partly because of the availability of some relatively easy-to-use tools for topic modeling.

The natural language processing tool for topic extraction we use here is called MALLET, a package of Java code. It's run using the Java command line. For those who aren't quite ready for that, there's a Topic Modeling Tool, which implements MALLET in a graphical user interface (GUI), meaning you can plug files in and receive output without entering a line of code. We introduced MALLET in Chapter 2, where we discussed its origins [McCallum02], [Shawn12]. We present how to install to tool in Chapter 16.

Exercises

An academic department of a university that teaches business wishes to analyze one of its graduate programs' courses. They want to group the courses by topics covered.

What are the most significant topics covered by these courses, and can they be logically grouped by these extracted topics?

We must first create a folder for the input and output files for this project. In that folder, we will create two empty folders called *input* and *output*. We will transfer all text files (they must be in UTF-8 format) into the input folder. Make sure the *output* folder is left blank to be populated by the program's output. Follow the instructions and analyze the results.

Exercise 11.1 - Case Study Using Dataset G: University Curricula

1. Create a *University Curricular Topic Extraction* folder on your desktop.

2. In that folder, create two folders, one called *input* and one called *output*.

3. Open the folder *Dataset G: University Curricula*. Under the folder *Course Files*. Locate and copy all 37-course description text files into the *input* folder of the *University Curricular Topic Extraction* folder.

4. Find and run the Topic Modeling Tool program installed earlier. You should see an interface that looks like that shown in Figure 11.1.

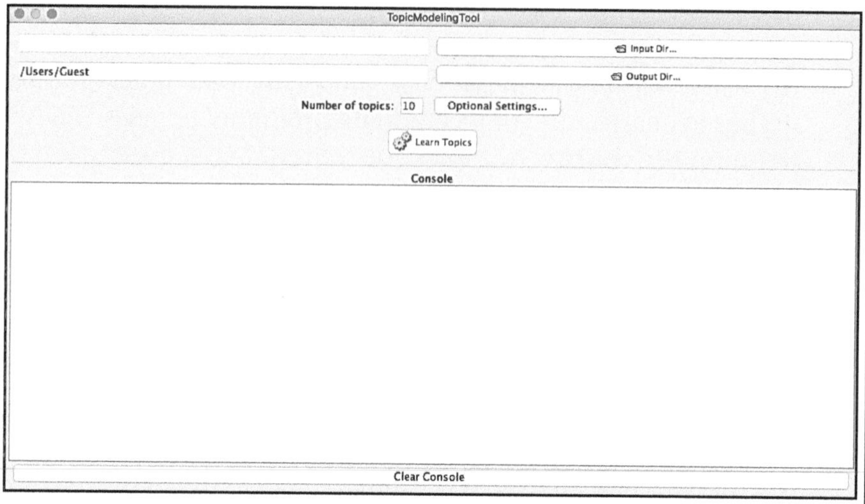

FIGURE 11.1 Topic Modeling Tool data entry screen

5. Click on *Input Dir...* and follow the prompts to accept the *input* folder of the *University Curricular Topic Extraction* folder.

6. Repeat for the *Output Dir...* and follow the prompts to accept the *output* folder of the *University Curricular Topic Extraction* folder. You should see an interface like that shown in Figure 11.2.

FIGURE 11.2 The Topic Modeling Tool interface screen showing the tool ready to run with the input and output directories properly selected as well as the desired number of topics.

7. Make sure you enter the desired number of topics for the analysis. The default is 10, but in this case, we want a simple structure, and we have set it to five. You should now be ready to run the program.

8. Press the *Learn Topics* button and watch the program compute the topics and align the courses to the topics. The output files are in the *output* directory. Note how long it takes (It should be less than a minute; if it appears to take longer, be patient, it may take several minutes, but if it is much longer than 5-10 minutes, the program may not have converged, and you need to stop the process.)

9. Figure 11.3 shows the end screen after the processors run. You will typically see a screen like this at the end of every process.

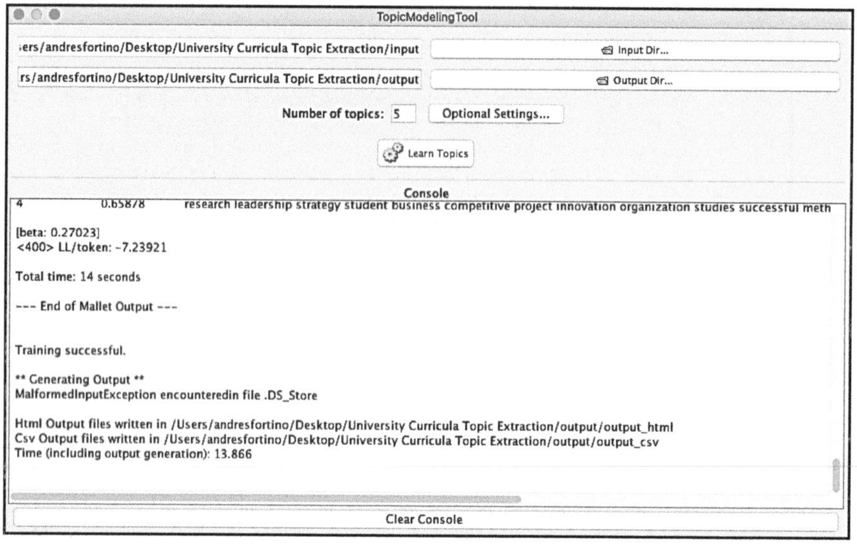

FIGURE 11.3 The Topic Modeling Tool interface screen showing the tool having completed learning and producing the output files with the analysis

10. Review some of the output files to see the rich information set provided by the program.

11. The first output file of interest is the keywords that characterize each unique topic. That file can be found in the *output* file folder under the *output_csv* folder and is named *topic-words.csv*. Figure 11.4 shows this compilation.

Topic Id	Top Words...
0	risk management financial change operational fundamental understand practices expected student insurance industry risks products concepts manage include today students professionals
1	database crisis management business plan development applications sql processes web based programs operations oracle continuity manage including pl emergency technologies
2	data business students information systems completion design techniques technology management analysis topics concepts world process include development real oriented system
3	knowledge marketing ethical communications economy global practice organizational customer personal student risks key integrated focus strategic trade markets related km
4	research leadership student strategy business innovation project competitive organization plan methods mining topic effective understand thesis critical opportunities technology order

FIGURE 11.4 The contents of the *topic-words.csv* output file showing the keywords associated with each of the five topics

12. The next *output* file of interest is the one that lists the texts in our corpus (the course descriptions) and scores them (on a scale from 0 to 1) against the five topics we asked for. It is the *topics-metadata.csv* file also found under the *output_csv* folder. Figure 11.5 shows the scored course descriptions. We highlighted the large scores to show which topics each course covers.

filename	0 change ethical marketing	1 database knowledge applications	2 crisis manageme nt business	3 data students business	4 risk manageme nt financial
1 Strategic Communications.txt	0.62229246	0.00209515	0.15382047	0.17217076	0.04962115
2 Financial Services and Trading Institutions.txt	0.00974862	0.00286812	0.00204297	0.0833051	0.90203519
3 Applied Project.txt	0.00471714	0.07349606	0.55281081	0.1616933	0.20728269
4 Strategic Marketing.txt	0.65443536	0.01054993	0.00197947	0.32938641	0.00364883
5 Business Analytics.txt	0.0019828	0.05849617	0.02074566	0.83164638	0.087129
6 Data Mining and Data Warehousing.txt	0.00284734	0.00472502	0.00336564	0.95643238	0.03262961
7 Application Architecture Design Development.txt	0.00300622	0.38164066	0.11515403	0.47969881	0.02050028
8 Enterprise Risk-Assessment and Mitigation.txt	0.01128762	0.00332091	0.00236549	0.05931075	0.92371523
9 Leadership.txt	0.00191241	0.00317356	0.04663232	0.18092003	0.76736168
10 Quantitative Models for Decision Makers.txt	0.54592104	0.14235701	0.02427678	0.259012	0.02843318
11 Crisis Management and Business Continuity.txt	9.22E-04	0.00153031	0.97676571	0.01877248	0.00200932
12 Systems Development and Analysis.txt	0.00257514	0.00427332	0.0030439	0.98449671	0.00561093
13 Management of Telecommunications .txt	9.30E-04	0.00154352	0.95930027	0.02756697	0.01065911
14 Innovation and Entrepreneurship.txt	0.42406684	0.04161421	0.43694702	0.07915837	0.01821356
15 Financial Management.txt	0.0048227	0.11989939	0.00570058	0.38910457	0.48047276
16 Database Applications.txt	0.00254473	0.67731173	0.00300795	0.28797376	0.02916183
17 Information Technology and Data Analytics.txt	0.0483004	0.04163378	0.00975043	0.83449888	0.06581652
18 Operational and Financial Risk Analysis.txt	0.00158824	0.01737571	0.0092474	0.13551194	0.83627671
19 Knowledge Management.txt	0.02560581	0.56635519	0.06016532	0.17373379	0.17413989
20 Database Technologies for Web Applications.txt	0.00284734	0.90319511	0.00336564	0.08438789	0.00620402
21 Managing Big Data.txt	0.02416445	0.00390045	0.15547634	0.74589539	0.07056336
22 Database Design & Management.txt	0.00181573	0.43272487	0.00214625	0.55935689	0.00395627
23 Data Process and Structure.txt	0.00254473	0.51199165	0.00300795	0.46510241	0.01735325
24 Managing in a Global Economy.txt	0.72993853	0.14466605	0.03485744	0.05235947	0.0381785
25 Research Project Thesis.txt	0.03478882	0.19404511	0.08251222	0.32012379	0.36853006
26 Managing Complex Change Initiatives.txt	0.79460361	0.01365272	0.03042968	0.15859488	0.0027191
27 Research Process and Methodology.txt	0.06291623	0.01183781	0.07197788	0.56142716	0.29184093
28 Auditing.txt	0.00155388	0.00978922	0.00183673	0.55800751	0.42881267
29 Enterprise Ethics and Sustainability.txt	0.90461293	0.00235759	0.00827196	0.07506932	0.0096882
30 Business Analysis in the Enterprise.txt	0.00230027	0.00381718	0.0240673	0.92210661	0.04770864
31 Project Management in The Information Age.txt	0.05071623	0.07686094	0.00583108	0.8558431	0.01074865
32 Business Strategy and Ethics .txt	0.54331491	0.02115907	0.00160524	0.29862348	0.13529731
33 Information Security Management.txt	0.00237636	0.00394346	0.12410899	0.22481125	0.64475993
34 Object-Oriented Systems Design.txt	0.00201997	0.00335204	0.00238766	0.9784656	0.01377473
35 Advanced Database Applications.txt	0.00163648	0.89879879	0.00193437	0.08647074	0.01115963
36 Strategic Management of Technological Innovation.txt	0.04116929	0.19227029	0.00201072	0.71348142	0.05106829
37 Enterprise Application Integration.txt	0.00222889	0.03472759	0.00263462	0.8934947	0.0669142

FIGURE 11.5 The contents of the *topics-metadata.csv* output file showing the course descriptions scored against the keywords associated with each of the five topics

13. Figure 11.6 shows the Excel conditional formatting rules used to highlight the highest-scoring topics for each course.

Manage Rules				
Show formatting rules for: Current Selection			Change rule order: ⬆ ⬇	
Rule (applied in order shown)	Format	Applies to		Stop if true
Graded Color Scale		'topics-metadata 5 topics'!$ 🔣		☐

| + | − | Edit Rule... | | | Cancel | OK |

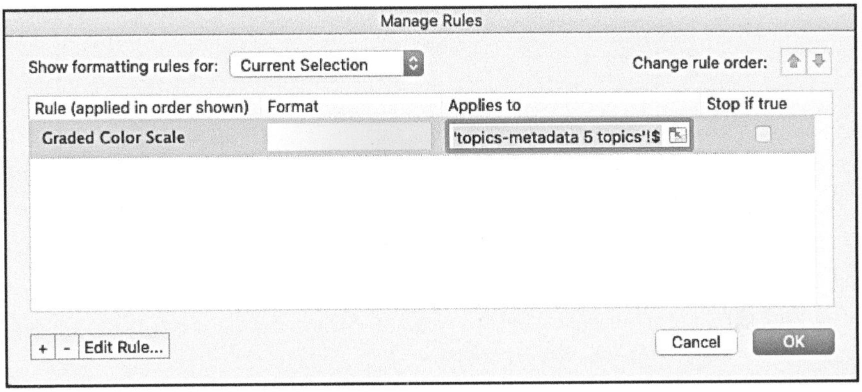

FIGURE 11.6 The Excel conditional formatting rule to highlight the high scoring topics for each course

14. Lastly, let's see what information some of the other output files yield. In the *output file* folder, under *output_html* files, find the webpage *doc3.html*. It corresponds to the Applied Project Capstone file. It scores 88% on topic 0. Check the keywords and their resonance with the course description. Figure 11.7 shows the results for the Applied Project course.

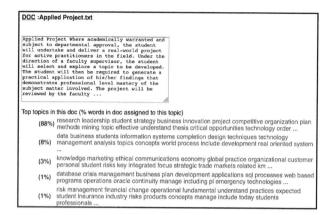

FIGURE 11.7 The results for the Applied Project course description scored against the five topics

15. Explore some of the other Webpages in the folder to review what information the output files can yield.

Exercise 11.2 - Case Study Using Dataset E: Large Text Files

We will extract topics from some large text files comprising over a million words. We have five books written by travelers. Each is around 200,000 words. Some traveled by ship (Darwin, Magellan, and Twain), some traveled to desert areas in the middle of large continents (Marco Polo), and some went to one place and stayed there for the entire book.

What topics do they have in common, and which topics make each book unique? What are the extracted topics?

As in the previous exercise, we must first create an empty folder to hold the *input* and *output* files for this project. In that folder, we will create two empty folders called input and output. We will transfer all of the text files (they must be in the UTF-8 format) into the input folder. Make sure the *output* file is left blank, because it will be populated by the output of the program. Follow the instructions and analyze the results.

1. Create a *Travel Book Topic Extraction* folder on your desktop.

2. In that folder, create two folders, one called *input* and one called *output*.

3. Open the folder *Dataset E: Large Test Files*. Under the folder, *Travel Books*, locate and copy all five books' text files into the *input* folder of the *Travel Book Topic Extraction* folder.

4. Find and run the Topic Modeling Tool program installed earlier. You should see an interface that looks like that shown in Figure 11.1.

5. Click on *Input Dir…* and follow the prompts to accept the *input* folder of the *Travel Book Topic Extraction* folder.

6. Repeat for the *Output Dir…* and follow the prompts to accept the *output* folder of the *Travel Book Topic Extraction* folder. You should see something similar to what is shown in Figure 11.2 in the previous exercise, but now pointing to the folders in the *Travel Book Topic Extraction folders*.

7. Make sure you enter the desired number of topics for the analysis. The default is 10, and in this case, we will want to obtain ten. We have complex texts with many topics, so a larger number of topics make sense. You should now be ready to run the program.

8. Press the *Learn Topics* button and watch the program compute the topics and align the courses to the topics. The output files will be found in the *output* directory. Note how long it takes (it should be less than a minute; if it appears to take longer, be patient, it may take several minutes, but if it is much longer than 5-10 minutes, the program may not have converged, and you need to stop the process.).

9. You will see something similar to what we saw in Exercise 1. It should look like Figure 11.3. This is the end screen after the processors run. You will typically see a screen like this at the end of every process.

10. We now review some of the output files to see the rich information set provided by the program.

11. The first output file of interest is the keywords that characterize each unique topic. That file can be found in the *output* file folder under the *output_csv* folder and is named *topic-words.csv*. Figure 11.8 shows this compilation.

Topic Id	Topics	Top Words...
0	King, Moors,	alhambra tower granada moorish love heart aben prince thou prophet thy city time aaron involuntary palace hamet moor life court
1	Travel, Kahn	1 city 2 de khan 3 grand province country people polo marco place king author named la inhabitants chapter part
2	Chrsitian, Death, Gener	made make night put long left house sun general called people high christian full give set hands god death fell
3	Honor, Beauty, Fortune	fortress beauty replied rose days door passed dis length father con ahmed honour half led page drew pride favourite fortune
4	Animals, River, Birds	river account sea horses men emperor majesty great likewise body handsome countries birds silver return greater qui animal tion observed
5	Captain, Voyage, Port	islands south made latitude cape place called sun port note voyage told twenty remained strait arrived captain time line set
6	Sea, Coasts, Indians	sea species island islands miles feet coast trees parts south land mr animals birds common water indians long horses country
7	City, Church, Ship	hundred city thing time people man years ship feet sea good st church half thousand chapter ancient long place looked
8	Islands, King, Magellan	king de island men tho ships ship magellan day captain named west people gave degrees 1 leagues found ho north
9	Water, Mountains	great day found time water side man country men small part place good distance head large white mountains made hundred

FIGURE 11.8 The contents of the *topic-words.csv* output file showing the keywords associated with each of the ten topics in the travel books

12. The next *output* file of interest is the one that lists the texts in our corpus (the travel books) and scores them (on a scale from 0 to 1) against the five topics we asked for. It is the *topics-metadata.csv* file also found under the *output_csv* folder. Figure 11.9 shows the scored course descriptions. We highlighted the larger scores to show which topics each course covers.

docId	Author	Book	Topic Number and Some Keywords									
			0 alhambra tower granada	1 city	2 made make night	3 fortress beauty replied	4 river account sea	5 islands south made	6 sea species island	7 hundred city thing	8 king de island	9 great day found
0	Twain	Innocents Abroad	0.040	0.000	0.178	0.001	0.000	0.000	0.012	0.537	0.000	0.231
2	Magellan	Magellan Voyages	0.000	0.003	0.138	0.004	0.017	0.263	0.001	0.000	0.488	0.086
3	Polo	Travels Of Marco	0.000	0.542	0.062	0.018	0.183	0.000	0.001	0.000	0.000	0.194
4	Irving	The Alhambra	0.469	0.000	0.157	0.154	0.007	0.000	0.004	0.034	0.000	0.175
5	Darwin	Voyage Of The Beagle	0.000	0.000	0.027	0.007	0.000	0.000	0.572	0.014	0.000	0.380
			Most Representative Keywords for Each Topic									
			King, Moors	Travel, Kahn	Chrsitian, Death	Honor, Beauty, Fortune	Animals, River, Birds	Captain, Voyage, Port	Sea, Coasts, Indians	City, Church, Ship	Islands, King, Magellan,	Water, Mountains

FIGURE 11.9 The contents of the *topics-metadata.csv* output file showing the travel books scored against the keywords associated with each of the ten topics

13. Figure 11.10 shows the Excel conditional formatting rule used to highlight the highest scoring topics for each travel book. Note that each book has a prominent topic, but there are some topics in common, as you would expect since they are travel books.

FIGURE 11.10 The Excel conditional formatting rule used to highlight the high scoring topics for each travel book

14. Lastly, let's see what information some of the other *output* files yield. In the *output* file folder, under *output_html* files, find the webpage *doc3.html*. It corresponds to *The Voyage of The Beagle* book by Darwin Capstone file. It scores 57% on topic 0 and 38% on topic 1. Check the keywords and their resonance with the topic keywords in Figure 11.11.

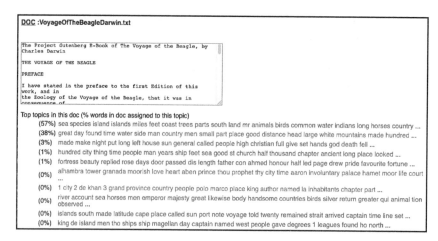

FIGURE 11.11 The results for *The Voyage of the Beagle* book scored against the ten topics

15. Explore some of the other Webpages in the folder to review what information the output files can yield.

Exercise 11.3 - Case Study Using Dataset E: Large Text Files

We will extract topics from several books we pulled off the shelves of a library. We want to see if this tool would differentiate between disciplines. We took a well-known book in each of the ten Dewey Decimal System's categories (General Works, Philosophy and Psychology, Religion, Social Sciences, Language, Science, Technology, Arts and Recreation, Literature, History, and Geography). We have nine books written by famous workers in each field:

- *Practical Cinematography and Its Applications*, by Frederick Arthur Ambrose Talbot

- *Science in the Kitchen*, by Mrs. E. E. Kellogg

- *The Foundations of Geometry*, by David Hilbert

- *The History of the Decline and Fall of the Roman Empire*, by Edward Gibbon

- *The Principles of Chemistry*, by Dmitry Ivanovich Mendeleyev

- *The Varieties of Religious Experience*, by William James

- *Three Contributions to the Theory of Sex*, by Sigmund Freud

- *Grimm's Fairy Tales*

As in the previous exercise, we ask

What topics do they have in common, and which topics make each boom unique? What are the extracted topics?

We hypothesize that these books are so far apart that they will yield some substantial topical differences, perhaps enough to distinguish each discipline.

As in the previous exercise, we must first create a folder for the input and output files for this project. In that folder, we will create two empty folders called *input* and *output*. We will transfer all text files (they must be in the UTF-8 format) into the *input* folder. Make sure the *output* is left blank, because it will be populated by the output of the program. Follow the instructions and analyze the results.

1. Create a *Dewey Decimal Topic Extraction* folder on your desktop.

2. In that folder, create two folders, one called *input* and one called *output*.

3. Open the folder *Dataset E: Large Test Files*. Under the folder, *Dewey Decimal Text Files* locate and copy all seven books text files listed above and copy into the *input* folder of the *Dewey Decimal Topic Extraction* folder.

4. Find and run the Topic Modeling Tool program installed earlier. You should see an interface that looks like that shown in Figure 11.1.

5. Click on *Input Dir…* and follow the prompts to accept the *input* folder of the *Dewey Decimal Topic Extraction* folder.

6. Repeat for the *Output Dir…* and follow the prompts to accept the *output* folder of the *Dewey Decimal Topic Extraction* folder. You should see something similar to what is shown in Figure 11.2 in the previous exercise, but now pointing to the folders in the *Dewey Decimal Topic Extraction folders*.

7. Make sure you enter the desired number of topics for the analysis. The default is ten, and in this case, we will want to obtain ten topics. We have complex texts with at least seven complementary topics, so a larger number of topics make sense. You should now be ready to run the program.

8. Press the *Learn Topics* button and watch the program compute the topics and align the courses to the topics. The output files will be found in the *output* directory. Note how long it takes (It should be less than a minute; if it appears to take longer, be patient, it may take several minutes, but if it is much longer than 5-10 minutes, the program may not have converged, and you need to stop the process).

9. The results should look like those shown in Figure 11.3. This is the end screen after the processors run. You will typically see a screen like this at the end of every process.

10. We now review some of the output files to see the rich information set provided by the program.

11. The first output file of interest is the keywords that characterize each unique topic. That file can be found in the *output* file folder under the *output_csv* folder and is named *topic-words.csv*. Figure 11.12 shows this compilation.

Topic Id	Top Words...	Topic Name
0	2 water acid 3 hydrogen oxygen 4 _ solution 1 heat sodium h_ substances salt temperature gas air 0 salts	Science
1	sexual object life impulse infantile pleasure child normal excitement note 1 erogenous gutenberg activity psychic aim project children development childhood	Sociology
2	years imperial palace return power chapter west title romans 1 law monarch subject interest honor 2 africa made honorable restored	History
3	iii age greek country iv sea twenty received christians year capital christian important enemies great century years europe found nation	History
4	straight 1 points theorem line point geometry axioms plane segments 2 0 number 17 lines parallel triangles axiom system segment	Math
5	life religion world god nature religious men mind spirit human state presence man truth day sense power moment fear part	Religion
6	fruit water bread cream stewed milk wheat graham soup fresh food sugar add boiling half cup flour baked hot cold	Food
7	return emperor tom roman empire rome hundred thousand ii people public war constantinople city de son italy barbarians part reign	History
8	king man good day woman home time eyes back _ thought house great long give door mother asked cried daughter	Stories
9	work film time made light camera make things case subject great good gutenberg pictures picture project life hand 1 moving	Film

FIGURE 11.12 The contents of the *topic-words.csv* output file showing the keywords associated with each of the ten topics in the library books

12. The next *output* file of interest is the one that lists the texts in our corpus (the library books) and scores them (on a scale from 0 to 1) against the ten topics we asked for. It is the *topics-metadata.csv* file also found under the *output_csv* folder. Figure 11.13 shows the scored course descriptions. We highlighted the larger scores to show which topics each course covers.

docId	Author	Book	Science	Psychology	History 1	History 2	Math	Religion	Food	History 3	Stories	Art	Dewey Decimal Category
0	Freud	Three Contributions to the Theory of Sex	0.000	0.845	0.000	0.004	0.000	0.025	0.000	0.000	0.003	0.122	100 Psychology
1	Mendeleyev	The Principles of Chemistry	0.960	0.001	0.001	0.000	0.005	0.005	0.002	0.000	0.002	0.025	500 Science
2	Talbot	Practical Cinematography and Its Applications	0.034	0.005	0.010	0.004	0.001	0.006	0.006	0.002	0.012	0.921	700 Arts
3	Gibbons	The History Of The Decline And Fall Of The Roman Empire	0.000	0.000	0.215	0.257	0.000	0.119	0.000	0.401	0.008	0.000	900 History
4	Grimm	Grimm's Fairy Tales	0.000	0.000	0.002	0.004	0.000	0.012	0.011	0.002	0.942	0.026	800 Literature
5	Kellogg	Science in the Kitchen	0.006	0.002	0.002	0.002	0.000	0.010	0.931	0.002	0.010	0.035	600 Technology
6	Hilbert	The Foundations of Geometry	0.000	0.000	0.000	0.000	0.955	0.002	0.000	0.000	0.000	0.042	500 Science
7	James	The Varieties of Religious Experience	0.000	0.060	0.003	0.015	0.001	0.408	0.000	0.007	0.057	0.449	200 Religion

FIGURE 11.13 The contents of the *topics-metadata.csv* output file showing the travel books scored against the keywords associated with each of the ten topics

13. Figure 11.14 shows the Excel conditional formatting rule used to highlight the highest scoring topics for each travel book. Note that each book has a prominent topic, and there are a few topics in common, as you would expect since they are books from different disciplines.

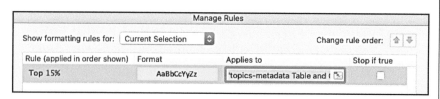

FIGURE 11.14 The Excel conditional formatting rule to highlight the high scoring topics for each library book

14. Lastly, let's see what information some of the other output files yield. In the *output* file folder, under *output_html* files, find the webpage *doc3.html*. It corresponds to the cookbook by Mrs. Kellogg, *Science in the Kitchen*. It scores 93% in topic 0, and scores insignificant amounts in the other topics. Check the keywords and their resonance with the topics in Figure 11.15.

DOC :Science in the Kitchen Kellogg.txt

```
The Project Gutenberg eBook, Science in the Kitchen., by Mrs.
E. E. Kellogg

This eBook is for the use of anyone anywhere at no cost and
with
almost no restrictions whatsoever.  You may copy it, give it
away or
re-use it under the terms of the Project Gutenberg License
included
with this eBook or online at www.gutenberg.net
```

Top topics in this doc (% words in doc assigned to this topic)

(93%) fruit water bread cream stewed milk wheat graham soup fresh food sugar add boiling half cup flour baked hot cold ...

(4%) work film time made light camera make things case subject great good gutenberg pictures picture project life hand 1 moving ...

(1%) king man good day woman home time eyes back _ thought house great long give door mother asked cried daughter ...

(1%) life religion world god nature religious men mind spirit human state presence man truth day sense power moment fear part ...

(1%) 2 water acid 3 hydrogen oxygen 4 _ solution 1 heat sodium h_ substances salt temperature gas air 0 salts ...

(0%) iii age greek country iv sea twenty received christians year capital christian important enemies great century years europe found nation ...

(0%) sexual object life impulse infantile pleasure child normal excitement note 1 erogenous gutenberg activity psychic aim project children development childhood ...

(0%) years imperial palace return power chapter west title romans 1 law monarch subject interest honor 2 africa made honorable restored ...

(0%) return emperor tom roman empire rome hundred thousand ii people public war constantinople city de son italy barbarians part reign ...

(0%) straight 1 points theorem line point geometry axioms plane segments 2 0 number 17 lines parallel triangles axiom system segment ...

FIGURE 11.15 The results for *Science in the Kitchen* cookbook scored against the ten topics

15. Explore some of the other webpages in the folder to review what information the output files can yield.

Exercise 11.4 - Case Study Using Dataset E: Large Text Files

The prior exercise using foundational texts in the various disciplines could be used to discover what discipline a new entry into the list belongs in. Suppose we want to classify a new text as to which Dewey Decimal category it belongs in. We can add the text to the orthogonal set and rerun the topic modeling software. It should tell us which topics most align with the new text, thus helping us classify it. We first do it with a text in mathematics, which should relatively easy to classify. Then, in the next exercise, we classify a text in several topic areas using nine books written by famous workers in each field:

- *Practical Cinematography and Its Applications*, by Frederick Arthur Ambrose Talbot

- *Science in the Kitchen*, by Mrs. E. E. Kellogg

- *The Foundations of Geometry*, by David Hilbert

- *The History of the Decline and Fall of the Roman Empire*, by Edward Gibbon

- *The Principles of Chemistry*, by Dmitry Ivanovich Mendeleyev

- *The Varieties of Religious Experience*, by William James

- *Three Contributions to the Theory of Sex*, by Sigmund Freud

- *Grimm's Fairy Tales*

We add a mathematics book:

- *A Treatise on Probability*, by John Maynard Keynes

As in the previous exercise, we ask

What topics do they have in common, and which topics make each book unique? What are the extracted topics? Can we also identify the Dewey Decimal classification of this book by associating it with our known book set?

We hypothesize adding this new book will yield some substantial topical differences and associations, perhaps enough to distinguish it with one and only one discipline.

As in the previous exercise, we must first create a folder for the *input* and *output* files for this project. In that folder, we create two empty folders called input and output. We will transfer all text files (they must be in the UTF-8 format) into the input folder. Make sure the *output* is left blank, because it will be populated by the output of the program. Follow the instructions and analyze the results.

1. Create a *Dewey Decimal Topic Extraction II* folder on your desktop (a new one, as not to confuse it with the analysis in Exercise 3).

2. In that folder, create two folders, one called *input* and one called *output*.

3. Open the folder *Dataset E: Large Test Files*. Under the folder, *Dewey Decimal Text Files* locate and copy all seven books text files listed above and copy into the *input* folder of the *Dewey Decimal Topic Extraction II* folder.

4. Find and run the Topic Modeling Tool program installed earlier. You should see an interface that looks like that shown in Figure 11.1.

5. Click on *Input Dir…* and follow the prompts to accept the *input* folder of the *Dewey Decimal Topic Extraction II* folder.

6. Repeat for the *Output Dir…* and follow the prompts to accept the *output* folder of the *Dewey Decimal Topic Extraction II* folder. You should see something similar to what is shown in Figure 11.2 in the previous exercise; it is now pointing to the folders in the *Dewey Decimal Topic Extraction folders*.

7. Make sure you enter the desired number of topics for the analysis. The default is ten, and in this case, we want to obtain ten topics. We have complex texts with at least eight complementary topics, so a larger number of topics make sense. You should now be ready to run the program.

8. Press the *Learn Topics* button and watch the program compute the topics and align the courses to the topics. The output files will be found in the *output* directory. Note how long it takes (It should be less than a minute; if it appears to take longer, be patient, it may take several minutes, but if it is much longer than 5-10 minutes, the program may not have converged, and you need to stop the process.).

9. You will see something similar to what we saw in Exercise 91, and it should look like Figure 11.3. This is the end screen after the processors run. You will typically see a screen like this at the end of every process.

10. We will now review some of the output files to see the rich information set provided by the program.

11. The first output file of interest is the keywords that characterize each unique topic. That file can be found in the *output* file folder under the *output_csv* folder and is named *topic-words. csv*. Figure 11.16 shows this compilation.

Topic Id	Top Words...	Classification
0	return emperor roman tom empire hundred rome ii thousand public constantinople reign city great arms son italy time provinces long	History
1	part general life church power state religion christian character history spirit world iv laws christians private head nature holy sovereign	History
2	war enemy country received royal year sea god court equal latin mahomet brother hand virtues original field franks 3 side	Literature
3	fruit water bread cream stewed milk wheat graham soup fresh food sugar add boiling half cup flour baked hot cold	Cooking
4	straight points theorem 1 line point geometry axioms plane segments lines 0 2 17 number axiom parallel equal triangles system	Math
5	people twenty day command subject reason strength authority hope loss man title exposed ancient obtained safety passed dangerous maintained weight	Art
6	2 water acid 3 hydrogen oxygen 4 _ solution heat sodium h_1 substances salt temperature gas air 0 salts	Chemistry
7	god man king life good time religious thought day world religion things great mind give back long find woman home	Religion
8	sexual life work film object 1 fact gutenberg camera project light picture pictures subject means time case hand made impulse	Psychology
9	probability 1 pp knowledge 0 5 probabilities argument theory 2 number de vol series evidence instances probable case di des	Math

FIGURE 11.16 The contents of the *topic-words.csv* output file showing the keywords associated with each of the ten topics in the library books

12. The next *output* file of interest is the one that lists the texts in our corpus (library texts) and scores them (on a scale from 0 to 1) against the five topics we asked for. It is the *topics-metadata. csv* file also found under the *output_csv* folder. Figure 11.17 shows the scored library books. We also highlighted the larger scores to show which topics each book covers.

docId	filename	0 return emperor roman	1 part general life	2 war enemy country	3 fruit water bread	4 straight points theorem	5 people twenty day	6 water acid	7 god man king	8 sexual life work	9 probability 1 pp	Classification
0	Three Contributions to the Theory of Sex Freud	0.000	0.007	0.001	0.000	0.000	0.020	0.000	0.016	0.942	0.014	Psychology
2	The Principles of Chemistry Mendeleyev	0.000	0.000	0.000	0.002	0.004	0.004	0.956	0.003	0.026	0.005	Chemistry
3	Practical Cinematography and Its Applications Talbot	0.000	0.002	0.001	0.008	0.000	0.040	0.023	0.026	0.898	0.001	Art
4	The History Of The Decline And Fall Of The Roman Empire Gibbon	0.386	0.227	0.213	0.000	0.000	0.172	0.000	0.002	0.000	0.000	History
5	Grimm's Fairy Tales	0.002	0.001	0.016	0.026	0.000	0.005	0.000	0.936	0.013	0.000	Fairy Tales
6	Science in the Kitchen Kellogg	0.001	0.002	0.001	0.927	0.000	0.010	0.006	0.014	0.039	0.000	Cooking
7	The Foundations of Geometry Hilbert	0.000	0.000	0.000	0.000	0.936	0.000	0.000	0.000	0.034	0.029	Math
8	The Varieties of Religious Experience James	0.004	0.105	0.008	0.002	0.001	0.059	0.000	0.541	0.241	0.039	Religion
9	A Treatise on Probability Keynes	0.000	0.005	0.001	0.000	0.023	0.013	0.000	0.005	0.044	0.909	Math
		History	History	Literature	Cooking	Math	Art	Chemistry	Religion	Psychology	Math	

FIGURE 11.17 The contents of the *topics-metadata.csv* output file showing the library books (including the Keynes book on Probability) scored against the keywords associated with each of the ten topics

13. Figure 11.18 shows the Excel conditional formatting rule used to highlight the highest scoring topics for each travel book. Note that each book has a prominent topic, and there are a few topics in common, as you would expect since the books are from different disciplines.

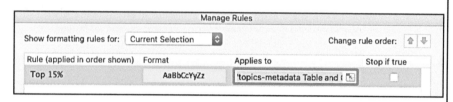

FIGURE 11.18 The Excel conditional formatting rule to highlight the high scoring topics for each library book

14. Lastly, let's see what information some of the other *output* files yield. In the *output* file folder, under *output_html* files, find the webpage *doc11.html*. It corresponds to the book by John Maynard Keynes. It scores 93% in topic 0, and insignificant amounts in any of the other topics. Check the keywords and their resonance with the topics in Figure 11.18.

Exercise 11.5 - Case Study Using Dataset E: Large Text Files

The prior exercise using foundational texts in the various disciplines could discover what discipline a new entry into the list belongs in. Suppose we want to classify a new text as to which Dewey Decimal category it belongs in. We can add the text to the orthogonal set and rerun the topic modeling software. It should tell us which topics most align with the new text, thus helping classify it. We first do it with a text in mathematics, which should relatively easy to classify. Then, in the next exercise us, we classify a text in several topic areas using nine books written by famous workers in each field:

- *Practical Cinematography and Its Applications*, by Frederick Arthur Ambrose Talbot

- *Science in the Kitchen*, by Mrs. E. E. Kellogg

- *The Foundations of Geometry*, by David Hilbert

- *The History of the Decline and Fall of the Roman Empire*, by Edward Gibbon

- *The Principles of Chemistry*, by Dmitry Ivanovich Mendeleyev

- *The Varieties of Religious Experience*, by William James

- *Three Contributions to the Theory of Sex*, by Sigmund Freud

- *Grimm's Fairy Tales*

We add a book on government and philosophy:

- *The Republic*, by Plato

As in the previous exercise, we ask

What topics do they have in common, and which topics make each book unique? What are the extracted topics? Can we identify the Dewey Decimal classification of this book by associating it with our known book set?

We hypothesize that adding this new book will yield some substantial topical differences and associations, perhaps enough to distinguish it with one and only one discipline.

As in the previous exercise, we must first create a folder for the input and output files for this project. In that folder, we will create two empty folders called *input* and *output*. We will transfer all text files (they must be in the UTF-8 format) into the *input* folder. Make sure the *output* folder is left blank, because it will be populated by the output of the program. Follow the instructions and analyze the results.

1. Create a *Dewey Decimal Topic Extraction III* folder on your desktop (a new one as not to confuse it with the analysis in Exercise 3).

2. In that folder, create two folders, one called *input* and one called *output*.

3. Open the folder *Dataset E: Large Text Files*. Under the folder, *Dewey Decimal Text Files*, locate and copy all nine text files listed above (including Plato's *Republic*) and copy into the *input* folder of the *Dewey Decimal Topic Extraction III* folder.

4. Find and run the Topic Modeling Tool program installed earlier. You should see an interface that looks like that shown in Figure 11.1.

5. Click on *Input Dir…* and follow the prompts to accept the *input* folder of the *Dewey Decimal Topic Extraction III* folder.

6. Repeat for the *Output Dir…* and follow the prompts to accept the *output* folder of the *Dewey Decimal Topic Extraction III* folder. You should see something similar to what is shown in Figure 11.2 in the previous exercise, but now pointing to the folders in the *Dewey Decimal Topic Extraction folders*.

7. Make sure you enter the desired number of topics for the analysis. The default is ten, and in this case, we want to obtain ten topics. We have complex texts with at least eight complementary topics, so many more topics make sense. You should now be ready to run the program.

8. Press the *Learn Topics* button and watch the program compute the topics and align the courses to the topics. The output files will be found in the *output* directory. Note how long it takes (it should be less than a minute; if it appears to take longer, be patient, it may take several minutes, but if it is much longer than 5-10 minutes, the program may not have converged, and you need to stop the process.).

9. You will see something similar to what we saw in Exercise 11.1, and it should look like Figure 11.3. This is the end screen after the processors run. You will typically see a screen like this at the end of every process.

10. We now review some of the output files to see the rich information set provided by the program.

11. The first output file of interest is the keywords that characterize each unique topic. That file can be found in the *output* file folder under the *output_csv* folder and is named *topic-words. csv*. Figure 11.19 shows this compilation.

Topic Id	Top Words...	Classification
0	2 water acid 3 hydrogen oxygen 4 solution _ heat 1 sodium h_ substances salt temperature gas air 0 salts	Chemsitry
1	king man good woman back time day home eyes thought house _ mother daughter long door great give gold forest	Story
2	film work camera light picture pictures moving movement 1 gutenberg made hand illustration time means small subject project motion apparatus	Art
3	day general human present world presence personal strong experience man act union natural years christ short immediately active part faith	Philosophy
4	fruit water bread cream stewed milk wheat graham soup fresh sugar food add boiling half cup baked flour hot breakfast	Cooking
5	life state man good _ god sidenote true men soul nature mind things world religious great justice time truth 3	Religion
6	iv law 1 equal 2 made numbers 3 side 5 measure 4 7 introduced 6 fall free real 9 10	Math
7	return emperor de rome arms hundred life age death ii thousand people italy tom long provinces time religion christian troops	History
8	sexual 1 straight points theorem point line geometry gutenberg axioms 2 plane object project segments life impulse number infantile 0	Psychology
9	empire roman city return reign constantinople public great barbarians tom country constantine iii army war king greek years throne part	History

FIGURE 11.19 The contents of the *topic-words.csv* output file showing the keywords associated with each of the ten topics in the library books, which includes Plato

12. The next *output* file of interest is the one that lists the texts in our corpus (library texts) and scores them (on a scale from 0 to 1) against the five topics we asked for. It is the *topics-metadata.csv* file also found under the *output_csv* folder. Figure 11.20 shows the scored library books. We highlighted the larger scores to show which topics each book covers.

docid	filename	0 water acid	1 king man good	2 film work camera	3 day general human	4 fruit water bread	5 life state man	6 iv law	7 return emperor	8 sexual straight	9 empire roman city
0	Three Contributions to the Theory of Sex Freud	0.000	0.005	0.046	0.062	0.000	0.085	0.000	0.000	0.801	0.000
1	The Republic Plato	0.000	0.020	0.022	0.039	0.000	0.847	0.051	0.005	0.004	0.011
3	The Principles of Chemistry Mendeleyev	0.954	0.001	0.021	0.015	0.001	0.005	0.000	0.000	0.003	0.000
4	Practical Cinematography and Its Applications Talbot	0.018	0.015	0.894	0.042	0.002	0.019	0.001	0.004	0.005	0.000
5	The History Of The Decline And Fall Of The Roman Empire Gibbon	0.000	0.007	0.000	0.116	0.000	0.000	0.093	0.397	0.000	0.387
6	Grimm's Fairy Tales	0.000	0.941	0.010	0.015	0.014	0.016	0.000	0.001	0.000	0.003
7	Science in the Kitchen Kellogg	0.006	0.010	0.026	0.018	0.924	0.014	0.000	0.002	0.001	0.001
8	The Foundations of Geometry Hilbert	0.000	0.000	0.010	0.000	0.000	0.003	0.000	0.000	0.986	0.000
9	The Varieties of Religious Experience James	0.000	0.065	0.077	0.229	0.001	0.573	0.000	0.018	0.035	0.003
		Chemsitry	Story	Art	Philosophy	Cooking	Religion	Math	History	Psychology	History

FIGURE 11.20 The contents of the *topics-metadata.csv* output file showing the library books (including the Keynes book on probability) scored against the keywords associated with each of the ten topics

13. Figure 11.21 shows the Excel conditional formatting rule used to highlight the highest scoring topics for each travel book. Note that each book has a prominent topic, and there are a few topics in common, as you would expect since the books are from different disciplines, including Plato.

FIGURE 11.21 The Excel conditional formatting rule to highlight the high scoring topics for each library book

14. We can see that the topic for this book is Religion.

Additional Exercise 11.6 - Case Study Using Dataset P: Patents

This is a real-world case study. You just searched the USPTO (the United States Patent and Trademark Office) patent database (*https://www.uspto.gov/patents-application-process/search-patents*). You were looking for patents on text data mining and found over a dozen such patents. You now want to extract the topics covered by the set of patents in question so you can further categorize them.

Use the set patent documents (already in text form) found in the *Case Data* text file repository, under the *Dataset P: Patents*. Use all the patents found there to extract ten topics.

Additional Exercise 11.7 - Case Study Using Dataset F: Federalist Papers

This is an example of searching for authorship and for topics each author covers in similar documents. You have a database of all 74 of the *Federalist Papers* published by James Madison, Alexander Hamilton, and John Jay. You want to know if there are themes covered by each author. Run the Topic Modeling Tool with a random set of 70 papers to train the dataset and extract topics. Then run it with the full set, noting if the four articles left out of the training set have an affinity for any one author or themes.

Additional Exercise 11.8 - Case Study Using Dataset E: Large Text Files

Occasionally, you will find that the results do not make sense. One reason may be that the corpus contains too much non-text information, such as financial reports with many tables of numbers. Let's say you want to analyze financial reports filed by public corporations. You have downloaded the annual financial reports of major corporations such as Apple, Amazon, and Google from the US SEC's (Securities Exchange Commission) Edgar website (*https://www.sec.gov/edgar.shtml*). Now you want to extract topics to see if an annual report from a company could be categorized after training the model with the major corporate reports. The Topic Modeling Tool will converge, but the results do not make sense. Try it. Use the set of corporate annual reports (already in text form) found in the *Case Data* text file repository, under the *Dataset H: Corporate Financial Reports*. Use all the reports found there to extract ten topics.

Additional Exercise 11.9- Case Study Using Dataset N: Sonnets

The topic extraction model is keyed to each individual language. We have been using the English language version of the tool, based on modern English. What if we tried it on a different version of English, such as Shakespearean English? Will it still work? Try it. Use the set of 12 Shakespearean sonnets found in the *Case Data* text file repository, under the *Dataset N: Sonnets* file folder. Use all of the sonnets found there to try to extract five topics. You will find that the model will try to converge for a long time. You will have to stop it churning on the texts after a couple of hours if you have that much patience (it is suggested you only wait 30 minutes to assure yourself it is not converging).

References

1. [McCallum02] McCallum, Andrew Kachites. "MALLET: A Machine Learning for Language Toolkit." *http://mallet. cs.umass.edu* (2002).

2. [Shawn12] Graham, Shawn, Scott Weingart, and Ian Milligan. *Getting started with topic modeling and MALLET*. The Editorial Board of the Programming Historian, 2012.

## CHAPTER 12

TEXT SIMILARITY SCORING

In this chapter, we use a popular way to compare two documents by seeing how similar they are to each other. The method is called TF-IDF (Term Frequency–Inverse Document Frequency). It is easy to implement and yields beneficial results in many circumstances. It is based on a Bag-of-Words approach and uses counts of the frequency of words for comparison, which is similar to what we have done in earlier chapters, but here we carry it a bit further. It matches the frequency words that are exactly the same or have the same root (such as "clean," "cleaning," "cleans," and "cleaned") in the two documents. It does not perform well when we want to associate two words in the two documents with similar meanings (such as "cleans" and "scrub"). We can refer to this type of word association as a *semantic similarity*. Nonetheless it does a very serviceable job for most business applications. Even with this limitation, the TF-IDF method is an excellent way to score a set of candidate resumes against a job description, for example. The algorithm scores the resumes and returns an ordered list sorted by the resumes that are most similar to the job description. Or you can score a resume against a group of possible jobs to see which ones are more similar to the resume. We perform both these tasks in this chapter.

This technique has requirements that make it unsuitable for Excel implementation. We use an open-source implementation in Python accessible via a Web interface. We show how to set up the proper files and run the program to return scored results. We also demonstrate how SAS JMP can be programmed to perform the TF-IDF analysis and compute similarity scores between documents. Lastly, we offer R routines that can be used to perform the TF-IDF and the similarity scoring computation as well.

What is Text Similarity Scoring?

This is an elementary explanation of the TF-IDF (Term Frequency–Inverse Document Frequency) algorithm with cosine similarity scoring.

Take, for example, these three texts:

- Most mornings, I like to go out for a run.
- Running is an excellent exercise for the brain.
- The lead runner broke away from the pack early in the race.

We want to compare these statements against this one-sentence document:

- The sergeant led the platoon in their daily run early in the day.

Which of the three texts above is most similar to the fourth text? Can we produce a ranked order list? The three sentences are the target, and the fourth is our source. In the first step, the algorithm extracts all the terms and produces a Bag-of-Words for each (as we did in early chapters).

Text A	Text B	Text C		Source
Most	Running	The		The
mornings	is	lead		sargeant
I	great	runner		led
like	exercsie	broke		the
to	for	away		platoon
go	the	from		fin
out	brain	the		their
for		pack		daily
a		early		run
run		in		early
		the		in
		race		the
				day

FIGURE 12.1 The three target texts and the source document sorted into a Bag-of-Words

In the next step, the algorithm removes all the stop words (*I, to, a*). Then tokenizes and lemmatizes all terms (*run* and *runner* get converted to *run*). The TF, or *term frequency*, is computed next (essentially, it performs a word frequency analysis). But if some words are too frequent, they may not be too interesting (like the word "lawyer" in contracts: we all know they will be there, so they are commonplace and should be downplayed). The algorithm downplays them by using the inverse of the frequency (the IDF part). We are left with lists of words and their inverse frequencies. Now we compare the list of words and their score to see if they have words in common and compute a common score normalized to 1 (the *cosine similarity score*). For this set of documents, the score is shown in Figure 12.2.

TEXT	description	similarity_score
Text A	Most mornings I like to go out for a run.	0.099
Text C	The lead runner broke away from the pack early in the race.	0.091
Text B	Running is great exercsie for the brain.	0.083

FIGURE 12.2 Similarity scoring of the three target texts against the source text scored and sorted by cosine similarity

For this demonstration, we used the Web-based tool demonstrated in the exercises below. The scores are pretty low, but even so, the ordering of the texts is uncannily accurate. A sergeant taking the platoon for a morning run is most similar to me going out for my morning run.

Text Similarity Scoring Exercises

Exercise 12.1 – Case Study Using Dataset D: Occupation Description

---

Analysis Using an Online Text Similarity Scoring Tool

The online scoring tool requires two data files. The first is a simple (UFT-8) text data version of the source file. It could be a resume, a job description, a contract, or any source text file. It must be a text version of the document. It can be called "*Source*," but the name is not critical.

As an exemplar, we converted the resume of a job applicant (Dr. Andres Fortino) into a text data file. It is called "resume," and we saved it as a UTF-8 text file. Any other such text-based credential would do as well (e.g., a LinkedIn profile or a curriculum vitae converted to UTF-8 text).

The target file is a simple Excel flat file exported into the CSV file format with job titles in the first column and the text of job descriptions in the second. The first row should have column titles. Additional information can be added in separate columns (such as the company and location), but the tool will use the column labeled "description" for the texts to use to compare to the exemplar. That column title must be the variable name for the rows of data to be used for comparison. It preserves the additional information columns in the output document.

As our exemplar here, we used the text file called "O*NET.csv" with 1,100 jobs downloaded from the Bureau of Labor Statistics O*NET database [ONET21]. You can use this file against your resume to see the kinds of career jobs your resume is similar to. You can build a similar target CSV file from job descriptions downloaded from any job search engine (such as Monster.com, Indeed.com, or Glass Door).

We will use similarity scoring to answer the following questions:

Which occupations from the O*NET database is this person most suited for?

1. Use a browser and an Internet connection and invoke the online similarity scoring tool at *https://text-similarity-scoring. herokuapp.com/.* It may take a minute to set it up. You will see a data entry screen that like that shown in Figure 12.3.

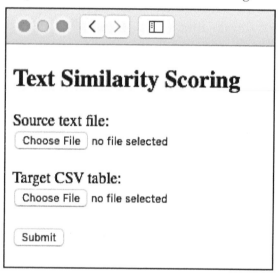

FIGURE 12.3 Similarity Scoring tool data entry screen found at *https://text-similarity-scoring.herokuapp.com/*

2. For the source text file, use the *resume.txt* file found in the *Case Data* repository folder under *Dataset L: Resumes* folder.

3. For the *Target CSV* table, use the *O*NET JOBS.csv* file found in the *Case Data* repository folder under the *Dataset D: Occupation Descriptions* folder.

4. Press the *Submit* button. A table such as in Figure 12.4 should appear.

RightJob

Source text file:
Browse... resume.txt

Target CSV table:
Browse... O*NET JOBS.csv

Submit

job	description	similarity_score
Training and Development Specialists	Training and Development Specialists Design and conduct training and development progr...	0.2609276672341326
Training and Development Managers	Training and Development Managers Plan, direct, or coordinate the training and developm...	0.2324697365727887
Vocational Education Teachers, Postsecondary	Vocational Education Teachers, Postsecondary Teach or instruct vocational or occupational...	0.1745773140876692
Instructional Coordinators	Instructional Coordinators Develop instructional material, coordinate educational content,...	0.1434601812720495
Education, Training, and Library Workers, All Other	Education, Training, and Library Workers, All Other All education, training, and library w...	0.1401564050070442
Remote Sensing Scientists and Technologists	Remote Sensing Scientists and Technologists Apply remote sensing principles and method...	0.1389852320811925
Industrial-Organizational Psychologists	Industrial-Organizational Psychologists Apply principles of psychology to human resource...	0.1374728087229978
Education Teachers, Postsecondary	Education Teachers, Postsecondary Teach courses pertaining to education, such as counseli...	0.1303272098752070
Graduate Teaching Assistants	Graduate Teaching Assistants Assist faculty or other instructional staff in postsecondary in...	0.1241001648636717
Health Educators	Health Educators Provide and manage health education programs that help individuals, fa...	0.1192736642443547
Environmental Restoration Planners	Environmental Restoration Planners Collaborate with field and biology staff to oversee the...	0.1136094981611334
Special Education Teachers, Secondary School	Special Education Teachers, Secondary School Teach secondary school subjects to educati...	0.1100035828128121 9214
Special Education Teachers, Middle School	Special Education Teachers, Middle School Teach middle school subjects to educationally ...	0.1081569084678192 5

FIGURE 12.4 Similarity scoring of a resume versus O*NET occupation data

5. The occupations are sorted by similarity score to the resume. Note that the top 10 returned occupations fit with the information on the resume.

6. Scroll down to the bottom of the displayed table and use the *Download as CSV* button to obtain a copy of the table in CSV format. (See Figure 12.5.)

Precious Metal Workers

Millwrights

Maintenance Workers, Machinery

Home Appliance Repairers

Cutting and Slicing Machine Setters, Operators, and Tenders

Molding and Casting Workers

Download as CSV

FIGURE 12.5 The download button at the foot of the data table returned by the similarity scoring tool

Analysis using SAS JMP

To perform similarity scoring with SAS JMP, the program must be a version that has a text analysis capability. Once the program is invoked, the *Text Analysis* functions may be found in the *Analyze* pull down menu, as shown in Figure 12.6. The data file must also be prepared before loading it into JMP. We will use the O*NET Jobs CSV file. We add a row right below the variable names that include the source information, using the rest of the occupation data as the target. JMP gives us a similarity score of the first row against the rest of the target rows.

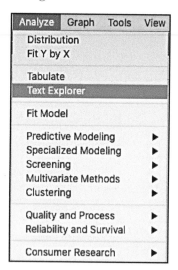

FIGURE 12.6 SAS JMP *Analyze* menu function showing the text analysis capability of this version of the program

1. Open the target CSV table use the *O*NET JOBS.csv* file found in the *Case Data* repository folder under *Dataset D: Occupation Descriptions* folder using Excel.

2. Insert an empty row in row 2. Insert a name (use applicant name, for example) into cell B2.

3. With a text editor, open the source text file *resume.txt* file found in the *Case Data* repository folder under *Dataset L: Resumes* folder. Scrape all of the text and paste it into cell B3 in the open spreadsheet. Save the file as a CSV file under the name *O*NET Plus Resume.csv.* on your desktop for now. The resulting file should look like that shown in Figure 12.7.

4. Run the SAS JMP program and load the *O*NET Plus Resume. csv* from your desktop into JMP. The resulting file should look like that shown in Figure 12.7.

	job	description
1	AFORTINO	ANDRS GUILLERMO FORTINO, PE, ...
2	Chief Executives	Chief Executives Determine and ...
3	Chief Sustainability ...	Chief Sustainability Officers ...
4	General and ...	General and Operations Managers Plan, ...
5	Legislators	Legislators Develop, introduce or enact ...
6	Advertising and ...	Advertising and Promotions Managers ...
7	Green Marketers	Green Marketers Create and implement ...
8	Marketing Managers	Marketing Managers Plan, direct, or ...
9	Sales Managers	Sales Managers Plan, direct, or ...
10	Public Relations and ...	Public Relations and Fundraising ...
11	Administrative ...	Administrative Services Managers Plan, ...
12	Computer and ...	Computer and Information Systems ...
13	Financial Managers	Financial Managers Plan, direct, or ...
14	Treasurers and ...	Treasurers and Controllers Direct ...
15	Financial Managers, ...	Financial Managers, Branch or ...
16	Industrial Production ...	Industrial Production Managers Plan, ...
17	Quality Control ...	Quality Control Systems Managers Plan, ...
18	Geothermal ...	Geothermal Production Managers ...

Columns (2/0): job, description

Rows: All rows 1,111; Selected 0; Excluded 0; Hidden 0; Labelled 0

FIGURE 12.7 SAS JMP with the *O*NET Plus Resume.csv* file loaded

5. Pull down the *Analyze* function from the top ribbon in JMP and invoke the *Text Analysis* functions. In the next screen, move the *description* variable to *Text Columns* entry box. Leave all other choices as displayed; see Figure 12.8. Click the OK button and run the function. You will obtain the familiar *Text Explorer For Description* table seen in Chapter 5.

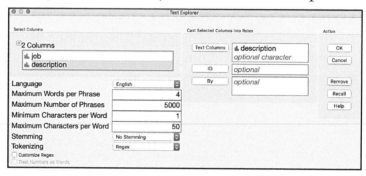

FIGURE 12.8 SAS JMP with the *O*NET Plus Resume.csv* file loaded

6. In the *Text Explorer For description*, right next to the title, use the red triangle button to invoke the functional choices and select *Save Document Term Matrix*. A *Specifications* dialog screen similar to that shown in Figure 12.9 will pop up. This is where you select TD-IDF for the *Weighting*. The resulting DTM matrix is very large and contains the scores of all the words in all the rows against each other.

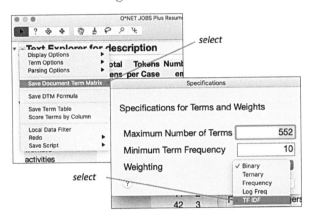

FIGURE 12.9 Saving the *Document Term Matrix* and selecting TF-IDF as the weighting method

7. It is now time to compute the cosine similarity between the rows in the DTM and produce a table of the similarity between all the rows to each other. We use a JMP script that computes the cosine similarity score:

```
// https://en.wikipedia.org/wiki/Cosine_similarity

NamesDefaultToHere(1);

dt = CurrentDataTable();

m = dt << getAsMatrix;

n = NRow(dt);

// Make some column headings for the final table

cols = {};

for(i=1, i<=n, i++,

        InsertInto(cols, "Document in
        Row "||Char(i));

);

// Get the modulus of each feature vector

modulus = J(n, 1, .);

for(i=1, i<=n, i++,

        modulus[i] = sqrt(ssq(m[i,0]));

);
```

```
// Get the cosine of the angle between each pair of
feature vectors

cosTheta = J(n, n, .);

for(i=1, i<=n, i++,

      for(j=1, j<=i, j++,

         cosTheta[i,j] = Sum(m[i, 0] :* m[j, 0])/
         (modulus[i] * modulus[j]);

      );

);

dt2 = AsTable(cosTheta, << ColumnNames(cols));

dt2 << setName("Cosine between feature vectors
in "||(dt << getName));
```

8. The script file may also be found in the *Tools* directory of the accompanying data store for this book under the *SAS JMP* folder. In the currently opened O*NET JOBS Plus Resume DTM file, go up to the JMP program ribbon and under *File*, open the *CosineSimilarity.jpl* script and press run in the script function ribbon (see Figure 12.10).

```
                                    CosineSimilarity
   Run Script  Debug Script  Reformat Script  Balance  Import as Data
   // https://en.wikipedia.org/wiki/Cosine_similarity
   NamesDefaultToHere(1);

   dt = CurrentDataTable();
   m = dt << getAsMatrix;
   n = NRow(dt);

   // Make some column headings for the final table
   cols = {};
   for(i=1, i<=n, i++,
       InsertInto(cols, "Document in Row "||Char(i));
   );

   // Get the modulus of each feature vector
   modulus = J(n, 1, .);
   for(i=1, i<=n, i++,
       modulus[i] = sqrt(ssq(m[i,0]));
   );

   // Get the cosine of the angle between each pair of feature vectors
   cosTheta = J(n, n, .);
   for(i=1, i<=n, i++,
       for(j=1, j<=i, j++,
           cosTheta[i,j] = Sum(m[i, 0] :* m[j, 0])/(modulus[i] * modul
       );
   );
   dt2 = AsTable(cosTheta, << ColumnNames(cols));
   dt2 << setName("Cosine between feature vectors in "||(dt << getName
```

FIGURE 12.10 The *CosineSimilarity.jpl* JMP script file loaded and ready to run. Press *Run Script* to execute.

9. The resulting table has the similarity scores of the first data row (the resume) against all the occupation descriptions, as Figure 12.11 shows.

	Cosine between feature vectors in O*NET JOBS Plus Resume

Data Filter Tabulate Graph Builder Distribution Fit Y by X Fit Model Recode		Document in Row 1	Docu
	1	1	
	2	0.1519944414	
Columns (1111/0)	3	0.0376088707	
Document in Row 1	4	0.2341714177	
Document in Row 2	5	0.1407195089	
Document in Row 3	6	0.1103894649	
Document in Row 4	7	0.0444994159	
Document in Row 5	8	0.1407195089	
Document in Row 6	9	0.093813006	
Document in Row 7	10	0.1243796488	
Document in Row 8	11	0.1597940311	
Document in Row 9	12	0.1655841974	
Document in Row 10	13	0.057448499	
Document in Row 11	14	0.0444994159	
Document in Row 12	15	0.057448499	
Document in Row 13	16	0.0497518595	
Document in Row 14	17	0.0861727484	
Document in Row 15	18	0.0629316776	
Rows	19	0.1379868312	
All rows 1,111	20	0.0827920987	
Selected 1			
Excluded 0			
Hidden 0			

FIGURE 12.11 The resulting table with the similarity scores. The first column contains what we are seeking: the similarity score of the resume against the occupation descriptions

10. While in the resulting similarity scores table, open the JMP file menu, select *Export,* and save the table as an Excel file. Copy the first column from the file. Open the *O*NET JOBS Plus Resume.csv* file (if not already open) and paste the similarity score from the first column of the previous file into column C. Label that column *Similarity Score*. Add a filter and sort by similarity score.

	A	B	C
1	job	description	Similarity Score
2	AFORTINO	ANDRÉS GUILLERMO FORTINO, PE, PHD 75 Grist Mill Lane	1
3	Middle School Teachers, Except Special and Career/Technical Education	Middle School Teachers, Except Special and Career/Techn	0.241331967
4	General and Operations Managers	General and Operations Managers Plan, direct, or coordina	0.234171418
5	Elementary School Teachers, Except Special Education	Elementary School Teachers, Except Special Education Tea	0.231225748
6	Secondary School Teachers, Except Special and Career/Technical Education	Secondary School Teachers, Except Special and Career/Te	0.228277187
7	Graduate Teaching Assistants	Graduate Teaching Assistants Assist faculty or other instru	0.223422228
8	Vocational Education Teachers, Postsecondary	Vocational Education Teachers, Postsecondary Teach or in	0.221841711
9	Command and Control Center Officers	Command and Control Center Officers Manage the operat	0.214657133
10	Career/Technical Education Teachers, Middle School	Career/Technical Education Teachers, Middle School Teac	0.205533998

FIGURE 12.12 The resulting occupation list scored against the resume and sorted by similarity scores

11. The resulting sorted occupations will seem very familiar as they should be the same as when this process was done with the Python code above. See Figure 12.12 for the results.

Analysis using R

Exercise 12.2 - Case D: Resume and Job Description

1. In the *Case Data* file folder under *Dataset D: Job Descriptions,* copy *O*NET JOBS.csv* and name the copy *cased.csv*. The text of the resume referenced in the exercise may also be found in that data repository.

2. Install the packages we need using Repository(CRAN): `dplyr, tidytext, textstem, readr, text2vec, stringr`

3. Import the library and read the case data:

```
> library(dplyr)
> library(tidytext)
> library(text2vec)
> library(readr)
> library(stringr)
> cased <- read.csv(file.path("cased.csv"),
stringsAsFactors = F)
> resume_f <- read_file("resume.txt")

# make resume content a dataframe
> resume_fdf <- tibble(job = "Fortino",
description= resume_f)

# combine resume and job description
> case_d_resume <- rbind(resume_fdf,cased)

# data cleaning function
➢   prep_fun = function(x) {
    # make text lower case
    x = str_to_lower(x)
    # remove non-alphanumeric symbols
    x = str_replace_all(x, "[^[:alnum:]]", " ")
    # collapse multiple spaces
    str_replace_all(x, "\\s+", " ")}
```

4. The cleaned resume document is shown in Figure 12.13.

```
# clean the job description data and create a new
column
```

➤ ```
case_d_resume$description_clean =
prep_fun(case_d_resume$description)
```

| description_clean<br><chr> |
|---|
| andrés guillermo fortino pe phd 75 grist mill lane pleasant valley ny 12569 agfortino gmail com 845 242 7614 educ... |
| chief executives determine and formulate policies and provide overall direction of companies or private and public s... |
| chief sustainability officers communicate and coordinate with management shareholders customers and employees t... |
| general and operations managers plan direct or coordinate the operations of public or private sector organizations d... |
| legislators develop introduce or enact laws and statutes at the local tribal state or federal level includes only workers... |
| advertising and promotions managers plan direct or coordinate advertising policies and programs or produce collat... |
| green marketers create and implement methods to market green products and services |
| marketing managers plan direct or coordinate marketing policies and programs such as determining the demand for... |
| sales managers plan direct or coordinate the actual distribution or movement of a product or service to the custome... |
| public relations and fundraising managers plan direct or coordinate activities designed to create or maintain a favor... |

1–10 of 1,111 rows | 3–3 of 3 columns          1  2  3  4  5  6 ... 100  Next

**FIGURE 12.13** Job description column after data cleaning

```
# use vocabulary_based vectorization
```

➤ ```
it_resume = itoken(case_d_resume$description_
clean, progressbar = FALSE)
```

➤ ```
v_resume = create_vocabulary(it_resume)
```

➤ ```
v_resume = prune_vocabulary(v_resume, doc_
proportion_max = 0.1, term_count_min = 5)
```

➤ ```
vectorizer_resume = vocab_vectorizer(v_resume)
```

```
# apply TF-IDF transformation
```

➤ ```
dtm_resume = create_dtm(it_resume,
vectorizer_resume)
```

➤ ```
tfidf = TfIdf$new()
```

➤ ```
dtm_tfidf_resume = fit_transform(dtm_resume,
tfidf)
```

5. The results of the computed cosine similarity are shown in Figure 12.14.

```
# compute similarity-score against each row
```

➢ resume_tfidf_cos_sim = sim2(x = dtm_tfidf_resume, method = "cosine", norm = "l2")

➢ resume_tfidf_cos_sim[1:5,1:5]

```
5 x 5 sparse Matrix of class "dsCMatrix"
            1          2          3          4          5
1 1.00000000 0.07695001 0.03867244 0.06228349 0.02184387
2 0.07695001 1.00000000 0.10397812 0.18452794 0.10054453
3 0.03867244 0.10397812 1.00000000 0.02833903 .
4 0.06228349 0.18452794 0.02833903 1.00000000 .
5 0.02184387 0.10054453 .          .          1.00000000
```

FIGURE 12.14 Cosine similarity score against each row(job)

```
# create a new column for similarity_score of data
frame
```

➢ case_d_resume["similarity_score"] = resume_tfidf_cos_sim[1:1111]

```
# sort the dataframe by similarity score
```

➢ case_d_resume[order(-case_d_resume$similarity_score),]

6. The results of the cosine similarity of the jobs against the resume ordered by similarity score are shown in Figure 12.15.

job <chr>	similarity_score <dbl>
Fortino	1.0000000000
Training and Development Specialists	0.2601687893
Education, Training, and Library Workers, All Other	0.2449726919
Training and Development Managers	0.2433782818
Education Teachers, Postsecondary	0.1786205110
Vocational Education Teachers, Postsecondary	0.1690794638
Adult Basic and Secondary Education and Literacy Teachers and Instructors	0.1594161953
Industrial–Organizational Psychologists	0.1546035291
Special Education Teachers, All Other	0.1543412842
Health Educators	0.1496801049

1–10 of 1,111 rows | 1–1 of 4 columns

FIGURE 12.15 Jobs against resume data ordered by the similarity score

Reference

1. [ONET21] *O*NET OnLine*, National Center for O*NET Development, *www.onetonline.org/*. Accessed 31 March 2021.

## CHAPTER 13

ANALYSIS OF LARGE DATASETS BY SAMPLING

This chapter presents techniques useful when dealing with datasets too large to load into Excel. One useful way is to randomly sample the "too-big-to-fit-into-Excel" dataset and analyze the sampled table made up of the sampled rows. Excel has a randomization function, and we could use it to extract the sample rows. The problem with that approach is that we can't get the entire table into Excel to do that. So, we must use a different tool to perform the sampling. We will do this in the R program. There is an exercise in this chapter where you are guided on how to set up and use R to extract a meaningful sample of rows for a large dataset. You are also shown how to compute how many rows your sample needs to obtain statistically significant results using the sample table. Once the sample rows are extracted, Excel may be used to get useful answers using the skills taught in earlier chapters. This technique answers the business question:

How do we work with datasets too large to load into Excel?

As in previous chapters, we demonstrate the technique in the first exercise and allow for more challenging work in subsequent exercises.

Using Sampling to Work with Large Data Files

Exercise 13.1 - Big Data Analysis

Analysis in Excel

This exercise's premise is that we wish to use Excel as our analysis tool but are aware of its limitations with respect to very large files. Typically, the problem is not that there are too many variables, but too many rows. Let's say we have a huge data file of hundreds of megabytes consisting of hundreds of thousands (or perhaps millions) of rows. How do we use Excel when we can't load the entire file in a spreadsheet? The answer is to make a tradeoff. We are willing to accept a slight decrease in accuracy in our statistical results for the convenience of using Excel for the analysis.

The technique is to randomly sample the large (or big data) file and obtain a random sample of manageable rows of data. We first use one tool to compute an adequate sample size, and then we use another tool to sample the original file. We use a free Web-based tool to compute sample size, and then we use a free cloud-based program, RStudio, to extract a random sample.

Name	Size (MB)	Rows	Columns	Source	Description
ORDERS.csv	1.8	8,400	22	Company	Office supplies orders
Community.csv	70	376,000	551	US Census	2013 ACS census file
Courses.csv	73	631,139	21	MIT	edX 2013 MOOC Courses
BankComplaints.csv	306	753,324	18	US FTC	Bank complaints to the FTC

FIGURE 13.1 Characteristics of the data files used to demonstrate the sampling of large datasets

1. The data files for this exercise (as listed in Figure 13.1) may be found in the Case Data repository, under the *Dataset E: Large Text Files*, the *Other Large Files* folder. First, let's compute an adequate sample size. The entire file is our population. For example, we wish to have 95% confidence in our statistical analysis using our sample and to have no more than a 1% margin of error in our results (these are very typical parameters in business). Let's take the 306 MB *BankComplaints.csv* big data file with 753,324 rows (see Figure 13.1). Using an online sample size calculator found at *https://www.surveymonkey. com/mp/sample-size-calculator/*, we see that we need a random sample of 9,484 rows to achieve our desired level of accuracy and margin of error (Figure 13.2).

Calculate Your Sample Size:

Population Size:	753,324
Confidence Level (%):	95
Margin of Error (%):	1

CALCULATE

Sample Size:

9,484

FIGURE 13.2 Using an online sample size calculator to reduce the 306 MB *Bank Complaints* file to a manageable set of rows that will yield significant results.

2. As an additional exercise, use the online calculator to compute the necessary number of random rows in the other sample files for various accuracy levels in Table 13.1. Note that the rightmost column has the answer.

Name	Size (MB)	Population Rows	Confidence Level %	Margin of Error %	Random Sample Rows
ORDERS.csv	1.8	8,400	95	1	4,482
Community.csv	70	376,000	95	1	9,365
Community.csv	70	376,000	99	1	15,936
Courses.csv	73	631,139	95	1	9,461
Courses.csv	73	631,139	95	2	2,394

TABLE 13.1 Computed elements of the sampling of the datasets

3. We now use a popular free cloud version of the R program: RStudio Cloud. (You may want to download and install RStudio on your computer so you have a permanently installed sample extraction tool for future use. Otherwise, proceed to learn the technique with the cloud version.)

4. We now use a popular free cloud version of the R program: RStudio Cloud. (You may want to download and install RStudio on your computer so you have a permanently installed sample extraction tool for future use. Otherwise, proceed to learn the technique with the cloud version.)

5. Navigate to *https://rstudio.cloud/*, create a free account, and then proceed to the next step.

6. In RStudio Cloud, create a new project. The typical RStudio interface appears. Note the ">_" prompt in the lower-left-hand corner of the left screen. It should be blinking and waiting for your R commands. The resulting screen in your browser should look like Figure 13.3.

FIGURE 13.3 Interface screen of RStudio Cloud

7. First, we upload all the files we are sampling.

8. Using the Case Dataset provided, open the *Exercises* folder and then open the Case Data repository, under the *Dataset E: Large Text Files*, the *Other Large Files* folder, and find the files *ORDERS.csv, Courses.csv*, and *Community.csv* files.

9. Click on the *Files* tab in the lower-right-hand pane of the RStudio desktop on your browser. Then, click *Upload* in the new row. You will get the interface shown in Figure 13.4.

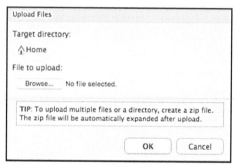

FIGURE 13.4 The RStudio Cloud tool used to upload files to the Web for analysis

10. Click the *Browse* button and upload each of the three files. Be patient, as some of the larger files take some time to upload. When done, the *File* area in the upper-right-hand screen should like that shown in Figure 13.5.

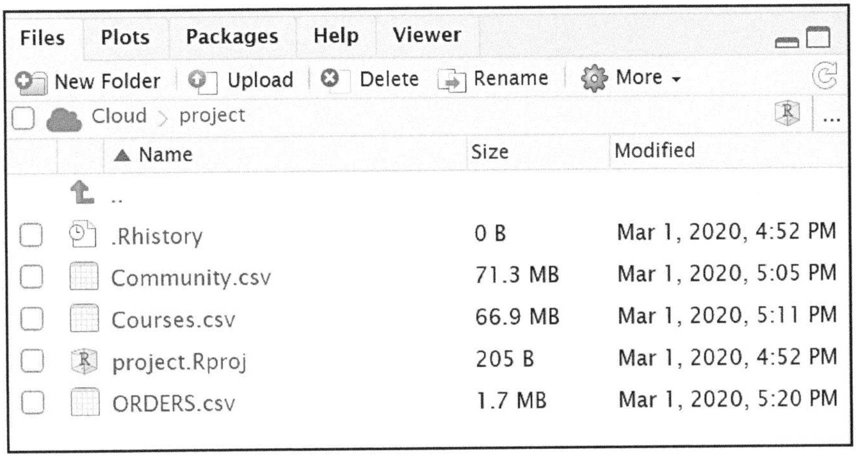
Files
Plots
Packages
Help
Viewer
New Folder
Upload
Delete
Rename
More
Cloud > project
Name
Size
Modified
..
.Rhistory
0 B
Mar 1, 2020, 4:52 PM
Community.csv
71.3 MB
Mar 1, 2020, 5:05 PM
Courses.csv
66.9 MB
Mar 1, 2020, 5:11 PM
project.Rproj
205 B
Mar 1, 2020, 4:52 PM
ORDERS.csv
1.7 MB
Mar 1, 2020, 5:20 PM

FIGURE 13.5 Screen of the uploaded data files ready to be processed with an R script

11. Now, we start with sampling the smaller file (*ORDERS*) and then move on to the larger files.
12. In the upper-left-hand panel, pull down the *File* > *Open* function and select the *ORDERS.csv* file from the list. That loads the file into the workspace (note the "Source" panel now appears and has information about the file).
13. Drop down to the lower-left-hand panel and click in front of the ">_" cursor. It should start blinking, ready for your command.
14. Enter the following sets of commands:

```
> set.seed(123)
> Y <- read.csv("ORDERS.csv")
> View(Y)
> index <- sample (1:nrow(Y), 4482)
> Z <- Y[index, ]
> View(Z)
> write.csv(Z,'Z.csv')
```

15. Enter the random number of rows required (4482), but without a comma, or the command will be interpreted as a part of the command and not as part of the number.

16. We are using Y and Z as temporary containers for our data.

17. Note that the *Source* upper-left-hand panel shows the original data in table form (the result of the *View* command).

18. Also, note that the upper-right-hand panel shows two files in the workspace, Y and Z, and their characteristics. Note that Y has the original set of rows, 8,399, and Z has the sample rows, 4,482. The random sampling was done with the `sample` command.

19. We outputted the sample rows to the Z file, and the program wrote it out to the disk as Z.*csv*. Now the lower-right-hand panel has that file in the directory as shown in Figure 13.6.

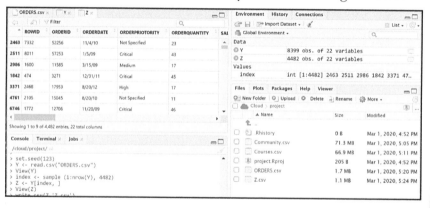

FIGURE 13.6 RStudio Cloud interface screen showing the data file (upper left), R script (lower left), details of the input and output data files (upper right), and files in a directory (lower right)

20. Now we need to download the file from the cloud directory to our computer. You should check the box next to the *Z.csv* file. In the lower-right-hand panel, click on the *More* icon (it looks like a blue gear). Select *Export* and follow the directions to download the file to your desktop for now. Rename the file to *ORDERSSample.csv* as you save it. (It is important to note that we only used *Y* and *Z* as temporary, easy-to-use containers.)

21. To check our work, we compute some result using both the original population and the sample rows and compare.

22. Open *ORDERS.csv* and *ORDERSSample.csv*. Notice that the sample dataset contains a new column (at the extreme left) that identifies each sample row uniquely (a random number). You need to label that column (for example, *SAMPLEID*).

23. Using pivot tables, tabulate the total sales by region for both files. Compare the results from both tables shown in Figure 13.7. Compute the difference between the total population and the sample. You will find it to be well within the 5% margin of error.

1 Using the sample

ORDERSSample.csv

Row Labels	Count of ROWID	Average of SALES
Atlantic	587	1858
Northwest Territories	211	2224
Nunavut	36	1246
Ontario	989	1715
Prarie	915	1759
Quebec	420	2125
West	1046	1900
Yukon	278	1671
Grand Total	**4482**	**1842**

2 Using the entire file

ORDERS.csv

Row Labels	Count of ROWID	Average of SALES
Atlantic	1080	1865
Northwest Territories	394	2033
Nunavut	79	1473
Ontario	1826	1678
Prarie	1706	1663
Quebec	781	1934
West	1991	1807
Yukon	542	1800
Grand Total	**8399**	**1776**
	Difference in total Sales	3.7%

FIGURE 13.7 Comparison of the same analysis using the entire file and the sample showing less than a 5% error difference

24. Note that whereas the computed total from the sampled file is accurate when compared to that computed using the entire original file, there is a much wider error in the individual regional results, especially for those regions with fewer rows. If you repeat for the *PROFIT* variable rather than *SALES*, you will see a much wider variation.

Repeat these steps using the two other data files as additional exercises.

25. Repeat the process for the *Community.csv* and *Courses.csv* files for a 95% confidence level and a 2% margin of error. Compute the summary of one of the variables for both the total population and the sampled files and compare the results.

Additional Case Study Using Dataset E: BankComplaints Big Data File

1. You will find that if you try to load the *BankComplaints.csv* 300 MB file in RStudio Cloud, it will give you an error. The free cloud version only allows smaller files to load. One solution is to get a paid subscription and continue, but since we are only using R for its easy sampling capability, let's use free version of RStudio.

2. Install RStudio on your PC or Mac computer. Then, you can use the techniques of the exercise above as they are given. (The interface to RStudio is identical, so just follow the instructions given, except now you can load a 300 MB or 3 GB or whatever size file you need to sample.)

3. As a first step, locate the free RStudio program on the Internet and download and install it. You may obtain it here: *https://www.rstudio.com/products/rstudio/download/*.

4. Once installed, try it out on the 306 MB *BankComplaints.csv* file. Compute the number of random rows to select for an adequate sample for a 95% confidence level and a 1% margin of error, as seen in Table 13.2.

Name	Size (MB)	Population Rows	Confidence Level %	Margin of Error %	Random Sample Rows
BankComplaints.csv	306	753,324	95	1	4,484

TABLE 13.2 Computed parameters of the sampling of the dataset

5. Use the R commands given earlier to sample the file and save it as *BankComplaintsSample.csv*. (Make sure to use the correct file name in the commands.)

6. Use the file of samples to tabulate the percentage of complaints by state to discover the states with the most and least complaints.

7. Add the size of the population of each state and normalize the complaints per million residents of each state. Get the states with the least and the most complaints per capita. Compute other descriptive statistics of this variable.

8. Use Excel and get summary descriptive statistics (Figure 13.8).

COMPLAINTS/MPERSON	
Mean	24.46
Standard Error	1.45
Median	24.25
Mode	#N/A
Standard Deviation	10.24
Sample Variance	104.91
Kurtosis	-0.53
Skewness	0.43
Range	41.82
Minimum	6.76
Maximum	48.58
Sum	1222.99
Count	50.00

FIGURE 13.8 Descriptive statistics of the sample extracted from the *BankComplaints.csv* data file

## CHAPTER 14

INSTALLING R AND RSTUDIO

R is a language and environment for statistical computing and graphics. It stems from a project at Bell Laboratories by John Chambers and his colleagues [Chambers08]. R provides a wide variety of statistical (linear and nonlinear modeling, classical statistical tests, time-series analysis, classification, and clustering) and graphical techniques. R is popular because it makes it easy to produce well-designed publication-quality plots and it is available as free software. It compiles and runs on various UNIX platforms and similar systems (including FreeBSD and Linux), Windows, and macOS. It is highly extensible and includes many packages and libraries. We use it extensively in this book for its versatility in text data mining.

RStudio is an integrated development environment (IDE) for R. RStudio is available in two formats. RStudio Desktop is a regular desktop application, which we use here. It is also available for servers (RStudio Server). There is a browser-accessible version, RStudio Cloud, available. It is a lightweight, cloud-based solution that allows anyone to use R, and to share, teach, and learn data science online. It has limitations in its uploadable database size.

In this chapter, we provide instructions for installing the latest version of R and RStudio.

Installing R

Install R Software for a Mac System

1. Visit the R project Website using the following URL: *https://cran.r-project.org/*.

2. On the R website, click on the *Download R* for the system that you use. This set of instructions is for the Mac OS X system, so click on Download R for (Mac) OS X (see Figure 14.1).

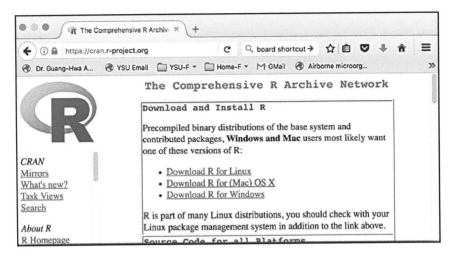

FIGURE 14.1 First installation screen showing the page to download the program for a Mac

3. On the *Download R for the MacOS* Webpage, click *R-3.4.0.pkg* or the most recent version of the package (see Figure 14.2).

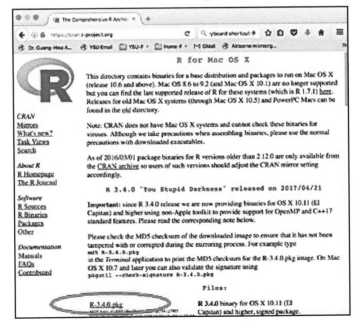

FIGURE 14.2 The location of the R program for a Mac

4. If you choose to *Save File*, you will need to go to the *Downloads* folder on your Mac and double click on the package file to start the installation (see Figure 14.3).

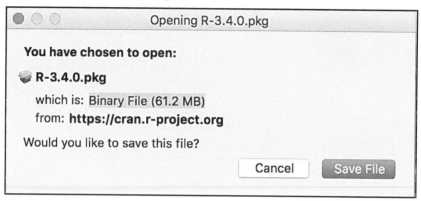

FIGURE 14.3 Opening the downloaded *dmg* file

5. From the installation page, click on *Continue* to start the installation (see Figure 14.4).

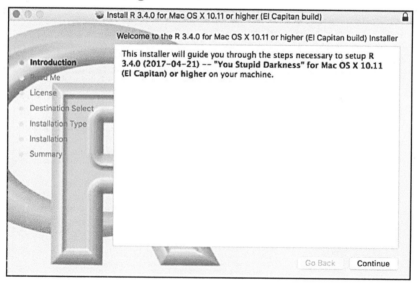

FIGURE 14.4 Executing on the *dmg* file

6. In the *Read Me* step, click on *Continue* to continue the installation process (see Figure 14.5).

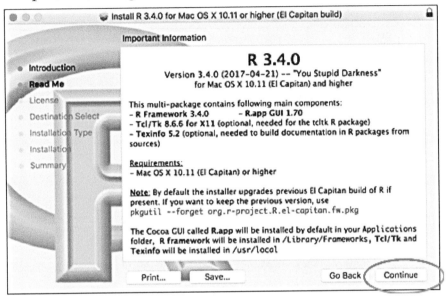

FIGURE 14.5 Click on *Continue* to move to the next step in the installation process

7. Click *Continue* in the Software License Agreement step, and click *Agree* to move to the next step in the process.

8. Click the *Install* button to start the installation (see Figure 14.6).

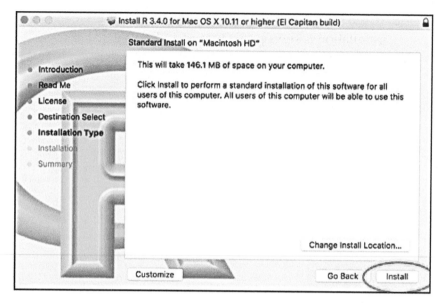

FIGURE 14.6 Click the *Install* button to start the installation

9. Wait until the installation is complete (see Figure 14.7).

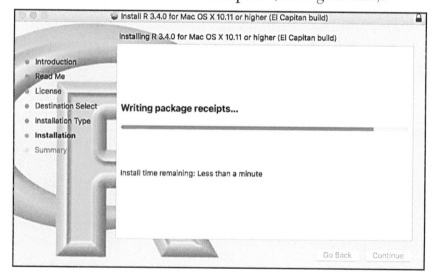

FIGURE 14.7 The installation screen

10. When you see the screen shown in Figure 14.8, then the installation is successful (Figure 14.8).

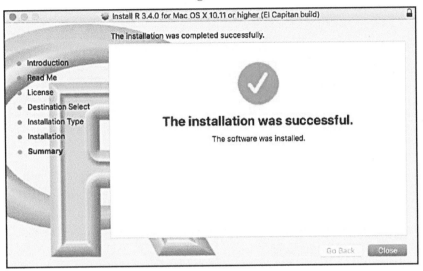

FIGURE 14.8 The successful installation screen

11. You should now be able to load and run R. It will be located on the *Applications* folder on your Mac.

Installing RStudio

1. Visit the RStudio website using the following URL: *https://rstudio.com/products/rstudio/download/*.

2. Select RStudio Desktop Free license from the *Choose Your Version* screen. Click *Download.* It will take you to a screen that allows you to select the version of RStudio for your operating system (see Figure 14.9).

3. Select MacOS10.13+ and click on the *RStudio-1.3.1093.dmg* file (see Figure 14.9).

4. Once the *dmg* file is downloaded into the *Downloads* folder, double click it, and it will begin installing (see Figure 14.10).

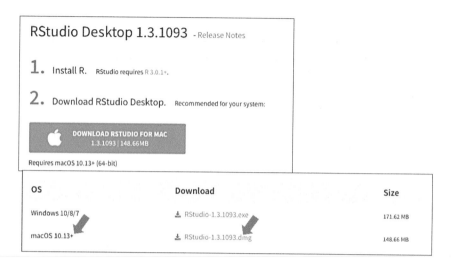

FIGURE 14.9 Details for the installation of RStudio

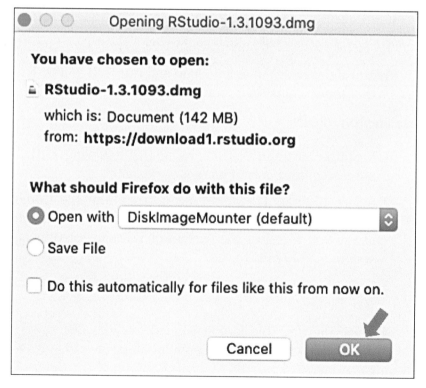

FIGURE 14.10 Run the downloaded *dmg* file to begin the installation

5. Once the program has been successfully installed, you are allowed to transfer it to the *Applications* folder, as shown in Figure 14.11.

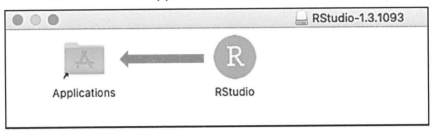

FIGURE 14.11 Transfer the RStudio application to the *Applications* folder on your Mac

6. RStudio is now ready to run. It will be located on the *Applications* folder on your Mac.

Reference

1. [Chanbers08] Chambers, John. *Software for data analysis: programming with R.* Springer Science & Business Media, 2008.

## CHAPTER 15

INSTALLING THE ENTITY EXTRACTION TOOL

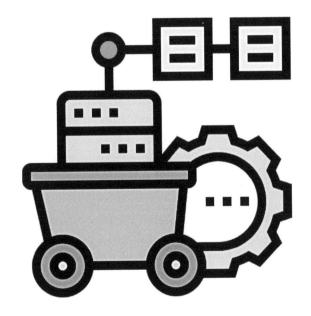

The Stanford NER is a Java implementation of a Named Entity Recognizer. Named Entity Recognition (NER) labels sequences of words in a text, which are the names of things, such as person and company names or gene and protein names. It comes with feature extractors for NER and many options for defining feature extractors. Included with the download are named entity recognizers for English, particularly for the three classes (person, organization, and location).

The Stanford NER is also known as a *CRF Classifier*. The software provides a general implementation of (arbitrary order) linear chain Conditional Random Field (CRF) sequence models. That is, by training your models on labeled data, you can use this code to build sequence models for NER or any other task.

The original CRF code was developed by Jenny Finkel. The feature extractors were created by Dan Klein, Christopher Manning, and Jenny Finkel. Much of the documentation was created by Anna Rafferty.

Downloading and Installing the Tool

You can try out Stanford NER CRF classifiers or Stanford NER as part of Stanford Core NLP on the Web. To use the software on your computer, download the zip file found at *http://nlp.stanford.edu/ software/CRF-NER.html#Download* and unzip it. You can unzip the file either by double-clicking it or using a program for unpacking zip files. It will create a stanford-ner folder.

You now have the program ready to run on your computer. There is no actual installation procedure. Downloading the files from the above link will install a running program, and you should be able to run Stanford NER from that folder. Normally, the Stanford NER is run from the command line (i.e., shell or terminal). The release of Stanford NER requires Java 1.8 or later. Make sure you have the latest version of Java installed.

The CRF sequence models provided here do not precisely correspond to any published paper, but the correct paper to use for the model and software is the paper by Finkel et al. [Finkel05].

The NER Graphical User Interface

Provided Java is on your *PATH*, you should be able to run a NER GUI by just double-clicking on the *stanford-ner.jar* archive. However, this may fail, as the operating system does not give Java enough memory for the NER system, so it is better to double click on the *ner-gui.bat* icon (Windows) or *ner-gui.sh* (MacOSX). Then, using the top option from the *Classifier* menu, load a CRF classifier from the *classifiers* directory of the distribution. You can then either load a text file or Webpage from the *File* menu, or decide to use the default text in the window. Finally, you can now create a named entity tag from the text by pressing the *Run NER* button. Refer to Chapter 10 for step-by-step instructions to load and run the NER for various cases.

Reference

1. [Finkel05] Jenny Rose Finkel, Trond Grenager, and Christopher Manning. 2005. Incorporating Non-local Information into Information Extraction Systems by Gibbs Sampling. *Proceedings of the 43nd Annual Meeting of the Association for Computational Linguistics (ACL 2005)*, pp. 363-370. *http://nlp.stanford.edu/~manning/papers/gibbscrf3.pdf*

## CHAPTER 16

INSTALLING THE TOPIC MODELING TOOL

In this chapter, we show you how to locate, download, and install the MALLETT Topic Modeling Tool. We also discuss how to set up and use the tool to perform all the exercises in Chapter 11: Topic Recognition in Documents.

Installing and Using the Topic Modeling Tool

Install the tool

The Topic Modeling Tool is built with Java, so it is possible to run it as a native application without installing Java. Currently, there are versions for Windows and Mac OS X. Follow the instructions for your operating system.

For Macs

1. Download *TopicModelingTool.dmg* to your computer from the *Tools* folder under the *Topic Modeling Tool* or download from the GitHub site: *https://github.com/senderle/topic-modeling-tool.*

2. Open the file by double-clicking on it.

3. Drag the app into your *Applications* folder – or into any folder you wish.

4. Run the application by double-clicking on it.

For Windows PCs

1. Download *TopicModelingTool.zip* to your computer from the *Tools* folder under the *Topic Modeling Tool* or from the GitHub site: *https://github.com/senderle/topic-modeling-tool.*

2. Extract the files into any folder.

3. Open the folder containing the files.

4. Double-click on the file called *TopicModelingTool.exe* to run it.

UTF-8 caveat

The tool is a native application to be used with UTF-8-encoded text. If you wish to analyze text with encodings other than UTF-8, the tool may have problems. Additionally, if you try to use the plain *.jar* file on a Windows machine or on any device that doesn't run Java using UTF-8 encoding by default, it won't work. All files in this book for use with this tool are provided in the UTF-8 format.

Setting up the workspace

Start with an organized workspace containing just the indicated directories and files. You may use any names you like, but we've chosen simple ones here for the sake of clarity. In the exercises in Chapter 11, we give explicit instructions on creating a file environment for each project.

Workspace Directory

1. *input* (directory)

   This directory contains all the text files you'd like to train your model on. Each text file corresponds to one document. If you want to control what counts as a "document," you may split or join these files together as you see fit. The text files should all be at the same level of the directory hierarchy. Although you may want to remove HTML tags or other non-textual data, the Topic Modeling Tool will take care of most other preprocessing work.

2. *output* (directory)

   This directory contains the output that the Topic Modeling Tool generates. The tool generates several directories and temporary files; this ensures they don't clutter up your workspace. If the tool runs successfully, you will see only two directories here when it's done: *output_csv* and *output_html*. If the tool fails, there may be other files here, but it's safe to delete all of them before trying again.

3. *metadata.csv* (file; optional)

This file is optional, but if it is present, the Topic Modeling Tool will join its own output together with the data in it. This will allow you to make use of some powerful visualization tools almost immediately. This is one of the biggest changes to the tool, and it's worth making use of! It does, however, add some complexity to the tool, and metadata files should follow these three rules:

1. The first line of the file **must** be a header, and the following lines *must* all be data.

2. The first column **must** consist of filenames precisely as they appear in the *input* directory. The tool treats filenames as unique identifiers and matches the names listed in the metadata file to the names as they appear in the directory itself. Even subtle differences **will cause errors**, so take care here – if something goes wrong, double-check file extensions, capitalization, and other easy-to-miss differences.

3. This must be a strictly formatted CSV file. Every row should have the same number of cells, and there should be no blank rows. If you want to have notes, put them in a dedicated column. Be sure that cells with delimiters inside them are double-quoted and that double-quotes inside cells are themselves doubled. For example, a cell containing the text

```
"The quick brown fox jumped over the lazy dog," he
said.
```

will need to look like this:

```
"""The quick brown fox jumped over the lazy dog,""
he said."
```

Using the Tool

Select the input and output folders.

1. Once you have your workspace set up, double-click the *TopicModelingTool.jar* file. A window should appear that looks like that shown in Figure 16.1.

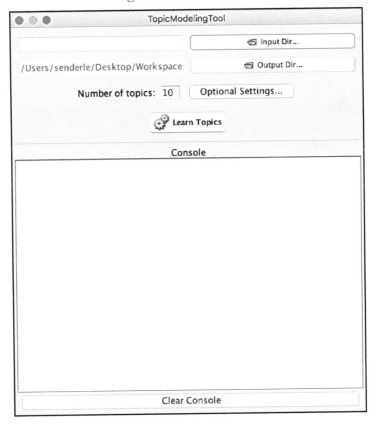

FIGURE 16.1 The Topic Modeling Tool starting screen appears as soon as you run the tool

2. For Mac users, you may need to hold down the *control* key while double-clicking and select *Open.* If that doesn't work, your version of Java may not be sufficiently up to date.

3. Next, select the input folder by clicking this button, as shown in Figure 16.2.

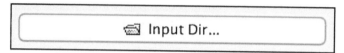

FIGURE 16.2 Using the *Input Dir...* button to indicate to the tool the location of the corpus of text files to be analyzed

4. Use the file chooser to select *input* by clicking once. (If you double-click, it will take you into the folder, which is not what you want.) Then click the *Choose* button, as seen in Figure 16.3.

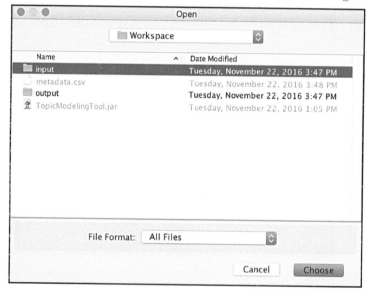

FIGURE 16.3 Location of the *input* directory

5. Then select the output folder by clicking the *Output Dir...* button, as shown in Figure 16.4.

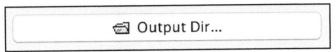

FIGURE 16.4 Using the *Output Dir...* button to indicate to the tool where it should place the output files after the tool runs

6. Use the file chooser to select *output* by clicking once and then click on the *Choose* button, as in Figure 16.5.

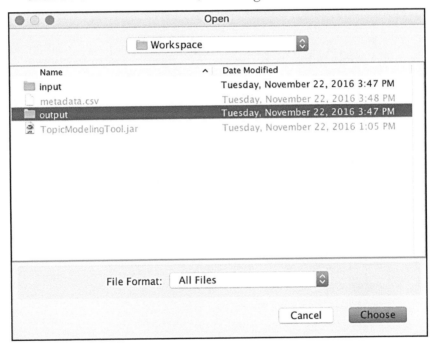

FIGURE 16.5 Location of the *output* directory

Select metadata file

1. Metadata files are optional, but they can help you interpret the tool's output. We do not use the metafile in this book, but it could be of use for more complex projects. If you'd like to include a metadata file, open the optional settings window by clicking this button shown in Figure 16.6.

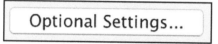

FIGURE 16.6 Using the *Optional Settings...* button to change some of the default parameters on the tool

2. A window like that shown in Figure 16.7 should open.

● ● ●	TopicModelingTool	
Mallet Default		🗁 Stopword File...
		🗁 Metadata File...
☑ Remove stopwords		
☐ Preserve case		
Tokenize with regular expression	[\p{L}\p{N}_]+	
Number of iterations	400	
Number of topic words to print	20	
Interval between hyperprior optimizations	10	
Number of training threads	4	
Divide input into n-word chunks	0	
Metadata CSV delimiter	,	
Output CSV delimiter	,	
	Default Options Ok	

FIGURE 16.7 Parameter setting screen for some of the tool options

3. Click on the button shown in Figure 16.8 to indicate the location of the metadata file.

FIGURE 16.8 Using the *Metadata File* button to indicate to the tool where it should place some of the data after the tool runs. This is an optional file.

4. Now use the chooser to select *metadata.csv* (if one was created) and click on the *Open* button, as shown in Figure 16.9.

	Open	
	Workspace	

Name	^	Date Modified
input		Tuesday, November 22, 2016 3:47 PM
metadata.csv		Tuesday, November 22, 2016 3:48 PM
output		Tuesday, November 22, 2016 3:53 PM
TopicModelingTool.jar		Tuesday, November 22, 2016 1:05 PM

File Format: All Files

Cancel   Open

FIGURE 16.9 The location of the *metadata* file with respect to all the other directories and files

Selecting the number of topics

1. You may want to adjust the number of topics. This will affect the "granularity" of the model; entering a higher number results in finer divisions between topics. However, it also results in a slower performance. We suggest running the tool several times and adjusting the number of topics to see how it affects the output. The number of topics is set in the input screen, as shown in Figure 16.10.

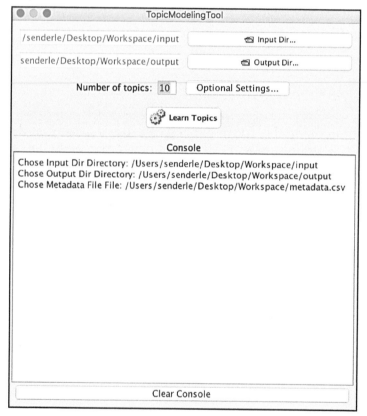

FIGURE 16.10 Input screen showing how to change the number of topics for each run

2. For more information on the other options, look at the MALLET documentation (*http://mallet.cs.umass.edu/*). Shawn Graham, Scott Weingart, and Ian Milligan have written an excellent tutorial on MALLET topic modeling. It can be found at this location: *http://programminghistorian.org/lessons/topic-modeling-and-mallet*.

Analyzing the Output

Multiple Passes for Optimization

1. You are likely to run the tool several times, looking at output and considering whether you've selected the right number of topics. You will have to rely on your intuition, but your intuition will become stronger as you change settings, compare results, and use the tool on different corpora. Remember that this tool does not eliminate your bias. Be skeptical of your interpretations and test them as best you can by running the tool multiple times to verify that the patterns that interest you are stable. Basic checks are important: check word frequency counts and look at the titles of works devoted to topics that interest you. You may find that a topic that the tool has discovered isn't what you thought it was based on the first ten or twenty words associated with the topic.

The Output Files

The tool outputs data in two formats: CSV and HTML. The HTML output comprises a browsable set of pages describing the topics and the documents. Inside the *output_html* folder, open the *all_topics. html* file to start browsing. That output is fairly self-explanatory.

The *output_csv* folder contains four files:

1. *docs-in-topics.csv*

This is a list of documents ranked by topic. For each topic, it includes the 500 documents that feature the topic most prominently. It's useful for some purposes, but the HTML output presents the same data in a more browsable form. The order of topics here is insignificant, but the order of documents is significant. For each topic, the first document listed has the highest proportion of words tagged with that topic label.

2. *topic-words.csv*

This is a list of topics and words associated with them. The words listed are those that have been tagged with the given topic most often. Here again, the order of topics is insignificant, but the order of words is significant. For each topic, the first word listed has been tagged with that topic label most often. A more browsable form of this data also appears in the HTML output.

3. *topics-in-docs.csv*

This is a list of documents and the topics they contain. Each row corresponds to one document, and the first topic label in the list is the one that appears most frequently in the document. The decimal fraction that appears after each topic label is the proportion of words in the document that was tagged with that label. This is, in some sense, the inverse of *docs-in-topics.csv*. Again, a more browsable form of this data appears in the HTML output.

4. *topics-metadata.csv*

This organizes the topic proportions from *topics-in-docs.csv* as a table and associates those proportions with any metadata that has been supplied. By arranging the data as a table, this file makes it possible to build a pivot table that groups documents by metadata categories and calculates topic proportions over those document groups. Pivot tables are useful tools for data analysis and visualization and can be easily generated using Excel or Google Sheets.

## CHAPTER 17

INSTALLING THE VOYANT TEXT ANALYSIS TOOL

Voyant is a powerful open-source text analysis tool [Sinclair16]. Throughout this book, we use it as an alternative to some of the other tools for essential functions, such as word frequency analysis, keyword analysis, and creating word clouds.

The program has a client-server architecture where the computations run on a server, and the data input and output are performed through a browser interface. A Web-based version of the Voyant server can be accessed on the Internet at *https://voyant-tools. org/*. For many, this will suffice, but be aware that your text files need to be uploaded to a non-secure server, and this could be a breach of security. There is, however, an open-source version of the server that can be downloaded and run on a private secure computer on the same computer as the browser's front end or some intranet server.

The instructions below allow you to download the server version of Voyant and load and run it on your computer or an intranet server. The exercises throughout the chapter can be done with any version of the server: Web-based, intranet, or locally stored.

Install or Update Java

Before downloading the Voyant server, you need to download and install Java if you don't already have it. If you do have Java installed, you should still download and update it to the newest version.

Installation of Voyant Server

Although Voyant Tools is a Web-based set of tools, you can also download it and run it locally. Downloading Voyant to your own computer has a number of advantages, but the main reason is so that we won't encounter loading issues resulting from overwhelming the server. Using Voyant locally also means that your texts won't be cached and stored on the Voyant Server, which allows you to restart the server if you encounter problems, and it allows you to work offline, without an internet connection. We show you how to install the server on the computer you will be doing the analysis from.

The Voyant Server

VoyantServer is a version of the Voyant Tools server that can be downloaded and run locally. This allows you to do your text analysis on your own computer. It means

- You can keep your texts confidential as they are not be cached on the server.

- You can restart the server if it slows down or crashes.

- You can handle larger texts without the connection timing out.

- You can work offline (without an Internet connection).

- You can have a group of users run their own instance without encountering load issues on the server.

Downloading VoyantServer

To download **VoyantServer,** go to the latest releases page (*https://github.com/sgsinclair/VoyantServer/releases/tag/2.4.0-M45*) and click on the VoyantServer. zip file to download it (this is a large file of about 200 MB – it includes large data models for language processing). This is a *.zip* archive file that needs to be decompressed before using.

- **Mac:** On the Mac, you just double click the file, and the OS will decompress it.

- **Windows:** In Windows, it's best to right-click on the file and choose a destination directory – it may not work correctly if extracted into a virtual directory.

Once you decompress the *.zip* file, you should see something like the following, which is shown in Figure 17.1:

- *_app:* this is the actual web application – you shouldn't need to view this folder's contents

- *License.txt:* this is the license for the VoyantServer

- *META-INF:* this is a part of the VoyantServer architecture – you shouldn't need to view this folder's contents

- *README.md:* this includes some of the same documentation as on this page

- *server-settings.txt:* this is an advanced way to set server options, including the port and memory defaults

- *VoyantServer.jar:* this is the most important file, the one you'll click to start the server

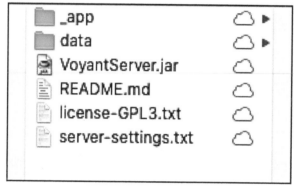

FIGURE 17.1 The downloaded and unzipped file structure for all the Voyant Server files

Running Voyant Server

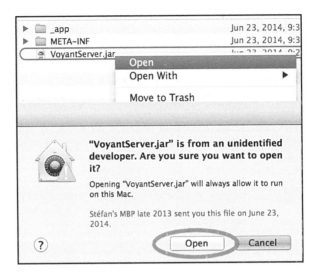

FIGURE 17.2 Running the Voyant Server on a Mac. Make sure to give the OS permission to open the program.

To run the server, you need to run the *VoyantServer.jar* Java JAR file. This Java Archive file is a package with all the resources needed to run the server (including an embedded JETTY server). To run this, you need to have Java installed.

- **Mac:** You should right-click (control-click) on the *VoyantServer.jar* file and choose *Open* from the menu. Click on Open in the next dialog (which isn't the default button).

- **Windows:** You should be able to simply click on the *VoyantServer.jar file*.

- **Command-line:** It should also be possible to launch the application from the command-line if you're at the prompt in the same folder as the jar file: *java -jar* VoyantServer.jar.

1. Once you run *VoyantServer,* you will see a control panel like that shown in Figure 17.3.

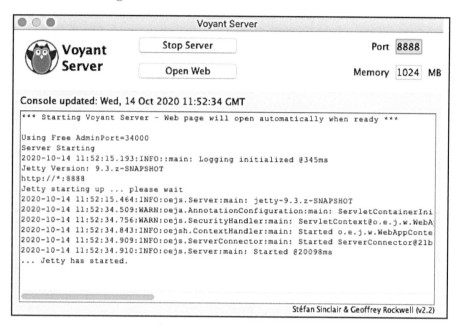

FIGURE 17.3 The Voyant Server running. Notice the JETTY has been started as the instructions indicate.

2. Typically, VoyantServer will automatically launch your browser with the Voyant Tools home screen, where you can define a text and get started.

3. You will see something like Figure 17.4 in your default browser.

FIGURE 17.4 Once the Voyant Server is running, it will open a browser session for data input.[1]

[1] Voyant is a web-based and downloadable program available at *https://voyant-tools.org/docs/#!/guide/about*. The code is under a GPL3 license and the content of the web application is under a Creative Commons by Attribution License 4.0, International License.

Controlling the Voyant Server

FIGURE 17.5 The various controls for the Voyant Server

Figure 17.5 Shows the major components of the VoyantServer. From the VoyantServer control panel you can

- **Stop Server / Start Server:** This button's label depends on the state of the server –it will say *Stop Server* if the server is already running and *Start Server* if it isn't. You can stop the server if it doesn't seem to be behaving and then restart it. **Note:** You should always stop the server to properly release resources when exiting (quitting) the Voyant server. Otherwise, re-launching the server may not work.

- **Open Web:** You can open your default browser with the Voyant Tools entry page that connects with this server. By default, the URL will be *http://127.0.0.1:8888*. You can always connect with a local server by typing this into the *Location* field of your browser if the browser launched is not the one you want to use.

- **File -> Exit:** You can quit the VoyantServer application (this also terminates the server, though quitting the application without using *Exit* won't).

- **Help:** You can access the *Help* page for the VoyantServer from the *Help* menu.

- **Port:** You can change the port that is used by the server (the default is port 8888). Normally this won't need to be changed – it's not recommended to make changes here unless you need to and know what you're doing. If the port specified is already in use, you can try a slightly different one (8889, for instance).

- **Memory:** You can increase the memory (in megabytes) allocated to the VoyantServer if you analyze larger texts. Make sure you stop and restart the server for the new memory setting to take effect. The default is 1024 (MB).

Testing the Installation

Once installed, test that the program is working:

1. Open the directory *Case Data* in the data repository associated with this book. In the *Case O: Fables* directory, open the *Little Red Riding Hood.txt* fable file with a text editor. Scrape the file into the buffer and paste into the open the *Add Texts* data entry portal, as shown in Figure 17.6.

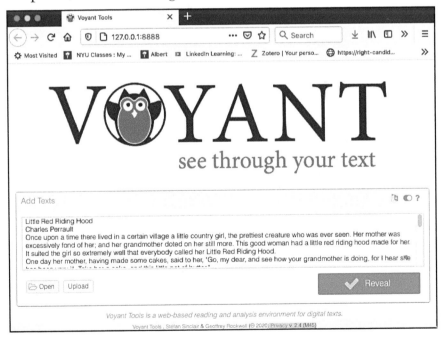

FIGURE 17.6 Pasting the *Little Red Riding Hood.txt* fable file into the Voyant data entry screen to test the installation

2. Press *Reveal* and, if the program is working correctly, you will see a screen similar to that shown in Figure 17.7.

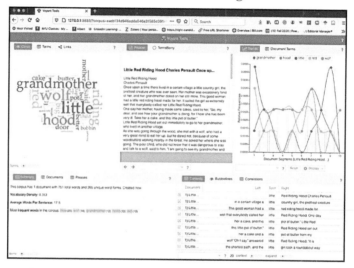

FIGURE 17.7 Pressing the *Reveal* for the *Little Red Riding Hood.txt* fable file into the Voyant data entry screen to test the installation

3. Click the refresh button on your browser and upload the file from the directory. You should achieve the same results.

4. The server should now be installed ready for use.

Reference

1. [Sinclair16] Sinclair, Stéfan and Rockwell, Geoffrey, 2016. *Voyant Tools*. Web. *http://voyant-tools.org/*.Voyant is a Web-based and downloadable program available at *https://voyant-tools.org/docs/#!/guide/about*. The code is under a GPL3 license and the content of the Web application is under a Creative Commons by Attribution License 4.0, International License.

INDEX

A

Ad-hoc analysis tool, 20
Adobe Acrobat file, 20, 41
    export tool in, 41
Adobe Acrobat Pro set, 20
Affinity analysis, 179–180
Affinity diagram process, 179–180
Aggregation, 43
    across rows and columns, 46
    new variable, 45
    O*NET data file with, 48
    process, 51
Analytics tool sets, 19–24
    Adobe Acrobat, 20
    Excel, 19
    Java program, 22
    Microsoft Word, 20
    R and RStudio, 21–22
    SAS JMP, 20–21
    Stanford Named Entity
        Recognizer, 23
    topic modeling tool, 23–24
    Voyant tools, 22
Applied Project course, 215–216
ASCII character set (UTF-8), 40

B

Bag-of-Words representation, 34, 39–40
Bag-of-Words text data file, 56, 60
Balagopalan, Arun, 24

Business
    context, 6
    data analysis in, 4–6
    decision-making process, 4
    environment, 3
    information needs, 2, 5
    intelligence analyst job, 113
    managers, 27
Business decisions, data visualization
    for, 140–141

C

Case Data repository, 264
Case study
data visualization
    consumer complaints, 147–153
    large text files, 161–162
    product reviews, 154–160
    training survey, 141–147
federalist papers, 53–54
keyword analysis
    customer complaints, 118
    job description, 87–101
    resume, 87–101
    university curriculum, 101–115
large data files, 49–53, 178–180
large text files, 200–203
    topic recognition, in documents,
        216–234, 236
NAICS codes, 46
occupation descriptions, 44–45, 47–48
onboarding brainstorming, 181–184

remote learning student survey, 14–15
resumes, 41–43
Titanic disaster, 10–12
word frequency analysis
  consumer complaints, 83
  job descriptions, 71–76
  product reviews, 77–82, 160
  training survey, 58–70, 146
Categorical data, 26, 30, 166
Categorical variables, 8, 44, 47
Chambers, John, 272
Chat systems, 188
Classifiers, 188, 190, 283
Client-server architecture, 298
Code, 167
  documenting, 179
Coding, 30, 166
  affinity diagram, 181–184
  analysis, 167
  deductive, 166, 176–177
  inductive, 166, 168–169
  onboarding brainstorming, 181–184
  process, 167
  of survey responses, 174
  text data
    authoritative reference for, 179
    common approaches to, 168
    qualitative data, 166
    quantitative data, 166
    remote learning, 172–176
    training department, 169–172
  types of, 166
Command-line, 301
Commercial products, 18
Commercial programs, 28–29
Communication, data visualization
  for, 140
Computerized data, 26
CONCATENATE excel function, 44–45
  formula, 72
Concept-driven coding, 168, 176

Conditional Random Field (CRF)
  sequence models, 188, 282–283.
  See also Stanford Named Entity
  Recognizer
Conjunctions, 56
Consumer complaints, 83
  data visualization
    using JMP, 147–150
    using R, 152–153
    using Voyant, 150–151
  narrative, 176, 177
  word frequency analysis, 83
Content characterization, 207
Conversion process, 4
CoNVO model, 6
Core NER process, 188
Corporate data, 35
Corporate financial reports, 30, 195–200
Corpus, 29, 30, 34
  of Facebook postings, 140
  words of text in, 162
CosineSimilarity.jpl script, 252
COUNTIF function, 19, 34, 49, 62, 87, 92,
  94, 107, 110, 121, 130, 140
  formula, 59, 116
CRF classifier, 282
CRF sequence models. *See* Conditional
  Random Field sequence models
CRISP-DM reference model. *See* Cross
  Industry Standard Process for
  Data Mining reference model
Cross Industry Standard Process for Data
  Mining (CRISP-DM) reference
  model, 2
CSV file, 29
Customer complaints, keyword
  analysis, 118
Customer conversational interactions, 27
Customer opinion data, 28–29

D

Data, 3–4, 173
  for analysis, 140
  computerized, 26
  distillation process, 4
  elements, 34, 40
    text data as, 56
  text, 26
  types, 26
Data analysis, 4, 34
  in business, 4–6, 180
  qualitative text, 167
  relate to decision making, 6–7
  survey responses for, 170
Database management system
    (DBMS), 206
Data-driven coding, 168
Data extraction, 206
Data file preparation
  case study
    Federalist Papers, 53–54
    large data files, 49–53
    NAICS codes, 46
    occupation descriptions,
        44–45, 47–48
    resumes, 41–43
  characteristics of, 261
  data shaping, 34–35
    Bag-of-Words model, 39–40
    essential and time-consuming
        process, 34
    flat file format, 34, 35–39
    single text files, 40
    text variable in table, 39
  large, 49–53
Data frame object, 34, 36, 96, 111
Data-mining programs, 18
Data retrieval system, 206
Dataset, 12, 15, 97

Data shaping, 34–35
  Bag-of-Words model, 39–40
  essential and time-consuming
    process, 34
  flat file format, 34, 35–39
  single text files, 40
  text variable in table, 39
Data sources, 26
Data visualization
  for analysis, 140
  for business decisions, 140–141
  for communication, 140
  consumer complaints, case study
    using JMP, 147–150
    using R, 152–153
    using Voyant, 150–151
  large text files, case study, 161–162
  product reviews, case study
    using Excel, 154–155
    using JMP, 156–157
    using R, 159–160
    using Voyant, 157–158
  training survey, case study
    using excel, 141–143
    using JMP, 143–144
    using R, 145–147
    using Voyant, 144–145
Data yields information, 6
DBMS. *See* Database
    management system
Decision-making process, 4
  data analysis relate to, 6–7
  data-driven, 7
Deductive approach, 177
Deductive coding, 166, 176–177
Dewey decimal system, 166, 167, 178,
    206, 207
  book classification coding scheme, 178
  categories, 220
  topic extraction folders, 222

Digital humanities, 22
docs-in-topics.csv, 295–296
Documents, 30
    characterization, 207
    collection, 208
    topic recognition in. *See* Topic
        recognition, in documents

E

E-commerce site, 86
Electronic research notebook, 140
Emails, 29, 189
    metadata, 29
Emotion AI, 120
Emphasis in analysis, 26
Enterprise platform, 20
Entities, 198
Entity chunking, 186
Entity classifier, 188
Entity extraction, 186
    downloading and installing, 282–283
Entity identification, 186
Excel, 19
    in big data analysis, 260–268
    conditional formatting rule, 215, 219,
        224, 230, 234
    data visualization
        product reviews, 154–155
        training survey, 141–143
    keyword analysis
        job description, 88–90
        product reviews, 77–82, 115–160
        university curriculum, 101–111
    pivot table analysis, 26
    spreadsheet, 35, 92
    techniques, 87
    word frequency analysis in
        job descriptions, 72–73
        product reviews, 77–79

    training survey, 58–64
    Windex customer comments, 79
Export tool, in Adobe Acrobat file, 41, 42

F

Facebook postings, 140
Federalist Papers, 53–54
Financial reports, 236
Finkel, Jenny, 23, 188, 282
Flat file format, 34, 35–39
    data file not in, 38
    elements of, 37
Foolproof conversion method, 20
Framed analytical questions, 6, 7–8
    business data analysis, 4–6
    data analysis to decision making, 6–7
    "data is the new oil," 3–4
    text-based analytical questions, 13–14
    well-framed analytical questions, 8–9
Functions
    COUNTIF, 92, 94
    JMP *Data Filter,* 90, 105
    Text Analysis, 246, 248
    Text Explorer, 90, 105

G

Gasoline-burning engine, 4
Google search engine, 206
Google Sheets, 19
Grammatical structure, 56
Graphical user interface
        (GUI), 21, 208, 283
GUI. *See* Graphical user interface

H

Histograms, 4
HTML output, 295–296

I

IDE. *See* Integrated development
    environment
Implicit coding, 176
In-depth linguistic analysis, 56
Index terms, 207
Inductive coding, 166, 168–169, 173
Information extraction, 187
Information needs, 5, 9
    parsing process, 7, 8, 10
Information retrieval (IR) system,
    39, 206–209
    document characterization, 207
    topic modeling, 208
Information Technology Project
    Manager occupation, 101, 110
Input directory, 288, 290
Integrated development environment
    (IDE), 21, 272
Intput files/folders, 216–217, 226, 231
IR system. *See* Information retrieval
    system

J

Java Archive file, 301
Java GUI front end, 24
Java program, 22
JMP
    analysis tool, 20
    data analysis fundamentals in, 144
    Data Filter function, 90, 105
    data visualization
        consumer complaints, 147–150

    product reviews, 156–157
    training survey, 143–144
  keyword analysis
    job description, 87–115
    university curriculum, 105–108
  sentiment analysis using, 125–129
Job description, case study, 71–76
  frequently used keywords in, 113
  keyword analysis, 87–101
    in Excel, 88–90
    in JMP, 90–93
    in R, 95–101
    in Voyant, 93–95
  text similarity scoring, 240–243
Job search engine, 243

K

Kawakita, Jiro, 179
Key performance indicators (KPIs), 2
Keyword analysis, 31, 71, 86–87
  customer complaints, 118
  definition, 87
  product reviews
    in Excel, 115–117
  resume and job description, 87–101
    in Excel, 88–90
    in JMP, 90–93
    in R, 95–101
    in Voyant, 93–95
  Rubbermaid, 115
  university curriculum, 101–115
    in Excel, 102–105
    in JMP, 105–108
    in R, 111–115
    in Voyant, 108–110
Keyword detection, 86
Keyword extraction, 86
Klein, Dan, 23, 188, 282
KPIs. *See* Key performance indicators

L

Language-based data, 167
Library of Congress subject coding, 207
Little Red Riding Hood.txt fable file, 305

M

Machine learning, 21
Mac System
    Java installed, 301
    R Software for, 272–277
    Topic Modeling Tool, 286
MALLETT, 24, 208
    Topic Modeling Tool, 286
Manning, Christopher, 23, 188, 282
McCallum, Andrew, 24
Medina, John, 141
Memory, 305
Metadata characterization, 207
metadata.csv file, 288
Metadata files, 292–293
Microsoft products, 18
Microsoft Word, 20
Monolithic file, 29

N

NAICS codes, 46
Named entities, 187
    extraction, 188, 192
    recognized, 201, 202
Named Entity Recognition
        (NER), 23, 186–187, 282
    algorithm forms, 189
    core function of, 188
    corporate financial reports, 195–200
    definition, 186
    extraction to business cases, 194–195
    File management tab in, 191

graphical user interface, 283
    large text files, 200–203
    mean for business, 188–189
    named entities tagged by, 191, 198
    primary objective, 186
    Stanford Named Entity Recognizer,
        188, 189–190
Natural language processing
        (NLP), 23, 30, 39, 186, 208
Negative words, 120, 123, 131
NER. *See* Named Entity Recognition
Newman, David, 23–24
NLP. *See* Natural language processing
Non-data elements, 36
Numerical data, 30, 166
Numerical summarization functions, 27
Numeric data, 26

O

Occupation descriptions, 44–45, 47–48
Oil distillates, 4
Oil industry, 3
Onboarding brainstorming, 181–184
O*NET.csv, 243
O*NET data file, 44, 48
    resume *vs.*, 245
Online text similarity scoring tool,
        243–245
Open coding. *See* Inductive coding
Open-ended questions, 57, 58
Open-source products, 18
Opinion mining, 120
Oracle corporation, 22
Ouput directory, 287, 291
output_csv folder, 295–296
Output files/folders, 216–219, 222,
        227, 231, 295–296

P

Parsing process, 7, 8
    information needs, 10–11, 13–15
Parts of speech (POS), 188
PDF document, 20
Pivot tables, 4, 27
Positive words, 122, 130, 131
Predictive analytic products, 4
Product feedback data, 86
Product reviews, case study, 77–82
    data visualization, 154–160
    keyword analysis, 115–117
    sentiment analysis, 120–122, 128–147
    word frequency analysis, 77–82, 160
Programming language, 36
Propositions, 56

Q

Qualitative data, 166
Qualitative text data analysis, 167
Quantitative data, 166
Quantitative questions, 8

R

Rafferty, Anna, 188, 282
Random sampling, 266
RapidMiner, 18
Raw materials, 7
Rcmdr program. *See*
    R-commander program
R-commander (Rcmdr) program, 21
RDBMSs. *See* Relational Database
    Management Systems
Relational Database Management
    Systems (RDBMSs), 35, 206
Remote learning, 172–176
Resume, case study, 41–43

keyword analysis, 87–101
    in Excel, 88–90
    in JMP, 90–93
    in R, 95–101
    in Voyant, 93–95
    text similarity scoring, 254–258
    vs. O*NET data file, 44–48
R program, 260–263, 273
    data visualization
        consumer complaints, 152
        product reviews, 159–160
        training survey, 141–147
    installation, 272–277
    keyword analysis
        job description, 95–101
        university curriculum, 101–115
    for Mac System, 272–277
    and RStudio, 21–22
    word frequency analysis in
        job descriptions, 75–76
        product reviews, 81–82
        training survey, 70
RStudio, 21–22, 272
    application, 279
    installation, 277–279
RStudio Cloud, 22, 263, 268, 272
    interface screen of, 263, 266
    tools, 252
RStudio Desktop, 272
RStudio Server, 272
Rubbermaid
    keyword analysis, 117
    product reviews, 121–124, 160

S

Sampling, large datasets by
    big data analysis
        bankcomplaints, 268–269
    in Excel, 260–268

computed elements of, 262
SAS JMP program, 18, 20–21
    with O*NET Plus Resume.csv file,
        247, 248
    online scoring tool, 243
    word frequency analysis in
        job descriptions, 71–76
        product reviews, 77–82
        training survey, 58–70
Search engine optimization (SEO), 27, 86
Search engines, 86
Sentiment analysis, 120–121, 130
    definition, 120
    positive and negative word lists to, 122
    in product reviews, 140
    by review date and brand, 136
    Rubbermaid product reviews, 121–
        124, 134–138
    using JMP, 125–129
    Windex product reviews, 129–134
SEO. *See* Search engine optimization
Single text files, 40
SMART
    goals and objectives, 8–9
    well-framed analytical questions, 9
Social media, 13
    data, 28
    postings, 49, 86
Social networks, 27
Sonnets, case study, 236
Spreadsheets, 36
    software, 19
    summarization tools in, 36
Stand-alone text documents, 40
Stanford Named Entity Recognizer
        (NER), 23, 188, 189–190, 282
    CRF classifiers, 282
Stanford NER. *See* Stanford Named
        Entity Recognizer
Stop word list, 62, 64, 88, 103, 149–158
    unwanted words using, 149

in Voyant, 158
Sun Microsystems, 22
Surveys, 30

T

Target file, 243
Term Frequency (TF) analysis, 19, 28,
        56, 65
    for financial management course, 106
    for resume, 91, 106
Text analysis, 56
Text analytics functionality, 18
Text-based analytical questions, 13–14
Text business data analysis, 57–58
Text data, 26
    field, 56
    file model, 34
    mining, 120
    sources and formats, 27
        customer opinion data, 28–29
        documents, 30
        emails, 29
        social media data, 28
        surveys, 30
        websites, 31
    types of, 86
Text Explorer function, 90, 105
    to JMP function, 125, 126
    for *review.title* variable, 129, 132–133
Text similarity scoring, 240–243
    exercises, 243–254
    occupation description
        using SAS JMP, 246–254
    online scoring tool, 243–245
    resume and job description, 254–258
Text string, 40
Text variable, 40, 47
    in table, 39
TF analysis. *See* Term Frequency analysis

Titanic disaster, case study, 10–13
  context, 10
  dataset, 12
  framed analytical questions, 12–13
  information need, 10
  key performance indicators, 10
  parsing process, 10–11
  performance gaps, 10
Tool sets, for text analytics. *See* Analytics
    tool sets
Topic extraction model, 236
Topic modeling, 208
Topic Modeling Tool, 23–24, 208
  data entry screen, 210
  installing and using, 286–295
  interface screen, 211, 212
  for Macs, 286
  MALLETT, 286
  metadata files, 292–293
  multiple passes for optimization, 295
  number of topics, 294–295
  output files, 295–296
  program, 227
  using tool, 289–291
  UTF-8 caveat, 287
  for Windows PCs, 286
  workspace, 287
Topic recognition, in documents
  case study
    Federalist Papers, 235
    large text files, 216–234, 236
    patents, 235
    Sonnets, 236
    University Curricula, 209–216
  Excel conditional formatting rule, 215,
    219, 224, 230, 234
  information retrieval system, 206–209
    document characterization, 207
    topic modeling, 208

topics-in-docs.csv, 296
topics-metadata.csv, 296
topic-words.csv, 296
Training department, case study, 169–172
Training survey, case study
  data visualization, 141–147
  word cloud of, 147
  word frequency analysis, 58–70, 146
Treemaps, 19
Twitter, 28

U

University curriculum,
    case study, 209–216
  keyword analysis, 101–115
Unstructured text data, 140
Unwanted words, 149, 150
US Bureau of Labor Statistics, 71
UTF-8 text file, 197, 243

V

Visualizing text data. See Data
    visualization
Voyage of the Beagle book, as text file, 50
Voyant, 29, 56
  data visualization
    consumer complaints, 150–151
    product reviews, 157–158
    text files, 161–162
    training survey, 144–145
  keyword analysis
    job description, 93–95
    university curriculum, 108–110
  stopword list in, 158
  Windex customer review word
      cloud in, 158
  word frequency analysis in

job descriptions, 74–75
product reviews, 80–81
training survey, 67–70
Voyant Server, 299
components of, 304
controlling, 304-305
downloading, 299–300
installation of, 298
running, 301-303
testing, 305-306
update Java, 298–305
Web-based version of, 298
VoyantServer.jar, 300
Voyant Tools, 22, 298

W

Web-based application, 22
Web-based text analytic tools, 56,
140, 162, 242
Web-based version, 109
Websites, 31
Weighting method, 249
Well-framed analytical questions, 4
characteristics of, 8–9
Windex consumer feedback, 154, 157
Windex product reviews, 129–134
filtering for, 156
treemap of, 155
Windows, 301

Windows PCs, Topic Modeling Tool, 286
Word frequency analysis, 19, 56–57,
146. *See* also Term Frequency
analysis
for attendee survey responses, 64
of bank complaints, 152
consumer complaints, 83
definition, 60
job descriptions, case study, 71–76
using Excel, 72–73
using R, 75–76
using SAS JMP, 73–74
using Voyant, 74–75
of Little Red Riding Hood table, 57
product reviews, case study, 77–82,
160
using Excel, 77–79
using R, 81–82
using SAS JMP, 79–80
using Voyant, 80–81
text business data analysis, 57–58
text data field, 56
training survey, case study, 58–70
using Excel, 58–64
using R, 70
using SAS JMP, 64–67
using Voyant, 67–69
Windex consumer feedback, 154
by word cloud, 146
Words, 56
Workspace directory, 287–288